To friends at Emory & Henry and Duke

A STUDY OF
THE LANGUAGE OF LOVE IN THE SONG OF SONGS
AND ANCIENT EGYPTIAN POETRY

SOCIETY OF BIBLICAL LITERATURE
DISSERTATION SERIES

Edited by
Howard C. Kee
and
Douglas A. Knight

Number 38
A STUDY OF
THE LANGUAGE OF LOVE IN THE SONG OF SONGS
AND ANCIENT EGYPTIAN POETRY

by
John Bradley White

SCHOLARS PRESS
Missoula, Montana

A STUDY OF
THE LANGUAGE OF LOVE IN THE SONG OF SONGS
AND ANCIENT EGYPTIAN POETRY
by
John Bradley White

Published by
SCHOLARS PRESS
for
The Society of Biblical Literature

Distributed by

SCHOLARS PRESS
Missoula, Montana 59806

A STUDY OF
THE LANGUAGE OF LOVE IN THE SONG OF SONGS
AND ANCIENT EGYPTIAN POETRY

by
John Bradley White
DePauw University
Greencastle, Indiana 46135

Ph. D., 1975
Duke University

Adviser:
Roland E. Murphy

Library of Congress Cataloging in Publication Data
White, John Bradley, 1947-
    A study of the language of love in the Song of Songs
and ancient Egyptian poetry.

    (Society of Biblical Literature dissertation series ;
no. 38)
    Originally presented as the author's thesis, Duke
University, 1975.
    Bibliography: p.
    Includes index.
    1. Bible. O.T. Song of Solomon—Criticism,
interpretation, etc. 2. Love poetry, Egyptian. 3. Love
in literature. I. Title. II. Series: Society of Biblical
Literature. Dissertation series ; no. 38.
BS1485.W43 1978   223'.9'06   77-13399
ISBN 0-89130-192-5

Printed in the United States of America
1 2 3 4 5
Printing Department
University of Montana
Missoula, Montana 59812
5959—UM Printing Services

TABLE OF CONTENTS

8

LIST OF TABLES

9

PREFACE

It does not take very long to become enamored with the
Song of Songs! While the book itself is particularly charming
in its use of imagery and while literary analysis of the love
poems can prove to be a rewarding locale for scholarly work,
my own initial interests in the Song grew from research in the
broader sapiential tradition of Israel. The preservation and
possible enhancement of the Song by the sages underscores that
this collection of love poems displays an important instruction
for the community of faith: the importance of fidelity and mutuality in human love.

Specific interest in the Song of Songs was kindled by a
graduate seminar on "Love Poetry in the Ancient Near East"
taught at Duke University by Professor Roland E. Murphy, O.
Carm. From that period of study, the idea arose for this project. Special acknowledgment and thanks go to Father Murphy,
my advisor, for his keen interest and thoughtful guidance in
the preparation of this work. I should also like to thank
Professor Orval S. Wintermute who made sacrifices of his time
to provide me directed study in Middle and New Egyptian. It is
impossible to measure the meaningful influences of these scholars upon my personal and academic life.

The writer is also indebted to others who have aided him
in this study: the members of my academic committee who have
provided helpful suggestions and encouragement at various
stages in this endeavor; my fellow graduate students who supported me with spirited conversation and consoling humor; and
my friends at Kansas Wesleyan for their interest and support
during the time of preparing the manuscript for publication.
Suggestions and comments on the translation of the Egyptian love
songs were received from Professor R. J. Williams during the
time prior to publication. I express my appreciation to Professor Williams for his interest in this project.

Finally, to my wife, Mary Margaret, who encouraged this
project and the years of study which preceded it, goes special

12

tribute. An Egyptian poet long ago captured her special
qualities: 〰 .

August, 1977
DePauw University

ABBREVIATIONS

AB	Anchor Bible
AbrN	*Abr-Nahrain*
AJSL	*American Journal of Semitic Languages and Literature*
AKM	Abhandlungen für die Kunde des Morgenlandes
AmiCl	*L'Ami du Clergé*
ANET	J. B. Pritchard (ed.), *Ancient Near Eastern Texts*
AO	*Archiv für Orientforschung*
AOAT	Alter Orient und Altes Testament
ASTI	*Annual of the Swedish Theological Institute*
ATD	Das Alte Testament Deutsch
BA	*Biblical Archaeologist*
BASOR	*Bulletin of the American Schools of Oriental Research*
BDB	F. Brown, S. R. Driver, C. A. Briggs, *Hebrew and English Lexicon of the Old Testament*
BdP	*Blatter für deutsche Philosophie*
BeO	*Bibia e oriente*
BHK	R. Kittel (ed.), *Biblia hebraica*, 3rd ed.
Bib	*Biblica*
BibOr	*Biblica et Orientalia*
BKAT	Biblischer Kommentar: Altes Testament
BO	*Bibliotheca orientalis*
BZ	*Biblische Zeitschrift*
BZAW	Beihefte zur Zeitschrift für die alttestamentliche Wissenschaft
CAH	I. Edwards, C. Gadd, N. Hammond (eds.), *Cambridge Ancient History*, 3rd ed.
CBQ	*Catholic Biblical Quarterly*

CE	*Chronique d'Égypt*
DAWBIO	Deutsche Akademie der Wissenschaften zu Berlin Institut für Orientforschung
DtVi	*Deutsche Vierteljahrs Schrift für Literaturwissenschaft und Geistesgeschichte*
Ex	*Expedition*
ETL	*Ephemerides theologicae lovanienses*
GKC	*Gesenius' Hebrew Grammar*, 2nd Eng. Ed.; ed. E. Kautzsch; trans. A. E. Cowley
Greg	*Gregorianum*
HAT	Handbuch zum Alten Testament
HSAT	Die heilige Schrift des Alten Testaments
HUCA	*Hebrew Union College Annual*
Int	*Interpretation*
JA	*Journal asiatique*
JANESCU	*Journal of the Ancient Near Eastern Society of Columbia University*
JAOS	*Journal of the American Oriental Society*
JARC	*Journal of the American Research Center in Egypt*
JCS	*Journal of Cuneiform Studies*
JEA	*Journal of Egyptian Archaeology*
JPOS	*Journal of the Palestine Oriental Society*
JSS	*Journal of Semitic Studies*
KAR	E. Ebeling (ed.), *Keilschrifttexte aus Assur religiösen Inhalts*
KAT	E. Sellin (ed.), Kommentar zum A. T.
KB	L. Koehler and W. Baumgartner, *Lexicon in Veteris Testamenti libros*
KBSup	L. Koehler and W. Baumgartner, *Supplementum ad Lexicon in Veteris Testamenti libros*
LXX	Rahlfs (ed.), *Septuaginta*
MDAI	*Mitteilungen des deutschen archäologischen Instituts*
NAB	*New American Bible*

NEB	*New English Bible*
Or	*Orientalia*
RB	*Revue biblique*
RechBib	Recherches bibliques
RSP	L. Fisher (ed.), *Ras Shamra Parallels*, **Vol. 1**
SaBi	La Sacra Bibbia
SAT	Die Schriften des Alten Testaments
SBE	*Semana Biblica Española*
SBJ	*La sainte bible de Jérusalem*
Scr	*Scripture*
SJT	*Scottish Journal of Theology*
ST	Studies and Texts
TLZ	*Theologische Literaturzeitung*
TRu	*Theologische Rundschau*
VT	*Vetus Testamentum*
WMANT	Wissenschaftliche Monographien zum Alten und Neuen Testament
ZA	*Zeitschrift für Assyriologie*
ZAS	*Zeitschrift für ägyptische Sprache und Altertumskunde*
ZAW	*Zeitschrift für die alttestamentliche Wissenschaft*
ZDMG	*Zeitschrift der deutschen morgenländischen Gesellschaft*
ZDPV	*Zeitschrift des deutschen Palästina-Vereins*
ZE	*Zeitschrift für Ethnologie*
ZTK	*Zeitschrift für Theologie und Kirche*

INTRODUCTION

The thesis of this study is that the language of love in the Hebrew Song of Songs is reminiscent of the language used to describe love in the corpus of ancient Egyptian love poetry. The Song, therefore, shares in the design, themes, and literary genres by which human love is expressed in the ancient world.

This thesis is supported by a literary analysis of both the Song of Songs and the Egyptian material. Emphasis will be placed upon an analysis of the cultural milieu of the 18th Dynasty in Egypt which provides a background for the *Geist* reflected in the Egyptian love poems (Chapter II). A systematic analysis of the variety of topoi (themes) which are characteristic of the Egyptian lyrics will then be presented (Chapter III). Chapter IV, then, purports to show the Song of Songs' participation in the love-language of the ancient world, by detailing the variety of themes which are held in common with the ancient Egyptian love songs. A summary (Retrospect) and a detailing of the significance of the Egyptian poems vis-à-vis the interpretation of the Song of Songs (Prospect) are contained in Chapter V.

Apart from providing the reader with a systematic analysis of the language of love in the Song and the Egyptian corpus of love lyrics, this study attempts to make two further contributions to the scholarly work in the area of love poetry in the ancient world. Chapter I of this work provides, for the first time in English in more than two decades, an extensive survey of scholarly work on the Song of Songs. This chapter should not, however, stand in isolation as a mere *Arbeitsbericht*, for it also illustrates how this writer deals with the variety of issues facing the interpreter of the Song as well as introduces the reader to issues of genre, structure, and text taken up in the latter portion of this study. Secondly, the Appendix of the study contains the writer's translations of the major collections of the Egyptian love poems with useful notations dealing with matters of text and interpretation.

CHAPTER I

A SURVEY OF SCHOLARLY OPINION ON
THE SONG OF SONGS

The extent of scholarly work on the Song of Songs in recent
years demands that an *Arbeitsbericht*, an attempt to survey major
developments, begin this study. In the last two decades, no
survey of the Song has appeared in English which attempts to
cover a broad spectrum of issues that have engaged recent scholarship. This chapter will not only seek to fill that void, but
also will seek to provide a foundation for addressing the wider
issue of this study: the relationship between ancient Egyptian
love poetry and the Song of Songs.

A section on meaning, i.e., the variety of interpretations
which have characterized the Song, is frequently emphasized in
surveys of scholarly opinion. A variety of positions is still
noted in this area, which will form the first section of the
chapter. With recent commentaries, moreover, issues arising
from the discipline of form criticism (life-setting, genre, and
structure) must be examined as well as the significance of research in the relationship between Ugaritic studies and the
Song (text) and of creative work in the area of the poetic quality of the Song. This chapter, then, will address both the new
emphases in the study of the Song as well as recent efforts by
scholars to solve old problems.

MEANING

Following the traditional schema, one may outline the
consensus of scholarship regarding the interpretation of the
Song of Songs as follows: 1) allegorical; 2) cult-mythological;
and 3) naturalistic.[1] Within the past two decades, the naturalistic interpretation has dominated scholarly work while the allegorical meaning is frequently used to exemplify the various
levels of interpretation in Jewish and Christian communities.
The cult-mythological interpretation has not gained a wide following.

19

1. The names of Robert, Tournay, Feuillet, Schneider, Krinetzki, Fischer, and van den Oudenrijn have been associated with the allegorical interpretation which achieved a classic presentation in the work of Cardinal Bea and most recently in the important commentary of Robert, Tournay, and Feuillet.[2] This latter work brings together A. Robert's thesis regarding the Song of Songs as an allegorical midrash (defined by Tournay p. 11) and his methodology which emphasizes words, phrases, and images taken from earlier biblical material, procédé anthologique. In the Song, Yahweh and Israel are personified as husband and wife, expressing, for example, in Cant 1:4 the same mutual commitment which is exemplified in Jer 31:1,3: "I will be the God of all the tribes of Israel and they will be my people. With age-old love I have loved you; so I have kept my faithfulness toward you."[3] Likewise, the imagery of the Song (wife, king, shepherd, flock, vineyard, garden, etc., for Robert; and marriage, morning, night, dew, the seek and find motif, the love of God theme, etc., for Feuillet) evokes certain theological ideas (Yahweh as king [Isa 52:7] or shepherd [Isa 40:9-11]--compare Cant 1:4,12; 3:7-9 and 1:7; 2:16; and 6:2.[4]

Many recent commentators have disassociated themselves from the allegorical interpretation of Robert and Feuillet. A. M. Dubarle, for example, warns against the uncritical use of anthological style, especially in drawing parallels between the Song and prophetic literature.[5] J.-P. Audet concurs and notes that the Song does not make use of prophetic ideas (for example, a betrothal between Yahweh and Israel [Hos 2:16, 21-22]) and should be understood at the "pre-literary stage" as a song of human betrothal.[6] R. E. Murphy has argued that the imagery in the Song does not necessarily have a definite, built-in theological meaning and cannot, therefore, evoke the theological claims which Robert and Feuillet propose.[7]

Another facet of the allegorical interpretation might be termed "typological-allegorical," for the literal meaning of the Song is noted (the Song speaks of human lovers, bride and bridegroom, etc.), but subordinated to a "higher" level of meaning reflecting the relationship between Yahweh and Israel. J. Fischer notes that the persons and their activities in the Song serve as types (Typen) for Yahweh's relationship to Israel

(and accordingly, Christ's relationship to the Church).[8] Working on two levels causes severe exegetical problems for Fischer,
problems which have not been overcome in the work of either
Krinetzki or van den Oudenrijn. Krinetzki is unable to divorce
himself from dogmatic concerns. Although he states that the
Song is a collection of human marriage and love songs, Krinetzki
also speaks of the "strong prophetic, eschatological, and mes-
sianic coloring" which characterizes the Song and leads the interpreter to "a wider, 'higher' sense."[9] In a similar fashion,
van den Oudenrijn points out that the human love relationship
"symbolizes" the long-standing relationship between God and his
people, and from this basis, one may speak of a "mystical sense"
which is an integral aspect of the meaning of the Song. Van den
Oudenrijn sees a variety of allegorical interpretations for the
Song including the relationship between Yahweh and his people,
Christ and the Church, a mystical union with Christ, and the
union of the soul with the Trinity.[10]

O. Loretz has recently urged commentators to distinguish
carefully between the theological meaning of the Song of Songs
and the variety of interpretations which have characterized the
history of scholarship on the Song. Loretz suggests that one
should begin with questions which result from an encounter with
the text rather than questions concerning the canonicity or the
spiritual inspiration of the Song. In so doing, one will not
become side-tracked by dogmatic considerations which can enter
into the exegetical process.[11]

Loretz's admonition to take seriously the literal meaning
of the text applies also to the so-called "parabolic" interpretation held by D. Buzy. Whereas allegorical interpretation demands a *precise* correspondence between a variety of details, a
parable aims only at a general correspondence. The Song, for
Buzy, develops the relationship between a new Israel and Yahweh
(particularly meaningful in Israel after the period of the exile) in terms of human marriage--a picture developed from prophetic imagery (Jer 2:2 and Isa 62:4).[12] Likewise, H. Schneider,
although not directly referring to *une tradition d'exégèse
parabolique*, interprets the Song as an ancient collection of
marriage and celebration songs which, when taken together, have
a religious purpose "so to create a *new Israel*, pure and holy,
dependent upon God alone in true love."[13] So for both Buzy and

Schneider, the Song takes on a different meaning within the context of the post-exilic community: a parable of the restored
relationship between Yahweh and Israel.

2. The numerous archaeological discoveries in the ancient
Near East in the first third of the Twentieth Century contri-
buted to knowledge regarding fertility cults and the ritual of
the *hieros gamos*. In Kuhl's *Arbeitsbericht* of 1937, the possible relationships between fertility ritual and the Song of
Songs were so noteworthy that Kuhl was led to report that the
cult-mythological interpretation should be the beginning point
of all future work on the Song.[14]

Building on the earlier work of Mowinckel, Wittekindt, and
Meek, several recent scholars have developed the cult-mythological interpretation. Haller hypothesized that the Song is a
festive hymn for a fertility celebration and should, therefore,
be seen as having reference to the gods of the fertility cycle:
the Canaanite Baal-Astarte; the Babylonian Tammuz-Ishtar; or
even the Egyptian Osiris-Isis.[15] Haller sees a reference to
the moon-goddess in Cant 1:5: one who is "dark but still shin-
ing." Likewise, Haller notes that Cant 6:10 provides us with
"the clearest piece of cultic mythology in the Song of Songs":
a reference to Nergal in the difficult word כַּנִּדְגָּלוֹת.[16]

Widengren has emphasized the contact between the Song and
divine kingship in the ancient Near East. The Song illustrates
the activity of the king in the cultic celebration of sacred
marriage and serves as a ritual text of such a celebration.[17]
Following Widengren is H. Ringgren who holds that the Song can
hardly be understood as anything but a collection of songs for
use in the sacred marriage. When taken literally, the Song
speaks of the intercourse between a divine bride and a royal
bridegroom taking place in the spring (therefore, excluding a
possible connection with the feast of booths, notes Ringgren) as
an equivalent to a New Year's festival.[18] As proof of the existence of cult-mythological ritual in Israel, Ringgren points
to the prophetic and Deuteronomic admonitions against such
activity. As time passed, these rites became popular custom
and their original cult-mythological meaning was lost. The Song
was then reinterpreted allegorically and was accepted into the
canon.[19]

H. Schmökel, in his *Heilige Hochzeit und Hohes Lied*, presents one of the most complete analyses of the cult-mythological
interpretation of the Song.[20] After a description of the Tammuz-Ishtar ritual of fertility, Schmökel notes that Tammuz was
known in Syria-Palestine and such knowledge is reflected in the
Bible (explicitly in Ezek 8:14 and indirectly in Isa 17:10; Hos
6:2; Jer 22:18, etc.,). The Song of Songs is a "textbook" for
the celebration of sacred marriage in Israel. The ritual is
divided and arranged into three scenes and has four speakers:
a male choir, female choir, priest, and priestess. The work is
a unity and the poetry exemplifies an artistic quality in spite
of the fact that the original order of the Song has allegedly
been disturbed.[21]

Because Schmökel's thesis requires a dramatic carving up
of the present order of the text to fit an hypothesized schema
reflecting the *hieros gamos* liturgy, his text analysis is somewhat suspect. Can one see evidence for such unharmonic and obscure metamorphosis taking place in the text of the Song as
Schmökel alleges? Equally unacceptable is Schmökel's attempt to
disprove the natural, literal meaning of the Song. He contends
that natural love poetry is not genuine in Israel and is not reflected in the Song of Songs for the following two reasons:
1) the close association of the role of the man (as king) with
that of Tammuz in the fertility cult, and 2) the judgment that
the woman, who often retains the initiative in love-making,
accurately parallels the role of Ishtar. The woman's role as
the initiator of love, however, is not limited to fertility
rites. The initiatory role of the woman in Egyptian love poetry
makes this fact clear. Moreover, one would expect Israel to
develop natural love poetry as did her Egyptian and Mesopotamian
neighbors.[22]

Most recently, the work of S. N. Kramer has developed the
cult-mythological interpretation of the Song. Like some earlier
scholars, namely T. J. Meek, Kramer has analyzed a variety of
ancient Near Eastern ritual love texts and has concluded that
these serve as "forerunners" to the Song of Songs.[23] Thus, the
lover in the Song is designated as both shepherd and king because these are epithets of Tammuz-Dummuzi. The woman is called
both "bride" and "sister," each designation to be found in

Sumerian love texts describing the priestess. Just as the dia-
logues in the Song are often interrupted by chorus-like refrains, so also is chorus-like material found in the ritual of
sacred marriage.[24]

For those scholars who adhere to the cult-mythological interpretation of the Song, at least two major difficulties must
be faced. First of all, the so-called literary parallels between the Song and the literature of the sacred marriage rite
are very general ones. For example, Kramer notes a "literary
parallel" between Cant 4:11 (see 5:1) and a Sumerian text entitled "The Honeyman." The coincidence of the word "honey" in
both texts seems to justify a literary parallel for Kramer. One
cannot, however, see any other element in the Sumerian text to
support a literary dependence or commonality of genre, structure, life-setting, etc. In the Mesopotamian texts, moreover,
there is a central emphasis upon the causal relationship between fertility and the natural cycle of vegetation--a theme
which is absent in the Song. Whereas the Song is characterized
by delicate imagery of sense and sound with the possibility of
a subtle level of *double entendre*, the sacred marriage texts are
quite explicit in their descriptions of sexuality.

Secondly, a cult-mythological interpretation of the Song
presupposes that the "institution" of sacred marriage would have
found an acceptable life-setting within the Israelite community.
Although the prophetic and Deuteronomic admonitions against sacred prostitution may point to its practice in Israel
(Schmökel), it is difficult to believe that sacred marriage
could have been deeply rooted in Israel to the extent that a
part of the ritual could have achieved inclusion into the Hebrew
canon.

3. A growing number of scholars have adopted the so-called
naturalistic interpretation which views the primary intention
of the Song as dealing with human sexual love.

The setting of a marriage rite and the more general wedding
milieu provides several scholars with a background for understanding the meaning of the Song. In the earlier part of this
century, K. Budde popularized the view of J. G. Wetzstein that
the Song bears similarities to modern Syrian wedding poetry.[25]
Budde, therefore, held that the Song was sung in the context of
a wedding celebration and that its imagery reflects the time

period of the week of celebration, the crowning of the bridal
pair, the singing of descriptive songs (*waṣfs*) in their honor,
and the performance of the bride's sword dance.[26] Due to the
lack of knowledge regarding *ancient* marriage customs, the particular elements of the recent Palestinian wedding rites are
held to be, by most commentators, immaterial to an interpretation of the Song. Yet, the position that human marriage is reflected in the Song is held by many recent commentators.

E. Würthwein, for example, posits that the primary setting
of the Song is marriage and that a majority of the units in the
Song speak of various aspects of an Israelite wedding. The dialogue of the poem is said to represent the mutual affirmation
and esteem of the bride and groom.[27] Likewise, A. M. Dubarle
notes that the meaning of the Song cannot be totally separated
from the marriage ceremony, for the atmosphere is festive, celebrating the personal love experiences of youth. For Dubarle,
this celebration of human love is sacred, thereby reflecting
God's sanction of human sexual love between a man and woman.[28]
A similar view is taken by H. H. Rowley who notes that the Song
deserved a place in the canon because of "the essential sacred-
ness of pure human love."[29]

J.-P. Audet understands the Song as an exchange of declarations of love and fidelity between a fiancé and his fiancée.
Audet remarks that the Song may be understood as the literary
embodiment of the declarations known as "the voice of the bridegroom and the voice of the bride" (see Jer 7:32-34; 25:10; and
33:10). The Song is not, therefore, a mere glorification of
human love nor a group of wedding songs; rather it reflects expressions of reciprocal love and trust that each partner has
for the other.[30] M. H. Segal has noted that the Song is unclear
whether or not the love between the man and woman has been consummated.[31] Although certain passages might support Audet's
premise of an engaged couple (e.g., in 4:12, the allusion to
"an enclosed garden" could be construed as a reference to the
woman's virginity), others, note Segal, allude to the consummation of the relationship (e.g., 4:16-5:1). At any rate, Segal
is quick to point out that the lovers' affair is "undoubtedly a
lawful love to be sanctioned by marriage."[32]

O. Eissfeldt has moved away from interpreting the Song
strictly within the context of marriage. Although he notes that
one may assume some of the songs were composed for wedding fes-
tivities (perhaps similar to those described originally by
Wetzstein), he contends that other songs seem to have no reference to marriage, even in the broadest sense (including engage-
ment). These poems express the desire of a man and woman for
each other and their longing for sexual union. To strictly con-
fine the meaning of the Song within the framework of a marriage
celebration, according to Eissfeldt, would be to fail to consider the Song's affirmation that love is a powerful force to be
extolled.[33]

W. Rudolph has also moved away from the classical position
of Budde and notes that the *majority* of the individual songs
have no reference to the marriage context. Consequently, these
songs celebrate human love without reference to a specific occasion and go so far as to suggest what Rudolph calls a context
of "*freie Liebe*."[34] Like Eissfeldt, however, Rudolph is cautious regarding the elimination of wedding references in the
Song. The unit 3:1-6, for example, is classified by Rudolph as
"the wedding procession" (*Der Hochzeitszug*).[35] Whereas one must
take note of the Song's display of openness and sensuous portrayal of the man-woman relationship, Rudolph also emphasizes
the reinterpretation of the Song which took place in the process
of canonization.[36] The emphasis upon "free love" could no longer stand, given the religious instruction of Israel (see Prov
31:3; Sir 9:5,8; Exod 22:16; and Deut 22:28-29).

For G. Gerleman, the Song consists of bold and outspoken
lyrics which extol the enjoyment of love and the praise of sensual beauty. Gerleman rejects attempts to moralize the poems
of the Song for they speak of a pleasurable attraction between
man and woman which at times may be highly erotic.[37] Using the
model of ancient Egyptian love lyrics, Gerleman denies that the
meaning of the Song is somehow related to marriage, even in
those cases where the text seems to allude to marriage. The
mention of "bride" in the Song (e.g., 4:9-11; 4:12-5:1) is not
to be an allusion to a wedding context, for, according to Gerleman, the word is but a synonym for the word "sister" (note the
parallelism in 4:9-11 of the words אחתי and כלה).[38]

While Gerleman's emphasis upon the Song's exclusive meaning apart from a marriage context provides an important balance
to other studies (Budde, Audet, Würthwein, etc.), which may
overemphasize the setting of marriage without textual foundation
or may moralize on the meaning of the Song, he may have over-
stated his case. In his exclusion of the marriage context altogether as an important backdrop for the Song, Gerleman has discerned a "secular," highly erotic character to individual units.
Although the Israelite social ethos did not exclude eroticism,
the social morality did exclude adultery and emphasized the ne-
cessity of virginity before marriage (see above, p. 26).[39]
While many of the individual songs may not demand the setting
of marriage or the wedding ritual, the Song does speak of the
mutuality and exclusiveness of the love relationship: "My lover
belongs to me and I to him" (Cant 2:16 and 6:3). The Song must
be interpreted in light of the Israelite social ethos and cannot, therefore, be understood as a tract justifying pre-marital
sexual intercourse.

A dramatic *reinterpretation* of the Song at the time of canonization from "free love" to a wedding context (Rudolph and
others) is somewhat suspect given the same demands of Israelite
morality. Would these songs have been preserved to the point of
canonization if they reflected unacceptable behavior on the part
of a man and woman? It is unlikely. J.-P. Audet has emphasized the role of the postexilic sages in the preservation of
the Song of Songs. Audet posits that the sages have left their
stamp upon the Song in Cant 8:6b-7, an addition which offers a
general comment on the value of love and its great power. These
sages, says Audet, recognized the Song as a betrothal song de-
serving preservation because of the lesson of mutual love and
faithfulness which was described.[40]

Recently, R. E. Murphy has developed Audet's insight into
the Song's preservation by the sages and has noted the following "...the sages understood the Song in the perspective of the
wisdom literature which was taking on such importance in the
postexilic period."[41] The ascription of the Song to Solomon is
understandable, then, given the sages' role in preserving the
love songs. The interest of the sages in the totality of nature
as well as human life is in the background of the sages' interest in the sexual relationship between a man and a woman.

Moreover, given the wonder of the wise men in "the way of a man with a maiden" (Prov 30:19), one may propose that the Song extols human sexual love--"the experience of it, its delights, its fidelity, and its power."[42]

It would be an exaggerated claim to hold that the naturalistic interpretation exhausts the meaning of the Song. The history of interpretation of Canticles points out that, in both Jewish and Christian communities, the book found various levels of meaning.[43]

STRUCTURE

The following two positions regarding the structure of the Song can be clearly defined in recent scholarship: 1) the Song is a *unity* of several short poems within the eight chapters or 2) the Song is a collection or anthology of disparate poems which possess little (if any) unity. Both positions have aspects which are beset with difficulties. Moreover, among those scholars who see unity, there is no unanimous agreement regarding criteria for understanding the Song as a literary whole. Likewise, for those who view the Song as a collection of short peoms, there is no agreement as to the number or demarcation of the songs in a loose unity.

Often scholars who propose a unity of construction base their conclusions on a "logical" analysis of the Song itself. Robert has noted that the Song is a book of "*cinq poèmes en progression constante*." There develops within the Song a movement of scenes picturing Israel's historical relationship with Yahweh. The literal sense provides the reader with the allegory of Yahweh and his people in five scenes along with a title, prologue, denouement, and conclusion which bind the work into a unity.[44] The scenes correspond to exile, the consolation of the message of II Isaiah, the return to Zion, etc.

Other scholars see development within the Song based upon a logical progression of human love, culminating in the fulfillment of love between a man and woman. Segal proposes three main parts to the Song based upon theme (although he warns that logical sequence is not often apparent) dividing the Song into the following: 1) 1:2-8, love has not yet "developed as a mutual passion"; 2) 1:9-8:6, "the celebration of mutual love"; and

TABLE 1

THE REFRAINS OF THE SONG OF SONGS

	1	2	3	4	5	6	7	8
A. Daughters of Jerusalem	1:5a	2:7a (=C)	3:5 (=C)		5:8b, 16d			8:4b (=C)
B. Embracing		2:6						8:3
C. Adjuration		2:7	3:5					8:4
D. Mutual Possession		2:16				6:3	7:11	
E. "To the Mountain"		2:17		4:6				
F. Eating/ Drinking					5:1 e-f			
G. "Like a Gazelle"		2:9 a-b (=E)						8:14
H. Mountain/ Hill				4:6 (=E)				

3) 8:6-14, concluding stanzas related to part two.[45] Yet, for the most part, theme is augmented by a number of duplications and repetitions scattered in various parts of the Song which aid in organization. These salient features give the Song not only the appearance of unity but also an artistic quality.[46] Among the elements which are often repeated are the following: 1) phrases (e.g., "come with me from Lebanon," 4:8; or "you whom my soul loves," 1:7; 3:1, 2, 3, 4); 2) themes (Lebanon, spices, wine, etc.); 3) situations (separation, admiration, searching, etc.); and 4) refrains. The refrains may best be seen in Table 1 (adopted from O. Loretz, *Das althebräische Liebeslied*, 60).

These elements of repetition aid scholars in discerning
"patterns" which may be inherent within the Song. These patterns may be hidden because of the Song's *aspetto frazionato*--
episodes which are unique and do not seem to fall naturally together. C. Carniti notes that the Song does indeed appear to
be a fragmented story, but with the aid of recurring motifs,
one is able to discern what Carniti calls "*un unico motivo in-
spiratore*."[47] Buzy had earlier noted that the unity of the
Song should be based not only upon the action and progression
of thought but also upon the "repetition of themes." The two
most important themes for Buzy are the lovers' description of
admiration (see the adjuration in 2:7; 3:5; and 8:4) and their
mutual possession (2:16; 6:3; and 7:11).[48]

Recently, J. Angénieux has sought to move away from the
formal criterion of basing structural analysis upon the sense
of the Song (noting that one could have as many structural analyses as interpretations!) to basing his analysis only upon the
form of the Song itself. Angénieux's methodological principles
are, therefore, somewhat rigid. He establishes the following
five principles for structural division: 1) initial and final
refrains; 2) circumstances of time and place; initial and final
themes; 4) distinctive themes; and 5) secondary refrains. Angénieux's emphasis in his research and his central categories
are *les refrains principaux* (embracing [2:6; 8:3]; mutual possession [2:16; 6:3; 7:11]; movement [2:17; 4:6]; and adjuration
[2:7; 3:5; 8:4]) and *les refrains secondaires* (the house [1:4;
2:4; 3:4; 8:2]; beauty [1:15; 4:1; 4:7; 7:7]; and a variety of
other short "refrains").[49]

Angénieux has coordinated his five principles with the present text of the Song and has achieved what he terms as "*texte
primitif reconstitué*."[50] Unfortunately, Angénieux's reconsitu-
tion of the text is very hypothetical and the imposition of his
rigid form analysis upon the present text has distorted it beyond recognition. The "refrains" are given more stress than
they should be; therefore, the reconstituted text lacks the
movement and flow of the Song. Moreover, Angénieux has been too
rigid in his designation of "refrain." Many of the secondary
refrains appear to be mere repetitions of words and phrases
(e.g., "O daughters of Jerusalem" [1:5; 5:8; etc.]; the "refrain"

of the watchmen [3:3; 5:7]; or the desert [3:6; 8:5]). Repeated words and phrases are not able to bear the weight of
being sophisticated structural principles.

J. C. Exum finds helpful two aspects of Angénieux's work
in her own structural analysis of the Song: 1) "the use of form
as a guide to meaning" and 2) "the establishment of methodological principles for the poetic division of the Song."[51] Exum
proposes a less rigid methodology than Angénieux and, therefore,
has greater respect for the integrity of the text. She seeks
to isolate poetic units, examine form and style of these units,
and seek parallels among the poems in order to support her contention of a unity of authorship and a high quality of poetic
style. Yet, unlike Angénieux, her criteria are not limited to
an analysis of the refrains, but include the occurrence of key
words, phrases, and motifs as well as "the contextual coherence
of the poems."[52]

Exum concludes from her analysis that the Song's structure
is that of a "ring composition," i.e., poems closely connected
with one another by means of catchwords and inclusio. Positing
that the Song is a unity of six poems, Exum notes that the first
poem (1:2-2:6) and the last (8:4-14) form an inclusio within
which the other poems occur. This contention is based primarily
upon the repetition of certain key terms such as כרם ("vineyard"); נטרים ("keepers"); שלמה ("Solomon"); etc., (see 1:5-6
and 8:11-13).

Although her analysis respects the text and underscores the
variety of poetic elements in the text (e.g., repetition, paronomasia, chiasmus, etc.), one must contend that neither Exum nor
Angénieux has been able to develop a significant pattern to the
variety of repetitions and refrains. The reason may well be
that these elements *do not* yield a significant pattern of orga-
nizing the discontinuous, fragmented Song. The use of "vineyard" as a formal inclusio for the entire Song seems question-
able. Is it not possible to see the vineyard references in 1:7
and 8:11-12 as examples of an often repeated image which occurs
throughout the poem (cf. 7:12; 2:15)?

In her attempt to find elements of unity in the poem, Exum
has on occasion failed to recognize what appear to be individual
units, discontinuous with what follows or precedes them. Canticles 3:6-11 is an example. Exum contends that 3:6-11 is

connected with the verses which follow (4:1-7) because of the
image of the *gibbôrîm* "who surrounded the litter of Solomon in
3:7 hang their shields upon the tower to which her neck is compared."[53]   This argument is simply not convincing.   Exum appears
to be contriving a unity between portions of material where
none exists.

Both Angénieux and Exum assume some relationship between
structure and meaning.   While few would doubt the existence or
importance of *double entendre* in the Song, Exum makes reference
to "the erotic level" of the Song in the context of discussing
structural analysis.   For example, while one would agree that
5:2-6:3 is a complex literary unit (perhaps even a secondary
composition),[54] Exum introduces the interpretation that the
unit speaks of a progression toward sexual intercourse--and argues this from the structure of the poem.   She notices a growing development of "ordered divisions" characterized by words
such as "sleeping," "arose," and "open"--the latter having sexual overtones.   From this progression of terms, she argues the
following: "The form of the story reflects the physical act it
describes.   When the climax is reached the pattern is broken."[55]
The question arises: Does the *structure* of this poem tell us
that intercourse is the proper interpretation?   One must be
cautious regarding the relationship between structure and meaning, lest one say that the structure of a given unit demands
that one read that unit with a given interpretation.

A growing number of scholars have proposed that a unified
picture of the Song cannot be gleaned from the internal evidence,
and these scholars propose that the Song is a collection or
anthology of units which have been brought together.   Eissfeldt
has noted that the principles of arrangement are difficult to
discern and notes that the order of the individual units "seems
to be based on catchwords."[56]   Rudolph follows Eissfeldt and
notes that "in most cases the bare *Stichwort* arrangement has
been the leading principle in the inter-relation of the songs."[57]
Most recent commentators have adopted this view that the Song's
units are loosely connected by catchwords (Loretz, Würthwein,
Gerleman).

One question which arises among these scholars is the problem regarding the number of units contained in the Song.   There

is no consensus (Gordis, 28; Gerleman, 32; Würthwein, 30; Eissfeldt, 25; Loretz, 30; etc.). What should be avoided, however,
is the radical atomization of the Song into very small units, a
thesis of F. Landsberger.[58] Such a proliferation of units makes
the text too fragmented for practical analysis. For example,
the series 4:12-5:1, usually taken to be a unit by most commentators (so Würthwein, Rudolph, Gerleman, and Loretz), is sub-
divided into four separate units by Landsberger. The significance of the "garden theme" pervading these verses (4:12, 15,
16, and 5:1) and the use of the catchword גן are items which
Landsberger does not develop.

The Song of Songs is characterized by the diversity of its
units. Seeing the Song as an anthology best explains the variety of geographical references[59] and linguistic characteristics[60] since the individual units in an anthology may come from
more than one provenance, from different periods of time, and
possess both archaic and later literary characteristics. Although there is diversity among the units and it is, therefore,
difficult to see the collection having unity of authorship
(against Rowley), one cannot deny that the internal, textual
evidence and thematic considerations point to some homogeneity.
In various stages of the preservation of the Song, the number of
repetitions evidence some effort to unify the poem.

Finally, mention should be made of the attempts to understand the Song as a drama. Two forms of the dramatic interpretation have enjoyed popularity. The first, presented in the
work of F. Delitzsch, sees two main characters, Solomon and a
Shulammite shepherd girl. Solomon falls in love with her and
takes her to be his bride in Jerusalem.[61] The second, developed
by Ewald and Pouget-Guitton, sees more complex action with Solomon and a rustic lover vying for the attention of the girl.[62]
Delitzsch notes that the Song falls neatly into six acts with
two scenes in each act. Pouget-Guitton, on the other hand, develop a drama around twelve scenes of dialogue between the Shulammite, the Beloved, his companions, Solomon, and the Daughters
of Jerusalem.

The utilization of the drama form to structure the Song has
not been advanced in recent decades for a variety of reasons:
1) drama as a literary form does not appear to have been known

in Israel; 2) the Song provides no stage directions; and 3)
there is no real conflict or catharsis in the Song. One may
most accurately say that the Song does have a quality of dramatic dialogue, but it is not of dramatic genre.

The dialogue character of the Song has long been recognized
and Codex *Sinaiticus* (400 A.D.) supplies the terms "bride" and
"bridegroom" to aid the reader in following the discourse in the
poem. Yet, as one reads the Song, he becomes quite aware of
one of the main difficulties--knowing who the speaker is! Certain passages are particularly ambiguous in this regard. Note,
for example, 1:2-4 (the change of person from first singular to
first plural) and 1:7-8; 2:7; 2:15; 3:4; 3:6-11; etc., (the
problem of designating the speaker). These problems of translation make the dramatic presentations suspect, for in some
passages there can be no universal agreement on the speaker.

TEXT

The question of the dating of the material within the Song
arises logically after a discussion of structure. Because the
problem of ascertaining a date to the material is intricately
involved with textual considerations, it seems appropriate to
address questions which arise out of recent scholarly research
in the area of textual criticism. This section will first seek
the *status quaestionis* regarding the dating of the Song. Secondly, it will analyze the recent work on the Song by Ugaritic
literature. Finally, a series of textual emendations will be
suggested in order to demonstrate the present state of textual
criticism on the Song and this writer's approach to various
textual problems.

1. One of the strongest arguments for the Song's characterization as an anthology of love lyrics stems from an analysis
of the text wherein commentators have discerned bits of evidence
which may reflect both late and early dating. The consensus of
recent opinion has neither endorsed Gerleman's proposal of an
early date in the period of the so-called Enlightenment under
the United Monarchy (tenth century)[63] nor accepted the opinion
of G. Fohrer who strongly endorses an unambiguous postexilic
date for the *entire* Song.[64] Most commentators (Eissfeldt, Gordis, Rudolph, Würthwein, etc.) conclude that, although a

postexilic date should be proposed for the *collection* of the
Song, some love songs may be substantially older. The internal
evidence is quite ambiguous.

One of the difficulties in dating the material is shown,
for example, in an argument often used for the conclusion that
the Song (or parts of the Song) is late: the presence of Aramaisms. Eissfeldt notes that the Song contains a whole series
of Aramaisms which is a strong indicator for later material.
Among those words which scholars have noted as having Aramaic
tendencies in either form or meaning are the following: חרכים
(2:9); כתל (2:9; סתו (2:11); סמדר (2:13, 15; 7:13); פג (2:13);
מנף (5:3); סנסנים (7:9); and סרוגה (7:3).[65] These Aramaisms are
joined with several words which are often classified as "late"
Hebrew (e.g., שש in 5:15 [see Esth 1:6 and 1 Chr 29:2]) and by
the relative particle ש to provide cumulative evidence in what
appears to be a strong case for the existence of a late flavor
in the Song.

W. F. Albright has shown, however, that caution should be
used in the evaluation of Aramaisms and has underscored by example what was already generally recognized--that Aramaic characteristics in a given word may not mean that the word is necessarily a late construction. The word סמדר, attested in the Song
and in other Aramaic dialects, has been discovered on a sherd
from eighth century Hazor.[66] Likewise, the relative particle
ש, usually regarded as an example of late Hebrew morphology, is
attested in such early biblical material as Gen 6:3; Jud 5:7; 6:17;
and 2 Kgs 6:11.[67] Many scholars have concluded that the presence of ש in these early texts is inconsequential because of its
alleged presence in glosses or in places of textual uncertainty.[68] Yet, the particle's occurrence cannot be easily dismissed
from earlier texts, given recent research in comparative Semitic
morphology and the recognition of a relative particle š in
Phoenician, akin to the Akkadian relative form ša.[69] Consequently, the presence of ש in a text cannot automatically signal its
late character, even though the preponderance of occurrences are
to be found in texts usually considered postexilic (i.e., Qoheleth, Ezra, certain Psalms, etc.). Nevertheless, given the existence of the particle in Northwest Semitic vocabulary and
given the continuing dialogue among scholars concerning the
significance of Ugaritic linguistics for the study of Biblical

Hebrew, one should be cautious and conclude that the use of שֶׁ
in the Song as well as the presence of alleged Aramaisms should
not be taken *singularly* as evidence of late material in the
Song.

Further evidence for the existence of late material in the
Song, however, comes from the presence of loanwords. Most commentators refer to the loanword פרדס (4:13) as a Persian word
which cannot antedate the sixth century. Krinetzki recognizes
two other Persian loanwords: נרד (1:12) and אגוז (6:11).[70]
Scholarly discussion still continues regarding the problem word
אפריון (3:9). Gordis has proposed that the word derives from
the Sanskrit *paryanka*, meaning "sedan, palanquin."[71] Widengren
has suggested that אפריון is a Persian word originally coming
from *upari-yana*, and this derivation is supported by Albright
and Koehler-Baumgartner.[72] Most recent commentators, however,
have followed the lead of their earlier counterparts and have
designated אפריון as a Greek loanword, from φορεῖον, "sedan
chair."[73] Such a derivation is given strong support in an
article by F. Rundgren who provides a cogent linguistic argument for the Greek origins of the word.[74] Indeed, the word appears to be a transcription into Hebrew of the Greek with the
addition of a prosthetic aleph.

If one supports the existence of a Greek loanword in the
Song, certainly a very late date is assumed for the final collection (perhaps as late as the third century). Rudolph wishes
to see the collection process taking place around 500, while
the Song became "modernized" over the course of the next few
centuries. This modernizing resulted in a growing number of
Armaisms in the text as well as loanwords like אפריון, a
"*modisches Prunkwort*" which may have replaced a Hebrew word in
later editing and transmission.[75] Rudolph's thesis of modern-
ization is not improbable; yet, one can say with some certainty
that the evidence of loanwords plus Aramaisms demands that the
Song reached its final, collected, and edited form perhaps as
late as the latter part of the fourth or sometime during the
third century.

2. The recent research in the area of Ugaritic studies is
now having an impact on scholarly discussion on the Song. Since
much of the Ugaritic work has been published within the last

decade, many recent commentaries on the Song either have not
had much of this material at their disposal or have not had
adequate time to evaluate its significance. A notable exception is O. Loretz's recent work on the Song, *Das althebräische
Liebeslied* (1971).[76]

In the dialogue between the Ugaritologists and Old Testament scholars, the Song of Songs has not been, thus far, a major
source for discussion. Nonetheless, a plethora of lexicographical and morphological notes have appeared which claim to support translations based upon Ugaritic parallels to Biblical Hebrew. M. Dahood and W. F. Albright have been major proponents
of the utilization of the alleged advances of Ugaritic phonol-
ogy, lexicography, and morphology to enlighten and, in some
cases, correct traditional interpretations and translations of
the Song. Below we shall note some of the recent proposals of
various scholars. Major sources for such textual discussion are
Dahood's notations published in *Biblica* and L. Fisher's edition
of *Ras Shamra Parallels* (Vol. I), the second part of which is
the work of Dahood.[77]

One contribution of Northwest Semitic philology is the
evidence provided for grammatical forms which were known in
Biblical Hebrew, but were not well attested. Among these forms
is the asseverative *kî*, recognized by Gesenius as occurring in
only isolated instances. Albright has asserted that an emphatic nuance to *kî* is a more common feature to Biblical Hebrew
than previously noticed.[78] Both Albright and Schoville have
noticed the presence of the asseverative *kî* in Cant 1:2, in
which the following phrase appears: כִּי טוֹבִים דֹּדֶיךָ מִיָּיִן ("Surely
your love is better than wine"). Schoville also notes the occurrence of the particle in 1:7b; 7:1; and 8:1.[79]

Likewise, Gesenius mentions the shaphel conjugation as one
of the "less common conjugations" in Biblical Hebrew.[80] In
Ugaritic texts, however, the š causative form is well represented as Gordon notes in the following: "The Š is the regular conj.
for expressing the causative [in Ugaritic]."[81] The š causative
form is attested in Akkadian, in South Arabian dialects, and
even in Egyptian. Dahood has argued for the existence of two
forms in the Song which are derived from the shaphel conjugation.
First, in 1:6, Dahood argues that the MT שֶׁזֵּפַתְנִי does not come

from the Aramaic שְׁדַף (thus, Hebrew שָׁזַף, meaning "to scorch"),
but he suggests that the form is a shaphel perfect of a denomin-
ative verb form from זֶפֶת ("pitch"). He, therefore, proposes
that the line be read, "that the sun has made me black as
pitch."[82] Secondly, Dahood, following Gesenius, notes in 8:6
that שַׁלְהֶבֶתְיָה reflects the shaphel conjugation, coming from the
root לחב.[83]

K. Schoville has pointed out a variety of other grammatical
elements which the study of Northwest Semitic languages has
underscored in connection with the Song of Songs. The emphatic
(pleonastic) waw (2:15; 6:9; 7:9), the lack of interrogative
particles (3:3), and the presence of a prosthetic aleph (8:10)
are grammatical features known from Biblical Hebrew and their
alleged presence in the Song is, therefore, not surprising.[84]

Other grammatical features which scholars know now exist
in Hebrew were not identified until the development of Ugaritic
studies. An example is enclitic mem. Schoville identifies five
occurrences of enclitic mem in the Song, two of which seem to
have some foundation. In 4:15, מַעְיַן גַּנִּים usually translates "a
garden fountain." *Biblia Hebraica*[3] suggests that one read "my
garden" but does not explain the reason for the deletion of the
mem.[85] Schoville proposes that one read as follows: מַעְיַן גַּנִּי-ם
("the fountain of my garden") with the mem understood as enclitic.[86] This reading is quite plausible for it does not require
the deletion of the mem. Moreover, גַּנִּי appears in a following
colon and forms a key-word repetition within a given unit of
material. The removal of the mem would take away from the alliteration of the line.[87] Another possible example is in 8:13,
חֲבֵרִים מַקְשִׁיבִים. Once again there is no reason to delete the mem
for its employment here adds alliteration.

Unfortunately, Schoville has not utilized the type of caution which is demanded when using the insights of Ugaritic pho-
nology. He is incorrect in his identification of enclitic mems
in 2:15 (מְחַבְּלִי-ם); 5:12 (אֲפִיקֵי-ם יָם instead of MT אֲפִיקֵי מָיִם,
based on analogy with Ps 18:16 and 2 Sam 22:16 and derivation
from Canaanite mythology); and in the textually corrupt verse
7:10.[88] In this last instance, the danger involved in a hypothetical interpretation of the text stands out clearly. Schoville recognizes in this verse examples of the Phoenician third

person singular -*y* suffix (e.g., לְדוֹדִי "for *its* lover").[89] Although certain examples of this suffix ending *may* be present in
Biblical Hebrew, Schoville's argument does not support such a
reading in this verse. His evidence is centered around what he
sees to be a demand for the third person suffix in the verse.
On the contrary, there is no *demand* for the suffix pronoun -*y* to
have כְּרָיִן as its antecedent. Moreover, in this context, parallelism with the following cola demands that לְדוֹדִי be first person singular (note לְדוֹדִי in verse 11 which follows).

To maintain harmony with the alleged -*y* third person singular ending in 7:10, Schoville finds it necessary to emend other
portions of v. 10. He proposes that MT שִׂפְתֵי וְשֵׁנִים have a closer
semantic connection with the preceding portions of the line.
Thus, the reading שִׂפְתֵי שָׁנִי-ם is proposed, "which is obtained by
deleting one of the yodhs after שׂפם as a copyist's reduplication
and reading a repointed וְשֵׁנִים as the adjective שָׁנִי, 'red, scarlet,' followed by an enclitic mem."[90] Schoville's verse 10
would then read as follows:

> And your kiss as the sweetest wine flowing for its
> lover;
> Even smooth liquor gliding o'er scarlet lips.

Not only would שָׁנִי-ם serve adjectivally, but Schoville also pos-
tulates a possible double-duty suffix (third person -*y*) to pro-
duce an alternative reading: "o'er his scarlet lips."[91] This
reading is imaginative but unlikely.

Likewise, Dahood's revocalization of 8:6 is unnecessary.
He proposes that a third person -*y* suffix be noted in the word
רֹשׁפִי. Moreover, this third person suffix is shared by the following word אֵשׁ based on the use of the double-duty suffix. Dahood, therefore, reads: "A divine spark is its spark, its fire
a divine flame."[92] The MT reading, however, would appear to
preserve a closer word-play on רֶשֶׁף: "Its flashes are flashes
of fire--a mighty flame."

If the insights of Ugaritic grammar possess some degree of
ambiguity regarding their value for the study of the Song of
Songs, one soon discovers that an analysis of the word parallels
between Hebrew and Ugaritic are equally ambiguous in their relative importance for translating the Song. In Table 2 is a
partial list of word parallels which have been collected in
Fisher's *Ras Shamra Parallels*.

TABLE 2*

PARALLEL PAIRS IN UGARITIC AND THE SONG

UGARITIC	HEBREW	CANTICLES	UT	FISHER
ṭb//ṭb	טוב//טוב	1:2-3	1084:1-2, etc.	II 203d
yn//šmn	שמן//יין	1:2-3; 4:10	126 III:15-16	II 249d
dd//ahbt	אהבה/דוד	1:4; 5:8	ᶜnt III:2-4	II 152e
šmḫ//gl	שמח + גיל	1:4	125:14-15	II 549h
krm//krm	כרם//כרם	1:6; 2:15; 8:11	1081:5-6, etc.	II 306d
ik//ik	איכה/איכה	1:7; 5:3	49 VI: 24-26; 51 II:21-23	II 22e
bt//ᶜrš	ערש//בית	1:16-17	Krt: 96-98	II 134f
tp//nᶜm	נעם//טף	1:16; 7:7	RS 22. 225:2	II 594f
ymn//smal	שמאל//ימין	2:6	137:40	II 240k
ᶜl/ᶜl	על//על	2:8	52:14-15	II 418d
lbnn + ᶜg̣	לבנון + ...	3:9	51 VI:18, 20	II 327f
yn//nbt	...	4:10-11	Krt: 71-72	II 246d
yn//šmn	שמן//יין	4:10	126 III:15-16	II 249d

TABLE 2 (continued)

UGARITIC	HEBREW	CANTICLES	UT	FISHER
špt//lšn	לָשׁוֹן//שָׂפָה	4:11	67 II:2-3	II 579f
kl//kl	לְכֹל//כֹל	4:14	49 II:15-16	II 283d
yn...škr	שֵׁכָר...יַיִן	5:1	601:3-4, 16	II 248g
lbš//ktnt	לְבוּשׁ...כֻּתֹּנֶת	5:3	2101:16-18	II 330e
yd//uṣbᶜt	אֶצְבַּע//יָד	5:5	68:13-14, etc.	II 213e
yd//špt	יָד//שָׂפָה	5:13-14	124:4	II 220f
ibnn..arṣ	אֶרֶץ//לְבָנוֹן	5:15	51 VI:18-19	II 326f
an//an	אָנָה//אָן	6:1	49 IV: 46-47	II 49e
km//k	כְּמוֹ//כְּ	6:10	51 IV:51, etc.	II 288f
brky//ᶜn	בְּרֵכָה + עַיִן	7:5	67 I:16-17	II 123f
bt//tǵr	שַׁעַר + בַּת	7:5	1007:5-6	II 137j
mgdl//ḥmt	מִגְדָּל//חוֹמָה	8:10	Krt:74-75	II 343f

Because both Hebrew and Ugaritic poetry are characterized
by parallelism and since *parallelismus membrorum* is sustained
by the existence of paired words, one would expect the use of
certain "stereotyped expressions" to be common to both languages given their classification as Northwest Semitic. While
one should be cautious about using the designation "fixed
pairs," i.e., stock phrases with a locked-in sequence, one
would be surprised *not* to find certain "parallel pairs" in existence within a common linguistic milieu.[93] The question
arises, however, regarding the extent to which "parallels" between two languages affect a literary dependence of one language upon another, i.e., in terms of source, locale, and data
for dating material.

From the list in Table 2, one may note that many "parallel
pairs" are the repetition of the same words in the two languages. Given the close association of the languages in terms
of lexicography and poetic structure (parallelism), the pairing
of words such as *kl//kl* in Hebrew and Ugaritic is a far too
general literary feature to be helpful in evaluating the question of "parallel pairs" and a literary dependence (note also
krm, $^c l$, *an*, etc., and their Hebrew counterparts). There are,
of course, other words that appear in parallel constructions
which are not identical in form and meaning. Yet, upon a close
inspection, one notices that the majority of these parallel
items are words whose meanings are closely related and are
often synonymous. One may again note that synonymous word association is to be expected between closely related languages,
and such a feature cannot demand a literary dependence between
the Ugaritic literature and the Song (see e.g., יין "wine"//
שמן "oil" [cf., Amos 6:6; Ps 104:15]; גיל "to be glad"//שׂמח "to
rejoice" [cf., Isa 25:9; Joel 2:21, 23, etc.]; and יד "hand"//
אצבע "fingers, arm" [cf., Isa 2:8; 17:8; Ps 144:11]). What is
needed for discussion is a "parallel pair" in which the words
are neither closely related in terms of meaning nor synonymous.

One of the "parallel pairs" which is mentioned by Fisher
does appear to be apt for discussion. Note the parallel pair
bt//^{c}rs in *Krt*: 96-98:

yḥd bth sgr	As for an only son, he closes his *house*,
almnt škr tškr	as for the widow, she surely hires,
zbl ^{c}ršm yšu	as for the invalid, he carries the *bed*.

One of two parallels with the Ugaritic pair occurs in Cant 1:16-17 (the other in Ps 132:3):

אַף-עַרְשֵׂנוּ רַעֲנָנָה   Even our *couch* is green,
קֹרוֹת בָּתֵּינוּ אֲרָזִים   the beams of our *house* are cedars.

The context of the parallels is quite different. In the *Krt* epic, a description of panic before an invasion is pictured; whereas in the Song, a scene describing the rustic trysting place of the lovers is portrayed. Because the elements of this pair are not closely related, given the radically different contexts, one may propose that the parallelism between these particular words may not be merely coincidental. Despite the occurrence of this striking parallelism, it cannot singularly bear the weight of a thesis claiming the Song's literary dependence on the Ugaritic literature.

The parallels which have been collected in Fisher's volume should be used with the utmost care. Although they are very helpful in pointing out pairs of closely associated words that occur in related languages, some of the "parallel pairs" are suspicious. For example, in Cant 7:5 שֵׂעָר is allegedly parallel to בת, based on a similar occurrence in Ugaritic texts (*bt// tǵr*). Although the Hebrew consonantal text (בת) is paralleled with the Ugaritic *bt* ("house"), the MT reads בַּת, "daughter." To recognize parallel *meaning*, one must repoint the consonantal text. Is there, however, justification? The MT should be read in this instance as a place name "Bathrabbim." Another occurrence of this alleged parallel is Ps 122:1-2. However, there appears to be reason to question whether or not בֵּית and בִּשְׁעָרַיִךְ are nouns in a strict parallel relation.

In certain instances, the Song has benefited from Ugaritic lexicography. For example, there is plausibility to Albright's and Dahood's translation of Ugaritic *ṭb* (UT 1084:1-3) as "sweet," in a context dealing with the word "wine." Thus Albright's translation for Cant 1:2, "for your love is sweeter than wine" makes use of Ugaritic data and enlightens a possible meaning for the word in the Song.[94]

On the other hand, the Ugaritic root *pḫd* (2 *Aqht* V:17, 22-23) has been taken to mean from context "flock." Albright has connected the Ugaritic root with the Hebrew פחד, extracting a meaning "kinsman" (note the reference in *RSP* III 99f).[95]

Dahood concurs, but proposes in certain Psalms (14:5; 64:2; 91:5) the meaning "pack (of dogs)."[96] This same meaning he applies to his understanding of Cant 3:8, מִפַּחַד בַּלֵּילוֹת. The translation "against a pack (of dogs) in the night" seems farfetched and unwarranted in this context. The more traditional meaning of פחד, "danger," should be retained.[97]

In a review of R. E. Murphy's *Seven Books of Wisdom*, Dahood contended that the Ras Shamra texts would take exception to the prevailing opinion that Egyptian literature provides the most important influence on the Song of Songs. In the Ugaritic literature thus far published, Dahood's conclusion has proven unfounded. Although there are numerous parallel pairs shared by the Song and the Ugaritic corpus of literature, these pairs are so general in nature that they cannot bear the burden of an argument that the Song of Songs is literarily dependent on Canaanite material. Northwest Semitic philology and lexicography are important in any attempt to translate and interpret the Song (and any portion of the Old Testament for that matter) but there is no cumulative evidence to support a systematic trend of "archaic style" (against Albright). Moreover, there is no evidence to support the associated hypothesis that an archaic trait within a certain unit of material in the Song suggests a Northern provenance.

3. Although there are numerous hapaxlegomena which provide an occasional uncertain reading, the text of the Song of Songs does not require the numerous emendations proposed by F. Horst in *BHK*.[98] The function of this section is to suggest a minimal number of proposals for textual emendation and revocalization which seem appropriate in achieving an accurate reading of the text. These recommendations appear below accompanied by brief evaluative arguments.

1:7d   MT: כְּעֹטְיָה   "as one veiled"
        Read: כְּטֹעֲיָה   "as one who wanders"

The MT reading appears to have suffered metathesis of the consonants ט/ע. From context, the roots עטה I., "to wrap oneself, to cover oneself" or עטה II., "to delouse" (Jer 43:12; cf. *NEB*) seem inappropriate. One should read the Qal feminine participle of the root טעה. In accepting such an emendation, one follows the witness of the following versions: Symmachus, the Syriac, and Vulgate (note the Syriac ‏ܐܟ‎).[99]

1:12   MT: בְּמְסַבּוֹ   "at his (round) table"
      Read: בִּמְסִבַּי   "round about me"

The MT reading, בְּמְסַבּוֹ, is a substantive form of the verb סבב. The meaning of the word is usually taken to be "round table," "banquet," or "circle of feasters." A revocalization of this word, however, preserves greater assonance within the following cola (viz., the words רַעְיָתִי; דּוֹדִי לִי; נִרְדִּי; etc.). Such a revocalization is proposed by Rudolph and is followed by Würthwein.[100]

1:17   MT (Ketib):   רָחִיטֵינוּ
      Read (Qere):   רַהִיטֵנוּ   "our rafters"

3:10   MT: אהבה
      Read: אהבה-ם   "leather"

This word is particularly problematic. Any connotation of "love" is unlikely. Most commentators follow *BHK's* proposed emendation of הָבְנִים, "ivory' (the mem coming from the initial consonant of the following word). The aleph preformative of the MT reading, however, goes unexplained. Hence, despite an explanation of the mem as an error in word division, the emendation to הָבְנִים is difficult to explain orthographically and does not offer an explanation of how MT became corrupt. Instead of resorting to textual emendation, one may explain the MT reading by referring to G. R. Driver's proposal that Hebrew אַהֲבָה is related to Ugaritic *ahbt*, thus having the connotation "leather."[101] Driver's recommendation has been included in the most recent edition of Köhler-Baumgartner as a second meaning for אַהֲבָה. This study proposes that one translate "leather" because such a meaning fits the context and because of the attestation of the word in Northwest Semitic lexicography. The problematic mem should be understood as enclitic (other solutions have not proved convincing).[102]

4:8   MT: אִתִּי   "with me"...   אִתִּי   "with me"
      Read: אֵתִי   "come"...   אֵתִי   "come"

Revocalization is necssary here to maintain a proper parallelism with תָּשׁוּרִי (understood as a verb). One should, then,

46

read with the LXX, Old Latin, the Syriac, and Vulgate. There
is no need to emend the verb חָשׁוּרִי to תָּשׁוּרִי as does Haller
(and Horst, *BHK*).[103]

4:12   MT: גַּל

     Read: גַּן   "garden"

Most commentators emend the text to גַּן noting scribal error caused by the presence of ל in the preceding and following
words.[104] Recent discovery of the word *gl*, "cup, bowl" in
Ugaritic texts provides Dahood no justification for his proposal that "the standard emendation of Cant. 4:12...is no longer
convincing."[105]

5:13   MT: כַּעֲרוּגַת   "as a bed"
              מִגְדְּלוֹת   "towers"
     Read: כַּעֲרוּגוֹת   "as beds"
              מְבַדְּלוֹת   "raising"

First of all, to maintain plural agreement, one should revocalize כַּעֲרוּגַת to agree with לְחָיָו, "cheeks" (see 6:2 for the
use of the plural construct). Secondly, to enhance the parallelism with the verbal form נֹטְפוֹת, one should revocalize
מִגְדְּלוֹת to מְבַדְּלוֹת, a Piel, feminine, plural, participle. In
adopting such a vocalic change, one reads with the witness of
LXX, Old Latin, Vulgate, and Targums.

6:12   MT: שָׂמַתְנִי מַרְכְּבוֹת עַמִּי נָדִיב
     Read: שָׂמַתְנִי מְבֹרֶכֶת עַמִּי נָדִיב

This verse is perhaps the most obscure in the Song and no
effective solution has been proposed by commentators. Rudolph's redivision of consonants, emendation, and revocalization only add to the obscurity of the verse. Gerleman and
Krinetzki follow the versions and read "Amminadab" for MT
עַמִּי נָדִיב.[106] Loretz follows another well-known idea and con-
siders the verse a gloss to be deleted.[107]

מַרְכְּבוֹת should be emended to מְבֹרֶכֶת (note the *NAB*, "the
blessed one"). MT has become corrupt due to metathesis. The
emendation should be vocalized as a Pual, feminine, singular,
participle. One may be justified in emending עמי נדיב in light
of בת־נדיב in 7:2 (see, e.g., *BHK*). If this emendation is
accepted, however, it becomes unclear how the text became

corrupt with the word עַמִי. Unfortunately, the identity of
עַמִּי נָדִיב remains obscure.

7:5b Read with MT: עֵינַיִךְ בְּרֵכוֹת   "your eyes are as pools"
      Read with MT: אַהֲבָה בַּתַּעֲנוּגִים   "O love, daughter of
                                               delights"

In each of these examples, emendations have been proposed
due to haplography in the text. In the first instance, a reading כִּבְרֵכוֹת could be justified because a kaph has allegedly
dropped out of the text due to the close proximity of the kaph
in the preceding word עֵינַיִךְ. Likewise, in 7:7b, a taw may have
dropped out of the line. The restored line would then read as
follows, אַהֲבָה בַּת תַּעֲנוּגִים (compare the Syriac حبا ف بت).
In each of these instances, however, the Song illustrates
the characteristic of a "shared consonant." This feature of
Northwest Semitic orthography is a frequent occurrence in
Ugaritic and has been recognized in Hebrew.[108] By recognizing
this feature, there is no need for textual emendation, for the
kaph in 7:5b and the taw in 7:7b perform double-duty functions.

7:10 MT: שִׂפְתֵי יְשֵׁנִים   "the lips of sleepers"
      Read: בְּשִׂפְתַים וְשִׁנַּים   "over the lips and teeth"

The MT reading is improbable given the context of the
poem. A proposed reading with LXX, Aquila, the Syriac, and
Vulgate seems cogent. The ב is deleted from MT because of haplography (note the preceding word, דּוֹבֵב). In reading the plural absolute, בְּשִׂפְתַים, one must also propose that mem likewise
dropped out of MT (note the final mem in יְשֵׁנִים). Commentators
differ on the particular aspects of this emendation. Würthwein
follows the above emendation, while Krinetzki and Rudolph propose בְּשִׂפְתַי וְשִׁנַּי, "over my lips and teeth."[109] It is difficult
to explain, however, the deletion of the mem if one accepts the
reading of Rudolph and Krinetzki.

8:5c-e MT: יְלָדָתְךָ; אִמֶּךָ; חִבְּלַתְךָ; עוֹרַרְתִּיךָ
        Read: יְלָדָתֵךְ; אִמֵּךְ; חִבְּלַתֵךְ; עוֹרַרְתִּיךְ

The revocalization of these words is necessitated by the
context of the unit. The man is speaking about the woman;
therefore, second person singular *feminine* suffixes are demanded
rather than second person masculine endings as in MT.

THE POETIC QUALITY OF THE SONG

Krinetzki's commentary is unique among recent studies on the Song insofar as his extensive work with the poetic-literary form is concerned. Relating his work to that of other scholars (viz., Alonso-Schökel), Krinetzki seeks to analyze the individual, unique elements of the Song's poetic structure, emphasizing characteristics of metric structure, parallelism, strophic construction, and the varieties of linguistic characteristics.[110]

In such a presentation, Krinetzki has augmented the more general task of form criticism by emphasizing the unique features of the various units in the Song. In many ways, then, Krinetzki's realization of the need for poetic analysis and for the evaluation of individual literary characteristics is a forerunner to the recent discussions in form-critical circles regarding the limits and scope of that discipline.[111]

While Krinetzki recognizes several metric patterns (3+2; 3+2+2; and 3+3) and a variety of types of parallelism, a main contribution in the analysis of the Song's poetic-literary form is in the area of the *sprachliche Formen* of the Song. He is quick to point out and exemplify the musical quality of the lines and a central feature: *rhyme*. For Krinetzki, rhyming consists of similarities of sound between two or more words. Normally these words have common features such as construction in a series or commonality of theme.[112] For example, one may note the following instances of rhyming words:

(2:7) בְּנוֹת - בִּצְבָאוֹת - בְּאַיְלוֹת

(2:14) הַשְׁמִיעִינִי - הַרְאִינִי

(7:12c, 13a) בַּכְּפָרִים - לַכְּרָמִים

Krinetzki notes several types of rhyme. *Alliteration* is a form of rhyming based on the similarity of consonantal sounds. Among the examples in the Song, one may note the following:

(1:4c) נַזְכִּירָה - וְנִשְׂמְחָה - נָגִילָה

(4:5a) כִּשְׁנֵי - שָׁדַיִךְ - שְׁנֵי

Assonance is the rhyming of vocalic sounds. The following may be noted:

(5:1e,f) אָכְלוּ - שָׁתוּ - וְשִׁכְרוּ

(6:12a,b) שָׂמַתְנִי - נַפְשִׁי - לֹא יָדַעְתִּי

Onomatopoeia is the vocal imitation of the sound suggested by a given word. Although this poetic quality is often difficult to recognize, the following two examples suggested by Krinetzki seem particularly interesting.

[the sound of kissing] יִשָּׁקֵנִי מִנְּשִׁיקוֹת (1:2a)
[the sound of knocking] קוֹל דּוֹדִי דוֹפֵק (5:2b)

Not only does the oral aspect of the Song reflect the importance of a study of poetic quality and characteristics, but the variety of rhetorical devices which one finds in the Song reflects this as well. The Song of Songs often uses paronomasia (word-play) as one such rhetorical device (see 2:7; 7:1; 7:14; 1:3, etc.). The use of hyperbole in comparisons is a frequent poetic device (see 1:4; 1:8, etc.). The variety of flora and fauna, spices, elements of nature, and geographical place names provides the Song with material for a plethora of metaphors which, for Krinetzki, refer to the *direct* identification between two items (e.g., 1:3 [name is oil]; 1:13-14 [lover is a sachet of myrrh]; and 4:12 [bride, sister is an enclosed garden]).[113] Likewise, the Song contains many similes which, according to Krinetzki's terminology, are more "intellectual" than simple metaphors, that is a subject is compared to an object and such a comparison presents a particular characteristic of the subject (e.g., 1:2b [love is like wine, costly]; 4:1 [hair is like a flock of goats, black and flowing]; and 6:4c [bride is like bannered troops, majestic]).[114]

Krinetzki's analysis of the poetry of the Song includes a host of other considerations: symbolic words, contrasts, items in a series, chiastic constructions, rhetorical questions, etc. Although his analysis of literary terms and features is at times unclear (e.g., the "complex" structure of the simile versus the "simple" structure of the metaphor), his work with the Song's typical features is an important prelude to wider classifications of literary genre into which the individual and poetically unique units of the Song may be placed.

GENRE

When discussing structure, the conclusion was reached that the Song of Songs is a collection of individual love songs.

Yet, the disignation "love song" is descriptive of a very general category of material, akin to "psalm." "Love song" is not
a classification of genre.

In 1935, F. Horst published a classic work on the literary
forms in the Song, "Die Formen des althebräischen Liebesliedes."[115] Recent commentators have not gone far beyond the
classifications of genre developed by Horst. In the Song he
discovered the following literary genres: song of admiration
(*Bewunderungslied*); self-description (*Selbstschilderung*); the
tease (*Scherzgespräch*); song of yearning (*Sehnsuchtslied*); the
description of a love-related experience (*Erlebnisschilderung*);
the descriptive song or *waṣf* (*Beschreibungslied*); the boasting
song (*Prahllied*); and comparisons and allegory (*Vergleiche und
Allegorien*).

The songs of admiration, like the other genre designations
of Horst, rely largely upon content analysis to distinguish
their distinctive characteristics. This genre is usually concerned with the adornment of the individual (clothing, decora-
tions, etc.) instead of the physical attributes of a person
(characteristics of the descriptive song).[116] An example of a
song of admiration is Cant 1:9-11 in which the man compares his
beloved with the extravagant finery of a royal steed. The beloved is described as adorned with fine jewels and spangles,
riches which he associates with Egyptian chariotry. In 4:9-11,
the man is captured by the sight of but one bead of his love's
necklace. Yet, as if that were not enough, the fragrance of
the beloved herself and the scent of her garments are especially delightful to the man. A second aspect of the songs of admiration, however, concerns the "effect" that the admiration
has upon the admirer. In 7:9, after a description of the delights of the woman in which comparisons are made to a stately
palm tree, the man longs to "climb" the tree and take hold of
its "branches." Likewise, in 1:15-17 the admiration that the
lovers express for one another in dialogue culminates in a
description of their trysting place where their mutual love
might be consummated.

The descriptive song (Arabic *waṣf*) usually gives a detailed picture of the physical features of the man or woman.
This genre, as has been shown by W. Hermann, has a long history

in the ancient Near East, being present in Mesopotamian mythological texts (associated with goddesses), in Egyptian love
lyrics which were detached from religion (detached in that they
were not associated with divine liturgy), and in Israel.[117]
The genre also makes an appearance in the Qumran material (the
description of Sarah in the Genesis Apocryphon, IQ IV, 20:2-8).
Horst discerns four instances of the genre in the Song of Songs:
4:1-7; 6:4a, 5b-7; 5:10-16; and 7:1-6. It is interesting to
note that the descriptions frequently display an order of portrayal (e.g., in 4:1-7, the description is from the top down
[facial features, neck, breasts]; in 7:1-6, the thighs are described first, then breasts, and facial features).

The comparisons that are made in the descriptive songs are
often foreign to the modern ear ("teeth like a flock of ewes,"
for example) or the elements of the comparison may escape the
modern ken ("eyes like the pools in Hesebon" or "nose like the
tower on Lebanon"). The occurrence of such remote and, for the
modern reader, bizarre comparisons has led R. N. Soulen to argue in favor of seeing the various descriptions as "lyrical
imagery" which is "to overwhelm and delight the hearer, just as
the suitor is overwhelmed and delighted in her [his] presence."[118] The comparisons are not intended, then, to convey
reality (i.e., representation) but are meant to convey the delight of the one who beholds (i.e., presentation). R. E.
Murphy has correctly questioned this interpretation, for, as he
notes, if one accepts Soulen's hypothesis, then "*any* pleasurable comparison [in a descriptive song] would do; on this premise the teeth could be just as easily compared to pomegranate
halves (v. 3, cheeks) as to the washed lambs (v. 2)."[119] However foreign the comparisons may be to a modern interpreter,
the *waṣf* should be viewed as an attempt to describe the beauty
of a man or woman, using comparative elements which would best
highlight a given feature. Such a description would also present the subjective feelings and delight of the suitor.

The genre of self-description in the Song of Songs is spoken only by the woman (1:5-6 and 8:8-10).[120] In both instances,
the self-description arises out of situations in which the woman must justify her physical features or defend herself. In
1:5-6, she defends herself to the daughters of Jerusalem saying

that her darkness is due to her work in the open vineyards
(she is dark, but lovely). In 8:8-10, the woman justifies her
independence to her brothers by affirming her physical attributes ("my breasts are like towers"). Another example of self-
description appears in the Song. In 2:1, the woman describes
herself as "a flower of Sharon, a lily of the valley." This
verse is part of a larger unit, 2:1-3, which is characterized
by a mixing of genres. Her self-description in 2:1 appears to
affect his *admiration* of her in 2:2. The unit is a dialogue
in which the woman describes herself and the man responds to
her description with his own admiration. In 2:3, to conclude
the unit, the woman responds to the man's admiration with her
own admiration of his unique delights (he is an apple tree
among the trees of the forest). Although Horst's genre designations are meaningful in this unit, it is necessary to sharpen
and refine his original work, for he does not recognize 2:1 as
a self-description.

W. Staerk, in his commentary written at the beginning of
this century, recognized a "teasing song" (*Scherzlied*) in Canticles. Such a song, he assumed, had its roots in the general
celebration of marriage in the ancient world.[121] Horst, following Staerk, describes the tease in 1:7-8 as a familiar theme
in love literature. In the Song, the man and woman engage in a
light dialogue in which she inquires concerning his whereabouts.
He responds (not his companions [Krinetzki] or the poet [Gerle-
man]) with an answer that Horst interprets as joshing--follow
your instincts![122] The tease, however, seems to cover up a
more serious theme which underlies the dialogue. In this instance, that theme is presence: the need of the woman for the
presence of the man. One may propose that tease-like passages
appear in other parts of the Song also. In the unit 2:14-15,
v. 15 is a coquettish response on the part of the woman to a
request by the man for her presence. Horst recognizes this
verse as allegory (foxes are suitors) and he may be correct;
yet, the verse is certainly curious and possesses the "underlying" theme of seeking and finding one's love partner. One
may also ponder the teasing manner in which the girl responds
to the man's address at her door in 5:3.

The song of yearning usually mirrors the *desire* of the
lovers to share in one another's presence. In 1:2-4, the woman

longs for the kisses of her lover. In 8:6, the woman is asking
for the presence of her lover over a period of time ("Set me as
a seal..."). Horst also recognizes songs of yearning in 2:4-5
and 2:10-13. In these last two instances, Horst's designations
must be refined. Based on a variety of considerations, one may
wish to see these passages as parts of larger units, viz., 2:4-
7 and 2:8-13, respectively.[123] When redefining the units, a
reconsideration of genre designations is also necessary. In
2:4-7, the theme appears to be the love-sickness of the woman
("for I am faint with love"). Although the woman yearns to be
with her lover, the song seems to hinge on the woman's feelings
without her love (faint) and with her love (sustained). The
unit, 2:8-13, is a complex one which seems to blend two of
Horst's forms--a song of yearning (the so-called "spring song"
in 2:10b-13) and a description of an experience (*Erlebnisschilderung*) in 2:8-9. The unit might well be termed "a spring
song" in which the man invites the woman to go with him.[124]
Horst cites another example of the *Erlebnisschilderung* in 5:2-
6, as the woman describes what Horst refers to as a dream experience ("I was sleeping, but my heart kept vigil," 5:2a).

Horst designates two units in the Song as "boasting
songs": 6:8-9 and 8:11-12.[125] Each of these units boasts of
the *uniqueness* of the woman (6:9a, "one alone is my dove, my
perfect one" and 8:11bc, "for its fruit one would have to pay
a thousand silver pieces"). Würthwein wishes to give 6:8-10 a
more precise designation, *Das Preislied* (song of praise).[126]
Such a classification may well arise out of the content of the
unit in which the women of the harem (verse 9) sing the praises
of the beloved (וַיְהַלְלוּהָ). Horst limits the boasting song to
6:8-9 (v. 10 is a song of admiration for him), while most recent commentators include verse 10 in the unit as the song of
praise about the woman sung by the women in the harem.[127]

Horst's final designation of genre for Old Testament love
songs is "comparisons and allegories."[128] These terms have not
been as helpful and, therefore, have not been utilized by recent commentators to the extent that Horst's other classifications have been. A "comparison" reflects an independent rhetorical device within a given genre rather than a specific form
itself. The term "comparison" is so general and its use in the
Song so widespread (see the comparisons in the songs of

admiration and descriptive songs) that it cannot serve as a
useful nomenclature for genre. Horst recognizes 1:13-14 as a
comparison. This unit should be more accurately designated as
1:12-14 and should be understood as a song of admiration in
which the woman is describing the scent of the man. Horst
notes 2:15 as an example of allegory. Again the question must
be raised whether or not this precise term refers to genre or
to a rhetorical device (with Krinetzki).

Content serves as a chief criterion for the determination
of genre; yet strong support for Horst's classifications of
genre have come from ancient Egyptian love poetry which contains
strikingly similar themes (topoi). Rudolph, Würthwein, and
most extensively, Gerleman have made use of a variety of Egyptian parallels to the Song. While Gerleman's contention that
the Egyptian influence is so thorough that the poet of the
Song of Songs had actual figures of Egyptian sculpture and bas
relief in mind as he explained the imagery of the descriptive
songs is exaggerated, the Egyptian love corpus is a valuable
aid in the study of the Song. The style, language, and literary genres of the Song participate in the world of love-language popular in the ancient world. If a genre is a typical
unit of human expression, then one would expect to find examples of a given genre in extra-biblical material. The corpus
of love poetry for the New Kingdom in Egypt provides a wealth
of material which typifies the atmosphere and language of love
found in the Song. The chapters which follow in this work will
investigate the salient features of the Egyptian love lyrics in
order to see how the Song of Songs participates in terms of
themes, style, and literary genre in the common milieu of love
expression.

The designations of genre in the Song of Songs lead one to
a consideration of the poetic character of the book. Rudolph
has recently championed the view that the various songs exemplify a *Volkspoesie* whose origins are to be found in the
general community. The consensus recently, however, favors
the view that the songs reflect a *Kunstdichtung*--an artistic
style which incorporates the variety of symbolism, repetitions,
rhetorical devices, etc. These literary characteristics would
point to a high poetic, artistic level of development for the

Song (Schmökel, Würthwein, Fohrer, Angénieux, Exum, Krinetzki).
Gerleman has emphasized the high quality of the Song because of
its parallels with the sophisticated Egyptian love lyrics. According to most commentators, an educated class would be presupposed in the construction and the preservation of this poetry.
Yet, there is a problem in determining the poetic character of
the Song. The internal evidence of the Song does not provide
an interpreter with an accurate way of distinguishing between
the established categories of "popular" and "artistic" poetry.
Therefore, such characterizations of the poetry of the Song
are neither descriptive nor helpful to the interpreter.

THE SETTING OF THE BOOK: שִׁיר הַשִּׁירִים אֲשֶׁר לִשְׁלֹמֹה

In part, the question of the original life setting for the
songs in Canticles has been addressed in the context of the
naturalistic meaning (see above, pp. 24-28). One may suspect
a variety of original settings within the sphere of the love
relationship between a man and woman. The Song passed through
various stages of development, both oral (with the possibility
of early written collections) and written. In the final stage
of development, the songs were edited into a book with the ascription "The Song of Songs by Solomon" (1:1). This final collection of material and title provide a key to ascertaining another life setting--one for the entire work.

The attribution of the Song of Songs to Solomon (note the
lamed *auctoris*, GKC §129c) suggests that the title may be based
upon Solomon's renown as a composer of songs in ancient Israel
(1 Kgs 5:12 mentions 1,005 songs which he composed) or as a
lover par excellence (1 Kgs 11:3 mentions his many wives and
harem). The editorial title is not unlike that in Prov 1:1,
מִשְׁלֵי שְׁלֹמֹה. Just as the proverbial collection was ascribed to
the patron of wisdom, so were the love songs ascribed to the
patron of love whose name is repeated in 1:5; 3:7-11; and 8:11-
12. The designation שִׁיר, like the repetition of Solomon's name,
provides a loose structure of unity to the collection.

The ascription to Solomon may denote the locale of the
Song's preservation: in the wisdom circles of Israel. Audet
has correctly noted that the Song was preserved by the postexilic sages who saw the function or intention of the collection

within their sphere of interests.[129]   The Song, to the sages,
was instructive of the mutuality of the human love relationship (see above, p. 25).   The setting of the book, then, is
didactic.   This setting reflects a *Nachleben* for the songs
whose original setting was in the love experience itself.

What is the title of the Song?   Audet has proposed that
the actual title may not be "The Song of Songs by Solomon."
This title, perhaps, is an "appreciative" one, given to the
Song by an editor who expressed his opinion of the collection,
"This is Solomon's best song!".   The original title, notes
Audet, *may* be found in the incipit, "let him kiss me with the
kisses of his mouth."   This line has been a difficult one to
explain due to the tendency of many translators to change pronominal suffixes to harmonize the line with the following
lines.   Audet notes that this is unnecessary if one assumes
that the line is an incipit, a short introductory phrase which
often, in ancient literature, begins a composition (note, e.g.,
Loretz's listing of incipits found in KAR 158).[130]   Audet would
assume that the title of the Song in its "pre-literary" period
would be something like "A Kissing Song for the Betrothed."[131]
Such titles are not foreign to the Egyptian love songs (see
below pp. 127-28).

[1]See for example the analysis of Curt Kuhl, "Das Hohelied und seine Deutung," *TRu* 9 (1937) 137-67. Kuhl's outline has been followed by recent surveys of current opinion regarding the Song including the following: D. Lerch, "Zur Geschichte der Auslegung des Hohenliedes," *ZTK* 54 (1957) 257-77; Edouard Cothenet, "L'interprétation du Cantique des Cantiques," *AmiCl* 73 (1963) 529-40, 545-52; and Ernst Würthwein, "Zum Verständnis des Hohenliedes," *TRu* 32 (1967) 177-212.

[2]Augustin Bea, *Canticum Canticorum Salomonis* (Rome: Pontifical Biblical Institute, 1953). André Robert, Raymond Tournay, and André Feuillet, *Le Cantique des Cantiques* (Paris: Gabalda, 1963).

[3]Robert et al., *Cantique*, 65. Cf. André Feuillet, "Note sur la Traduction de Jer XXXI, 3c," *VT* 12 (1962) 122-24.

[4]André Robert, *Le Cantique des Cantiques* (*SBJ*; 2d ed.; Paris: Les Editions du Cerf, 1958); "Le genre littéraire du Cantique des Cantiques," *RB* 52 (1943-44) 192-213; "La description de l'Epoux et de l'Epouse dans Cant. V, 11-15 et VII, 2-6," in *Mélanges É. Podechard* (Lyon: Facultés Catholiques, 1945) 211-23; and "Les appendices du Cantique des Cantiques," *RB* 55 (1948) 161-83. See also André Feuillet, *Le Cantique des Cantiques* (Paris: Les Editions du Cerf, 1953); "La formule d'appartenance mutuelle (2,16) et les interprétations divergentes du Cantique des Cantiques," *RB* 68 (1961) 321-53; and "Einige scheinbare Widersprüche des Hohenliedes," *BZ* 8 (1964) 216-39. Most recently, see Raymond Tournay, "Abraham et le Cantique des Cantiques," *VT* 25 (1975) 547-52.

[5]See André M. Dubarle, "L'amour humain dans le Cantique des Cantiques," *RB* 61 (1954) 67-86 and "Le Cantique des Cantiques dans l'exégèse récente," in *Aux grands carrefours de la Révélation et de l'exégèse de l'ancien Testament* (RechBib 8; Paris: Desclée de Brouwer, 1967) 139-52.

[6]Jean-Paul Audet, "Le sens du Cantique des Cantiques," *RB* 62 (1955) esp. pp. 201-202 where Audet points out that the prophetic interpretation of the Song speaks against the traditional interpretation which ascribed the Song to Solomon. See also Audet's "Love and Marriage in the Old Testament," trans. F. Burke, *Scr* 10 (1958) 65-83 (esp. pp. 79-81).

[7]Roland E. Murphy, "Recent Literature on the Canticle of Canticles," *CBQ* 16 (1954) 6.

[8]Johann Fischer, *Das Hohe Lied* (Würzburg: Echter-Verlag, 1950) 7.

[9]Leo Krinetzki, *Das Hohe Lied* (Düsseldorf: Patmos-Verlag, 1964) 39-40. But cf. Krinetzki's "'Retractationes' zu früheren Arbeiten über das Hohe Lied," *Bib* 52 (1971) 178, in which he notes his "overestimation" of the "higher sense" of the Song.

[10]M. A. van den Oudenrijn, *Het Hooglied* (Roermond: Romen & Zonen, 1962) 10-11.

[11]See Oswald Loretz, "Die theologische Bedeutung des Hohenliedes," *BZ* 10 (1966) 31-32. Also see Loretz's "Zum Problem des Eros im Hohenlied," *BZ* 8 (1964) 191-216.

[12]Denis Buzy, *Le Cantique des Cantiques* (Paris: Letouzey et Ané, 1949) 24. Roland E. Murphy seeks to differentiate parable and allegory by stating the following: "A parable differs from an allegory in that the words retain their proper meaning, but from them taken as a whole, a different meaning is adduced," *CBQ* 11 (1949) 381. Murphy warns that one not reduce the parabolic interpretation of the Song to the so-called "typical sense," as does, for example, Giuseppe Ricciotti, *Il Cantico dei Cantici* (Torino: Societa Editrice Internazionale, 1928) 62-63.

[13]Heinrich Schneider, *Die Heilige Schrift*, Bd. 7/1 (Freiburg: Herder, 1962) 264.

[14]Kuhl, "Hohelied," 166. Kuhl's work provides a bibliography of the pioneering work done in the area of cult-mythology and its relation to the Song.

[15]Max Haller, *Die Fünf Megilloth* (HAT 18; Tübingen: J.C.B. Mohr, 1940) 21-22. The Song's later entrance into the canon was based upon an allegorizing along the lines of Hosea 1-3 and Ezek 16 and 23 (p. 22). The oversimplified identification of Tammuz with other ancient Near Eastern fertility deities is critiqued by E. Yamauchi, "Tammuz and the Bible," *JBL* 84 (1965) 283-90.

[16]Haller, *Die Fünf Megilloth*, 40-41 and 27.

[17]Georg Widengren, *Sakrales Königtum im Alten Testament und im Judentum* (Stuttgart: Kohlhammer Verlag, 1955) 78-79.

[18]Helmer Ringgren, Artur Weiser, and Walther Zimmerli, *Prediger, Das Hohe Lied, Klagelieder, Das Buch Esther* (ATD 16; Göttingen: Vandenhoeck & Ruprecht, 1962) 59-60.

[19]Ibid.; see also Ringgren's *Israelite Religion* (trans. David E. Green; Philadelphia: Fortress, 1966) 197-98.

[20]Hartmut Schmökel, *Heilige Hochzeit und Hohes Lied* (AKM 32/1; Wiesbaden: Franz Steiner, 1956). See also Schmökel's "Zur kultischen Deutung des Hohenliedes," *ZAW* 64 (1952) 148-55.

[21]Schmökel, *Heilige*, 42-43.

[22]Ibid., 119. The existence of naturalistic love poetry in Israel would be expected based upon its presence even in Assyro-Babylonian texts (against Schmökel). See the texts published by Moshe Held, "A Faithful Lover in an Old Babylonian Dialogue," *JCS* 15 (1961) 1-21; 16 (1962) 37-39; Jerrold S. Cooper, "New Cuneiform Parallels to the Song of Songs," *JBL* 90 (1971) 157-62; and the incipits of KAR 158 in O. Loretz, "Zum Problem des Eros," 196-201.

[23]See Samuel N. Kramer, *The Sacred Marriage Rite* (Bloomington: Indiana University, 1969) esp. chap. 5. See also Kramer's "The Biblical Song of Songs and the Sumerian Love Songs," *Ex* 5 (1962) 25-31; and "The Sacred Marriage: A Panoramic View of the Sumerian Evidence," *Proceedings* of the XXVth International Congress of Orientalists 2 (1968) 28-32. The most recent work of Theophile J. Meek is his contribution to *The Interpreter's Bible*, "The Song of Songs: Introduction and Exegesis" (ed. G. A. Buttrick et al.; Nashville: Abingdon, 1956) 5. 91-148. This work is a culmination of Meek's earlier studies. See, for example, the following: "Babylonian Parallels to the Song of Songs," *JBL* 43 (1924) 245-52; "Canticles and the Tammuz Cult," *AJSL* 39 (1922-23) 1-14; and "The Song of Songs and the Fertility Cult," in *The Song of Songs: A Symposium* (ed. W. H. Schoff; Philadelphia: Commercial Museum, 1924) 48-79.

[24]Kramer, *Sacred Marriage*, 90. Kramer's works give helpful translations of Sumerian love texts. Many of these texts have been collected in Kramer's translation of "Sumerian Sacred Marriage Texts," in *The Ancient Near East: Supplementary Texts and Pictures Relating to the Old Testament* (ed. J. B. Pritchard; Princeton: Princeton University, 1969) 637-45. For other Assyro-Babylonian sacred marriage texts, see Wilfred G. Lambert, "Divine Love Lyrics from Babylon," *JSS* 4 (1959) 1-15. For further background on the ritual of sacred marriage and the characteristics of the particular deities involved, see Thorkild Jacobsen, "Mesopotamian Gods and Pantheons," in *Toward the Image of Tammuz and Other Essays on Mesopotamian History and Culture* (ed. W. L. Moran; Cambridge: Harvard University, 1970) 16-38.

[25]See Johann G. Wetzstein, "Die syrische Dreschtafel," *ZE* 5 (1873) 270-302. For another treatment of Middle Eastern marriage customs, see Stephen H. Stephan, "Modern Palestinian Parallels to the Song of Songs," *JPOS* 2 (1922) 199-278.

[26]Karl F. R. Budde, *Das Hohelied* (HSAT 2; 4th ed.; Tübingen: J.C.B. Mohr, 1923) 391.

[27]Ernst Würthwein, *Die Fünf Megilloth* (HAT 18; Tübingen: J.C.B. Mohr, 1969) 33.

[28]Dubarle, "L'amour humain," 81-82. A similar emphasis is to be found in the commentary of J. Winandy, *Le Cantique des Cantiques* (Maredsous: Casterman, 1960) 62.

[29]Harold H. Rowley, "The Interpretation of the Song of Songs," in *The Servant of the Lord* (2d ed.; Oxford: Blackwell, 1965) 244.

[30]Audet, "Le sens," 213.

[31]Morris H. Segal, "The Song of Songs," *VT* 12 (1962) 470-90.

[32]Ibid., 470.

60

[33]Otto Eissfeldt, *The Old Testament: An Introduction*
(trans. P. R. Ackroyd; New York: Harper and Row, 1965) 487-88.
Robert Gordis has developed a position similar to that of Eissfeldt. While he notes that there are some obvious wedding
parallels, he also states: "...it is clear that some of the
lyrics in the Song of Songs are not connected with wedding
ceremonies or with married love at all." See Gordis, *The Song
of Songs* (New York: Jewish Theological Seminary of America,
1954) 17.

[34]Wilhelm Rudolph, *Das Buch Ruth, Das Hohe Lied, Die
Klagelieder* (KAT 17/1-3; Gütersloh: Gerd Mohn, 1962) 103 and
105-106.

[35]Ibid., 138-39. Rudolph is followed by Loretz who notes
that Cant 3:6-11 is the only *direct* allusion to a marriage
celebration. See Oswald Loretz, *Das althebräische Liebeslied*
(AOAT 14/1; Neukirchen-Vluyn: Neukirchener Verlag, 1971) 63 and
23-25.

[36]Rudolph, *Das Hohe Lied*, 108.

[37]Gillis Gerleman, *Ruth, Das Hohelied* (BKAT 18; Neukirchen-
Vluyn: Neukirchener Verlag, 1965) 72. The claims of a marriage
context for the Song, according to Gerleman, are the result of
an imposition of a marriage-ethic upon the text (see p. 207).

[38]Ibid., 155.

[39]See, for example, Raphael Patai, *Sex and Family in the
Bible and the Middle East* (Garden City: Doubleday, 1959) 164-65.

[40]Audet, "Love and Marriage," 80-83. Würthwein is also
sympathetic to Audet's view; see *Die Fünf Megilloth*, 30-31.

[41]Roland E. Murphy, "Form-Critical Studies in the Song of
Songs," *Int* 27 (1973) 422.

[42]Ibid.

[43]For a comprehensive survey of the history of the Song's
interpretation in the medieval period, see Friedrich Ohly,
Hohelied-Studien (Wiesbaden: Franz Steiner, 1958).

[44]Robert et al., *Cantique*, 18-19.

[45]Segal, "Song of Songs," 471. See Leo Schwarz, "On
Translating the 'Song of Songs,'" *Judaism* 13 (1964) 73-74.
Donald Broadribb has likewise concluded that the Song is "a
connected poem, literarily unified." He discerns five "sub-
divisions" which break down both logically and with the internal cohesiveness of the text; see D. Broadribb, "Thoughts on
the Song of Solomon," *AbrN* 3 (1961-62) 11-36. Also cf. Daniel
Lys, *Le plus beau chant de la création* (Paris: Les Editions du
Cerf, 1968) 24.

[46]See Krinetzki, *Das Hohe Lied*, 80. Krinetzki discerns seven *Liedgruppen* in the Song.

[47]Cecilia Carniti, "L'Unita' Letteraria del Cantico dei Cantici," *BeO* 13 (1971) 106. Carniti posits seven episodes in the literary unity of the Song. Her analysis closely follows that of Gianfranco Nolli who describes eight episodes and two concluding comments; see Nolli, *Cantico dei Cantici* (SaBi; Rome: Marietti, 1968).

[48]Buzy, *Cantique des Cantiques*, 20-21.

[49]Joseph Angénieux, "Structure du Cantique des Cantiques en chants encadrés par des refrains alternants," *ETL* 41 (1965) 104-107. See also Angénieux's "Note sur les trois portraits du Cantique des Cantiques," *ETL* 42 (1966) 582-96.

[50]For Angénieux's reconstructed text, see his "Le Cantique des Cantiques en huit chants à refrains alternants," *ETL* 44 (1973) 96-107.

[51]J. Cheryl Exum, "A Literary and Structural Analysis of the Song of Songs," *ZAW* 85 (1973) 48-49.

[52]Ibid., 49.

[53]Ibid., 62.

[54]For example, see Würthwein, *Die Fünf Megilloth*, 25.

[55]Exum, "Analysis," 53.

[56]Eissfeldt, *The Old Testament*, 490. Herder in his commentary of 1776 wrote supporting the fragmentary nature of the Song. He noted that it was "a collection of pearls on a string" (quoted by Kuhl, "Hohelied," 58).

[57]Rudolph, *Das Hohe Lied*, 100.

[58]Franz Landsberger, "Poetic Units Within the Song of Songs," *JBL* 73 (1954) 203-16.

[59]See, e.g., A. González, "El lenguaje de la naturaleza en el 'Cantar de los Cantares,'" *SBE* 26 (1969) 397-433.

[60]For a summary of recent work, see below, pp. 48-49.

[61]Franz J. Delitzsch, *Commentary on the Song of Songs and Ecclesiastes* (trans. M. Easton; Edinburgh: T. & T. Clark, 1891) 8.

[62]Guillaume Pouget and J. Guitton, *The Canticle of Canticles* (trans. J. L. Lilly; n.p.: Delcom X. McMullen, 1946) 31-32.

[63]Gerleman, *Hohelied*, 76. Gerleman's thesis is based upon the contention that the Song has close connections with Egyptian love lyrics. The most advantageous time to see contact between Israel and Egypt, according to Gerleman, would be in the period of cultural exchange and growing humanism which characterized Solomon's reign. See Gerhard von Rad, *Old Testament Theology* (trans. D.M.G. Stalker; New York: Harper and Row, 1962) 1. 55. Cf. J. Audet's "pre-literary" stage of the Song which may have its origins in the monarchical period, "Love and Marriage," 79 and "Le sens," 215-16.

[64]Ernst Sellin and Georg Fohrer, *Introduction to the Old Testament* (trans. David Green; Nashville: Abingdon, 1968) 303.

[65]Quoted in Gordis, *Song of Songs*, 23 n. 78. Other lists of Aramaisms may be found in Krinetzki, *Das Hohe Lied*, 44 and in Rudolph, *Das Hohe Lied*, 111.

[66]William F. Albright, "Archaic Survivals in the Text of Canticles," in *Hebrew and Semitic Studies* (eds. D. W. Thomas and W. D. McHardy; Oxford: Clarendon, 1963) 2-3 n. 5.

[67]Cf. BDB, 979. For a complete listing of the occurrences of שׁ, see Gotthelf Bergsträsser, "Das hebräische Präfix שׁ," 29 (1909) 41.

[68]For example, Rudolph, *Das Hohe Lied*, 111 n. 4.

[69]Sabatino Moscati, ed., *An Introduction to the Comparative Grammar of the Semitic Languages* (Wiesbaden: Otto Harrassowitz, 1969) 113. Mitchell J. Dahood offers the presence of שׁ in Qoheleth as one example of a morphological influence of Phoenician on Biblical Hebrew; see Dahood, "Canaanite-Phoenician Influence in Qoheleth," *Bib* 33 (1952) 35-52 and 191-221.

[70]Krinetzki, *Das Hohe Lied*, 45. For a discussion of פרדס, see Alfred Jepsen, "Pardes," *ZDPV* 74 (1958) 65-68. Cf. J. P. Brown's discussion of the use of the word "nard" in the Song (1:12-14) as a love charm and parallels in Sanskrit in "The Mediterranean Vocabulary of the Vine," *VT* 19 (1969) 160-64.

[71]Gordis, *Song of Songs*, 21.

[72]Widengren, *Königtum*, 112. See Albright, "Archaic Survivals," 1 n. 2; and KBSup, 138.

[73]See Budde, *Das Hohelied*, 397 and Haller, *Die Fünf Megilloth*, 33. These earlier scholars are followed by Rudolph, *Das Hohe Lied*, 111; Loretz, *Liebeslied*, 24; Krinetzki, *Das Hohe Lied*, 45; and Würthwein, *Die Fünf Megilloth*, 30. Likewise, see Eissfeldt, *The Old Testament*, 490 and Sellin-Fohrer, *Introduction*, 303.

[74]Frithiof Rundgren, "אפריון 'Tragsessel, Sänfte,'" *ZAW* 74 (1962) 70-72.

[75]Rudolph, *Das Hohe Lied*, 111.

[76]See especially Loretz, *Liebeslied*, 55-56. One may look forward to forthcoming commentaries which may evaluate the Ugaritic material, viz., M. Pope in The Anchor Bible (Doubleday) and R. Murphy in Hermeneia (Fortress).

[77]See *RSP*. Specific section numbers will be utilized to refer the reader to a given citation. Section I of *RSP* consists of "Literary Phrases" compiled by Antoon Schoors; Section II, "Ugaritic-Hebrew Parallel Pairs" by M. Dahood; and Section III, "Flora, Fauna, and Minerals" by J. Sasson. Further citations will be made to numerical chapters and specific entries. The purpose of this series of volumes is to catalogue a list of possible parallels between Ugaritic literature and the Hebrew Bible. References to Ugaritic texts will utilize the enumeration of Cyrus H. Gordon in his *Ugaritic Textbook* (Rome: Pontifical Biblical Institute, 1965).

[78]Albright, "Archaic Survivals," 2 n. 3. See GKC, §159ee. J. Muilenburg has noted that כִּי developed from an original exclamatory interjection or cry; see his "The Linguistic and Rhetorical Usage of the Particle *Kî* in the Old Testament," *HUCA* 32 (1961) 135-60. See also Dahood, "Hebrew-Ugaritic Lexicography II," *Bib* 45 (1964) 287. Earlier, Gordis had recognized the value of the asseverative *kî* for Biblical Hebrew in his "The Asseverative Kaph in Ugaritic and Hebrew," *JAOS* 63 (1943) 176-78.

[79]Keith N. Schoville, "The Impact of the Ras Shamra Texts on the Study of the Song of Songs" (Ph.D. dissertation, University of Wisconsin, 1969) 48, 95, and 102. See Gordis, *Song of Songs*, 95.

[80]GKC, §55i.

[81]Gordon, *Ugaritic Textbook*, 83; see Moscati, *Comparative Grammar*, 125-26.

[82]Dahood, "Hebrew-Ugaritic Lexicography II," 406-407.

[83]Ibid., 407; GKC §55i; BDB, 529.

[84]Schoville, "Impact," 65, 68, 91, 97, and 109. See Paul Joüon, *Grammaire de l'hébreu biblique* (Rome: Pontifical Biblical Institute, 1947) §113m; Marvin H. Pope, "Pleonastic Waw Before Nouns in Ugaritic and Hebrew," *JAOS* 75 (1953) 95-98; P. Wernberg-Møller, "Pleonastic Waw in Classical Hebrew," *JSS* 3 (1958) 321-36; and Dahood, "Ugaritic Studies and the Bible," *Greg* 43 (1962) 65-66. See GKC, §150a for mention of the absence of the interrogative particles and §§19m and n for the prosthetic aleph.

[85]Friedrich Horst, "Canticum Canticorum," in *BHK* (Stuttgart: Württembergische Bibelanstalt, 1937).

[86]Schoville, "Impact," 81-82.

[87]Against Rudolph, *Das Hohe Lied*, 150; Würthwein, *Die Fünf Megilloth*, 54-55; and *BHK* who wish to delite the mem and Gerleman, *Das Hohelied*, 157, who understands גנים as a plural of generalization.

[88]Schoville, "Impact," 64, 86, and 99.

[89]For background on the third person -*y* ending, see Frank M. Cross and David N. Freedman, "The Pronominal Suffixes of the Third Person Singular in Phoenician," *JNES* 10 (1951) 228-30; M. Dahood, *Psalms I* (AB 16; Garden City: Doubleday, 1965) 10-11; and Dahood, "The Phoenician Contribution to Biblical Wisdom Literature," in *The Role of the Phoenicians in the Interaction of the Mediterranean Civilizations* (ed. W. A. Ward; Beirut: American University, 1968) 128-34.

[90]Schoville, "Impact," 99.

[91]Ibid. See below for another translation of this problematic verse, p. 47.

[92]Dahood, "The Phoenician," 134.

[93]For a discussion of "fixed pairs" employed in Ugaritic and Hebrew poetry, see Harold L. Ginsberg, "Ugaritic Studies and the Bible," *BA* 8 (1945) 41-58. For "parallel pairs," see *RSP*, II Intro. 5.

[94]See Albright, "Archaic Survivals," 2 and *RSP*, III 61d. Cf. Dahood, "Hebrew-Ugaritic Lexicography II," 410-11. Here Dahood wishes to emend דֹּדָיִךְ, "your love" to דַּדָּיִךְ, "your breasts." There is no justification for such an emendation.

[95]W. F. Albright, *From Stone Age to Christianity* (2d ed.; Garden City: Doubleday, 1957) 248 n. 71.

[96]M. Dahood, *Ugaritic-Hebrew Philology* (Rome: Pontifical Biblical Institute, 1965) 69; also *Psalms I*, 81-82.

[97]See William L. Holladay, *A Concise Hebrew and Aramaic Lexicon of the Old Testament* (Leiden: E. J. Brill, 1971) 124. Against Dahood, see Delbert R. Hillers, "Paḥad Yiṣḥaq," *JBL* 91 (1972) 90-92, esp. p. 92 n. 18.

[98]See Vinzenz Hamp, "Zur Textkritik am Hohenlied," *BZ* 1 (1957) 197-214. Hamp's work catalogues text critical work on the Song undertaken by a number of commentaries of the first half of the century.

[99]References to the Syriac are taken from *The Old Testament in Syriac, Sample Edition: Song of Songs, Tobit, 4 Ezra* (ed. Piet. A. H. de Boer and W. Baars; Leiden: Peshiṭta Institute, 1966).

100Rudolph, *Das Hohe Lied*, 127; Würthwein, *Die Fünf Megil-loth*, 41; see KB (1974) 2. 571.

101See Godfrey R. Driver, *Canaanite Myths and Legends* (Edinburgh: T. & T. Clark, 1956) 133 n. 2. See the *NEB* (this section under the editorship of Driver). See also KB (1967) 1. 18.

102See, e.g., Hamp, "Textkritik," 201.

103See Haller, *Die Fünf Megilloth*, 34. שׁוּר means "to descend" (see Isa 57:9; Ezek 27:25). Rudolph, *Das Hohe Lied*, 147 and Loretz, *Liebeslied*, 29 do not revocalize אתי.

104Rudolph, *Das Hohe Lied*, 151 and Würthwein, *Die Fünf Megilloth*, 54.

105Dahood, *Hebrew-Ugaritic Philology*, 54. Albright, on the other hand, supports the emendation based on his view that v. 12 contains an example of an archaic two-word repetition בַּ֫ן בְּעוּל//בַּ֫ן בְּעוּל. See Albright, "Archaic Survivals," 4. Lor-etz, *Liebeslied*, 31, supports the elimination of בַּ֫ל בְּעוּל as a gloss. This is reminiscent of Haller's position which reads בַּ֫ל in the first phrase, and eliminates the second colon because of dittography (Haller, *Die Fünf Megilloth*, 34).

106Gerleman, *Das Hohelied*, 188; Krinetzki, *Das Hohe Lied*, 308. Cf. R. Tournay, "Les chariots d'Aminadab (Cant VI:12): Israël, peuple théophore," *VT* 9 (1959) 288-309.

107Loretz, *Liebeslied*, 41.

108See W. Watson, "Shared Consonants in North West Semi-tic," *Bib* 50 (1969) 525-33 and "More on Shared Consonants," *Bib* 52 (1971) 44-50. See also Dahood, *Psalms II* (AB 17; Garden City: Doubleday, 1968) 81 and *Psalms III* (AB 17a; Garden City: Doubleday, 1970) 34.

109Würthwein, *Die Fünf Megilloth*, 64; Krinetzki, *Das Hohe Lied*, 311; and Rudolph, *Das Hohe Lied*, 174.

110See Luis Alonso-Schökel, *Estudios de poetica Hebrea* (Barcelona: J. Flors, 1963) esp. pp. 171-72.

111Two articles have appeared recently which focus on cer-tain limitations of the form-critical method. See James Muilen-burg, "Form Criticism and Beyond," *JBL* 88 (1969) 1-18 who notes that the very nature of form criticism concerns generalizations and that to stress the concreteness and specificity of given texts one needs another discipline (Muilenburg's "rhetorical criticism," see p. 5). Rolf Knierim's article "Old Testament Form Criticism Reconsidered," *Int* 27 (1973) 435-68 points out that form criticism must be prepared to deal with the individu-ality of texts as well as the general categories into which a text may fall. For a recent comprehensive work on developments in form criticism, see John H. Hayes, ed., *Old Testament Form Criticism* (San Antonio: Trinity University, 1974).

[112]Krinetzki, *Das Hohe Lied*, 55.

[113]Ibid., 63-64.

[114]Ibid., 64.

[115]Friedrich Horst, "Die Formen des althebräischen Liebesliedes," in *Gottes Recht* (ed. Hans W. Wolff; Munich: Chr. Kaiser Verlag, 1961) 176-87.

[116]Ibid., 176-77.

[117]Wilhelm Hermann, "Gedanken zur Geschichte des altorientalischen Beschreibungsliedes," *ZAW* 75 (1963) 176-96. Cf. Gillis Gerleman's recent treatment of the bride's song in the Acts of Thomas, "Bemerkungen zum Brauteslied der Thomasakten," *ASTI* 9 (1973) 14-22.

[118]Richard N. Soulen, "The *Waṣfs* of the Song of Songs and Hermeneutic," *JBL* 86 (1967) 190.

[119]Murphy, "Form-Critical Studies," 419-20.

[120]Horst, "Formen," 182-83.

[121]Willy O. N. Staerk, *Lyrik* (SAT 3/1; Göttingen: Vandenhoeck & Ruprecht, 1920) 305.

[122]Horst, "Formen," 183-84. Cf. Krinetzki, *Das Hohe Lied*, 95 and Gerleman, *Das Hohelied*, 102-103.

[123]For example, Rudolph, *Das Hohe Lied*, 130-33 and Würthwein, *Die Fünf Megilloth*, 44-45.

[124]See Horst, "Formen," 184.

[125]Ibid., 183. See also Gerleman, *Das Hohe Lied*, 184 and 222.

[126]Würthwein, *Die Fünf Megilloth*, 61 and 70.

[127]See ibid., 61; Loretz, *Liebeslied*, 39; and Rudolph, *Das Hohe Lied*, 164-65.

[128]Horst, "Formen," 178.

[129]Audet, "Love and Marriage," 80.

[130]Loretz, "Zum Problem des Eros," 196-201.

[131]Audet, "Love and Marriage," 82-83.

CHAPTER II

EGYPTIAN LOVE SONGS: THE CULTURAL MILIEU

Although it is reasonable to suppose that there was mutual
influence between the love-language of ancient Israel and that
of Canaanite fertility rites with which Israel was often involved, there is no evidence that portions of the Song were
originally composed for or modelled upon these rites. Moreover, Assyro-Babylonian literature provides only a few songs
portraying human love which are analogous to the Song. Mesopotamian literature, therefore, has not been as helpful as the
literature of Egypt in providing a corpus of parallel love
songs.

THE RECOGNITION OF PARALLELS

Recent commentators (e.g., Rudolph, Würthwein, and most
notably Gerleman) have discerned the importance of a group of
Egyptian love poems in the recognition of various themes and
validation of literary genres which appear in the Song. The
recognition of similarities between Egyptian love songs and
Canticles originates, however, among the scholars who first
published hieroglyphic transcriptions of the Egyptian songs.[1]
Soon, other Egyptologists were quick to point out interesting
parallels which appeared to exist between the Song and the
Egyptian poems. A. Erman, in his early yet still important
translation of Egyptian literature (including a segment of
Egyptian love songs), notes the following: "The resemblance of
these songs to the Song of Songs will strike every reader, and
a connection is favoured by another feature also, namely, that
the lovers call themselves there as here [i.e., in the love
songs of Egypt] 'brother' and 'sister'."[2] One of the classic,
earlier studies of ancient Near Eastern literature, that of
T. E. Peet, has elaborated the "resemblance" between the Egyptian love lyrics and the Song. Peet notes that both "breathe a
strong love of nature" and emphasize "the comparison between
the beauties of the beloved person and those of natural objects, more particularly of trees, flowers and gardens."[3]

In the post-World War II period, P. Gilbert, a French Egyptologist, recognized the affinity between the collection of Egyptian love poems and the Song. Not only were similarities of theme and imagery recognized, but Gilbert also noted a similar technique of composition: a collection of individual units.[4] On the other hand, the work of F. R. Schröder, while noting the close parallels between the Egyptian poetry and the Song, has not proved helpful.[5] Schröder contends that, while the Egyptian love poetry displays a profane and bucolic character, its origins lie in a sacred setting. The "sister-brother" terminology, for example, has roots in the legends of the divine brother-sister Osiris and Isis; the freedom of action which the woman displays in the Egyptian poetry reflects the search of the goddess for her lover; and the origins of the breast being offered to the man (see Harris, 2/2) has as its *Vorbild* the imagery of the goddess who allows the deceased to suckle at her breast as well as the imagery of Paraoh suckling the breast of Hathor.[6] To support his contention of a religious background to the Egyptian love lyrics, Schröder refers to the Song of Songs as a parallel. The Song, according to Schröder, also has its origins in a sacral, cultic setting.[7] A. Hermann, however, has correctly argued against Schröder's narrow limitation of the imagery of love poetry to the religious sphere, emphasizing, rather, the origin of the themes (topoi) of love poetry in the general life-experience of a people. The breast image to which Schröder refers, then, can also arise out of the human experience of nursing a child. Likewise, "brother-sister" terminology is characteristic of lovers' speech.[8] Hermann is therefore correct in his contention that one cannot speak of an *exclusive* sacral basis for the topoi of the Egyptian love songs.

There are four substantial collections of ancient Egyptian love poems which have come down to us: the Papyrus Harris 500; the Turin Papyrus; the Cairo love songs; and the Chester Beatty Papyrus I.[9] Several fragments of other love lyrics have also survived, but are very fragmentary in character and are, therefore, not as helpful in displaying the variety of themes and literary genres as the larger collections which have been translated and included in the Appendix of this work.[10] Other

translations of these love poems have been made and the following are the most accessible: A. Erman (1927); S. Schott (1950);
J. A. Wilson (1955); and W. K. Simpson (1972).[11]

The oldest collection of the love poems is generally
thought to be the poems of Papyrus Harris 500, dating from the
last half of the 18th Dynasty (14th Century B.C.).[12] This date
is supported by the variety of imagery in the collection of
twenty individual poems including a "harper song" and three
poems which appear to form a cycle about flowers. The *mater-
lactans* motif, for example, is a frequent scene depicted in
tomb art from the Old Kingdom. A form of this motif reappears
in the tombs at Thebes during the regnal years of Amenophis II
to Tuthmosis IV (1438-1402 B.C.).[13] Here the youthful prince
is depicted suckling the breast of his wet-nurse. Although the
motif does not convey the sexual connotation that is preserved
in the love poetry--the man being offered the breast of his
beloved (see Harris, 2/2 and 2/5)--its use in grave art does
provide a general backdrop for the breast imagery in love poetry. Likewise, the imagery of bird-snaring appears at Thebes
in Hatshepsut's temple of Deir el-Bahri and later on the wall
relief during the reign of Tuthmosis IV (see Harris, 2/12-4/1;
8/3-8/5).[14] A wealth of other images such as the Memphis trip
allusion (Harris, 4/8-4/9), geographical places (Harris, 4/6;
8/3; 4/3; 4/4), and the dove motif (Harris, 10/6 and 10/7) reflect the life-style preserved in the art work of the 18th
Dynasty.[15]

The Cairo love songs of Ostracon 25218 are a collection of
lyrics which date from the last of the 18th Dynasty or the
first part of the 19th Dynasty (circa 1300 B.C.). The poems
in this collection appear to be independent of one another; yet
the last three poems seem to be connected by the catchword of
the wish particle, 𓏲𓇋𓏤𓏤𓏤 𓐰 𓄿, which begins the first line
of each poem. Support for the dating of the collection at the
beginning of the 14th Century is found in the depiction of one
of the poem's themes--the woman catching a fish--on an ostracon from Deir el-Medineh, dating from the early 19th Dynasty.[16]

Quite recently, Georges Posener published the final fas-
cicle to the second volume of his *Catalogue des Ostraca Hiératiques littéraires de Deir el Médineh*. One text, Ostracon Deir

el-Medineh 1266, has proven particularly interesting in that
the new pieces discovered during the 1950's at Deir el-Medineh
augment the text of the vase known as Cairo 25218.[17] The fragments proved to be of the same ostracon! Unfortunately, the
text of Ostracon 1266 is fragmentary and, while it does add to
the text of Cairo Ostracon 25218, it does not add significantly
to our understanding of the themes and genres of Egyptian love
poetry. John L. Foster, a scholar in the English department at
Roosevelt University, has been the first to translate Cairo
25218 augmented by Ostracon Deir el-Medineh 1266.[18]

The third main group of Egyptian love poems are those of
the Turin Papyrus, a cycle of three "tree" poems, written down
on two sides of a papyrus sheet at the beginning of the 20th
Dynasty (ca. 1200 B.C.).[19] In each of the poems, the speaker
is a different kind of garden tree. The first tree speaks of
its role as the locale for the lovers' meeting (Turin, 9/2-
9/3). The second, the sycamore fig, describes itself as the
willing servant of the woman (Turin, 12/4). A third, the small
sycamore, invites the lovers to meet and enjoy one another in
the beauty of the garden spot (Turin, 15/3 and 16/3). In each
instance, the tree becomes an accomplice to lovemaking.

The imagery of the garden and trees is a familiar one and
is found in the literature of the 18th Dynasty. The garden
poems of the Harris 500 songs illustrate the earlier use of
this theme in love poetry (Harris, poems 18-20). On the temple
reliefs of Deir el-Bahri, the trading expedition of Hatshepsut
to Punt, the land of incense near the southern end of the Red
Sea, is pictured. Among the much prized cargo which was re-
turned to Egypt were live myrrh trees for replanting in the
temple groves of Amun (cf. Turin, 12/4).[20] Later, from the
Amarna period, there is preserved the so-called "Book of the
Sycamore and the Date Palm," a literary work which describes
the motif of the "dispute for precedence of the trees"--a familiar theme in ancient oriental literature (see Turin, 12/3).[21]
Although the affectation of the poem in terms of metaphor and
language may most accurately reflect the beginning of the 20th
Dynasty (with Müller), one would not go so far as to say that
the design of these poems is such that they reflect the work of
one author.

The latest group of Egyptian love poems that have been preserved are those of Papyrus Chester Beatty I. Gardiner is quite certain that the provenance of the Beatty Papyrus is Thebes, and his contention is supported by the following colophon: [hieroglyphs] , "It has come to a happy ending in Thebes, the Place of Truth."[22] Likewise, there is general consensus (Gardiner, Hermann, Schott) on a date in the late Ramesside period at the end of the 20th Dynasty (ca. 1160 B.C.).[23]

The Beatty songs are comprised of three separate sections of poems. The first, introduced by the title "The Beginning of the Pleasures" (Beatty, $C^1/1$), is a composition of seven songs or "stanzas" (the Egyptian word [hieroglyphs], "house")[24] which form a tight unity (i.e., a cycle) by means of paronomasia and word-repetition. A second cycle consists of three separate poems all introduced by the wish particle [hieroglyphs] (see Cairo, 13-16). The wish is that the man will come to his beloved like the messenger of the king (Beatty, $G^1/1$), like the king's horse (Beatty, $G^1/5$), and like a gazelle (Beatty, $G^2/1$). The final section of the Beatty songs is prefaced by an introductory phrase alluding to one Nakht-Sobek. Gardiner notes that the reference to Nakht-Sobek as the apparent writer of the collection appears to be an "impudent usurpation," an addition penned in over an erasure.[25] This third section of the Beatty material is particularly significant in that it utilizes more explicit sexual imagery--scenes which are more typical of the late portion of the 20th Dynasty.[26] The individual poems of the collection illustrate the night of love, filled with less than subtle sexual *double entendre* (see, e.g., Beatty, $R^{16}/9$-$R^{17}/1$). Beatty $R^{16}/9$ alludes to the woman's genitals while $R^{17}/5$-6 describes the male's penis.

THE CULTURAL MILIEU OF THE OLD AND MIDDLE KINGDOMS

Several aspects of the Egyptian cultural development provide an important backdrop for understanding the development of Egyptian love lyrics. Among these aspects is the position of women in Egypt during the Old and Middle Kingdoms--one of growing equalization with men. The ideal relationship was that a woman was a *companion* to man. Although the sources are at times ambiguous, one can discern that despite concubine-servant trade, monogamy was an ideal which was upheld.[27] At the same time, women and children possessed certain rights, and women had their own tombstones and awaited immortality, just as men.[28] Moreover, the position of woman as the beloved (to be respected and honored) and as mother (especially the mother of Pharaoh) began to take on greater significance through the centuries of Egyptian life.[29] A picture of the ideal is given in the following selection from the Instruction of Ptah-hotep (from the Middle Kingdom):

> If you are a smart man, you have found your
> house and love your wife as it is fitting.
> Fill her belly; clothe her back. Oil (*mrḥt*)
> is the prescription for her body. As long
> as you live, cause her heart to be glad.
> She is a field of profit for her lord.[30]

The goddess Hathor and her cult form a second important facet of cultural development which aids one's understanding of love poetry. Often pictured iconographically as a cow, [31] Hathor is the patroness of love. The symbol of the cow represents the maternal, divine essence which sustains life; hence, in the wider sense, Hathor is also goddess of health, plenty, and procreation. Dating from the Old Kingdom is the rite of "papyrus-gathering for Hathor" (*sšš wꜣḏw n Ḥ·t-Ḥr*), taking place in the delta region and having undertones of celebrating pleasures by bird-snaring and fish-catching--themes which are depicted erotically in the love poetry. Likewise, from the Middle Kingdom tomb of Amenemhet (12th Dynasty), a Hathor festival is described. Women were prominent in this festival, serving as musician-priestesses who paraded in the streets and moved from house to house bestowing Hathor's blessings on the inhabitants. A. M. Blackman has noted that singing and dancing accompanied the procession, while the priestesses touched the people with the emblems of Hathor, the sistrum and *mnꜣt* necklace, objects which would give life, health, and happiness.[32]

From the Beatty love songs, we have preserved an important aspect of the relationship between Hathor and humankind. Hathor (also known by the epithet, the Golden One), in her role as the goddess of love, is the addressee of the petitions made by lovers. Usually, the petitions concern the desire of one lover for the other, and Hathor is asked to entrust a lover to

the other.[33] Note in the following the desire that is expressed by the man:

> I make praises to Hathor,
> thanksgiving to the mistress.
> I report to her in order that she may
>   hear my petitions.
> May the mistress entrust her to me.
>   (Beatty, $C^3/5$-$C^3/6$)

A similar request is made in the following:

> I prayed to my goddess
> that she give to me a sister as a gift.
>   (Beatty, $C^3/9$)

Yet, the woman also petitions Hathor for the presence of the
brother in the following:

> Brother, would that I might be entrusted to you
> by the Golden One of women.
> O Golden One, place it in his heart,
> (and then) I will go speedily to the brother,
> (and then) kiss him in front of his companions.
>   (Beatty, $C^2/3$ and $C^4/4$)

When the beloved is finally present, the poet confesses the
following:

> It is the Golden One who has handed her over
> to you, my friend.
>   (Beatty, $G^2/5$)

While there is a "religious content" to the Hathor references that are contained in the love songs (with Bleeker),
there is no evidence for a systematic movement of seculariza-
tion taking place in Egyptian literature and being evidenced in
the love lyrics (against Schröder). Yet, through the worship
of Hathor, a veneration for love did grow in the individual
consciousness--manifesting itself in the enjoyment of pleasures
such as those found in the Hathor rites. The voyage to gather
papyrus in the delta swamp evidences to be not only a religious
rite, but also takes on sensual overtones as the individual
consciousness regarding pleasurable activities was raised.[34]
In the reliefs of the Old Kingdom, the female companion of the
hunter-fisherman who gathered papyrus in the swamp was not emphasized.[35] By the Middle Kingdom, however, the presence of
the woman in the swamp became an important image. From the
literary fragment known as the "Story of the Herdsman," a

woman, perhaps Hathor herself, attempts to seduce a herdsman who was tending his flock at the edge of a papyrus marsh. Her invitation was sexual in nature, evidenced by the herdsman's response: "I will never do what she said, awe of her is in my body."[36] By the time of the New Kingdom, the Ramesside period in particular, the boat-trip to the delta marshes for "papyrus-gathering" became an erotic adventure in which a man and woman would share the pleasures and enjoyment of human love. The growing awareness of the enjoyment of love and erotic pleasure fostered the development of the love lyrics.

Along with the growing equalization of the position of woman vis-à-vis man, and the experience of erotic enjoyment, A. Hermann has noted two other aspects of cultural movement in the Old and Middle Kingdoms which are significant in the development of love lyrics in Egypt: affection for living creatures and the growing belief that free choice could determine human relationships.[37] The former is noted in an emphasis upon the maternal feeling of a mother for her child or an animal for its offspring. In both literature and pictorial art, the tenderness of such a relationship is depicted. This feeling of affection Hermann notes as an important presupposition in the self-conscious feeling and tenderness exhibited between loving partners.[38] The latter is centered around a developing emphasis upon the conscious recognition of the love partner as a basis of the love relationship rather than the efficacy of the magical spell. While the "love spell" is known in the New Kingdom (as well as love potions and aphrodisiacs [Turin, 16/2-3]) and although the love spell is an important part of love literature, ancient Egyptian love lyrics reflect the power and force of the desire and choice of the individual person.[39] Indeed, despite even the petitions to Hathor, love-sickness can strike one partner and the accompanying need for prescriptions and love charms (see e.g., Beatty, $C^4/7$-$C^5/2$ and Harris, 4/10-11) is apparent because of the evasive behavior shown by the other partner.

THE CULTURAL MILIEU OF THE 18TH DYNASTY

H. Brunner has noted that ancient Egyptian love poetry, because of its freshness and spirit, is a child of the

Ramesside time (ca. 1300-1200 B.C.). It is in this period of
time that the new sense of the individual person and his freedom forms a proper foundation for preservation of this literature.[40] Although the later Ramesside period saw the writing
down of love lyrics, it is the 18th Dynasty (ca. 1550-1300
B.C.) which provides the most fertile ground within which the
roots of love poetry could grow. The cultural development at
the beginning of the New Kingdom provides the atmosphere and
the background for many of the images which appear in the love
poems.

Although admitting the danger of oversimplification, W. K.
Simpson has recently categorized the historical movements of
the 18th Dynasty in the terminology of European historiography:
renaissance, reformation, and counterreformation.[41] The first
part of the Dynasty is characterized by the expulsion of the
Hyksos under Ahmose (1558-1533) and a period which followed
largely devoid of military activity from the reign of Amenophis
I (1533-1512) to Hatshepsut's rule (1490-1469).[42] In contrast,
the reigns of Tuthmosis III (1469-1436) and Amenophis II (1438-
1412) were quite expansionistic and militaristic followed by a
period of general peace and luxury at the royal court under
Tuthmosis IV (1412-1402) and Amenophis III (1402-1363). These
years of the 18th Dynasty, Simpson equates with renaissance--a
transformation in artistic style from that of the Middle Kingdom, the "opening up" of Egypt (e.g., Hatshepsut's expedition
to Punt), and the penetration of Egyptian military prestige
into Western Asia.

As curious as the parallel may be and as dissimilar as the
characters Akhenaten and Luther may be, the period of Amenophis
IV (1363-1347) and his successors (the so-called Amarna Age)
may be designated "reformation." Indeed, Atenism in many characteristics represented a return to the worship of the sun god.
Akhenaten's reformation was open rebellion against the established power of the Amun priesthood who became in the years
preceding Akhenaten's reign less and less ecclesiastical in
their background and more favored courtiers of the reigning
Pharaoh, wielding strong political power.[43] Yet, the shifting
of the capital and religious power and the restructuring of the
Egyptian state was short-lived, largely due to a vacuum in the

political sphere after the death of Tutankhamun (1347-1338)
and the ascent to power of the aged Ay (1337-1333). Horemheb's
reign (1333-1303) represents the counterreformation in political, religious, and military policies. During Horemheb's rule,
the dismantling of Amarna begins along with the ignoring of the
reigns of the Amarna group in official documents. In the king
lists from the Ramesside period, the series passes from Amenophis III to Horemheb, omitting all the kings of Amarna!

One of the most striking features of the early 18th Dynasty is a matriarchal tendency which is seen in the important
roles played by the queens in the political sphere. So-called
matriarchal tendencies were not uncommon in the societies of
Western Asia,[44] although one would be in the realm of conjecture to suggest that the Hyksos influence in Egypt during the
15th to 17th Dynasties could be responsible for the roles
played by the queens, culminating in the *kingly* reign of Queen
Hatshepsut. D. B. Redford suggests that strong matriarchal
tendencies were found within the geographical area of Egypt itself, viz., Nubia and Kush.[45] Given the influx of Nubians into
Upper Egypt in the 17th Dynasty, one may hypothesize that a matriarchal tendency was exerted by Tetisheri and Ahhotpe, the
grandmother and mother of Kamose and Ahmose, respectively, and
by Ahmose-Nofretari, Ahmose's wife.[46] It is the strong-willed
Ahmose-Nofretari who delineates the exact status of the queen.
Her titles were "female chieftain of Upper and Lower Egypt"--a
designation which describes her political authority--and *ḥmt
nṯr* ("the god's wife")--a title which designates the queen's
role in future succession (the right of the throne passed
through her). The status and importance of the queen is noted
by Redford in the following: "The queen had her own palace and
her own estate, and presumably the king would be obliged to
present himself at her apartments if he wished to visit."[47]

The woman par excellence of the 18th Dynasty was Hatshepsut, the granddaughter of Ahmose-Nofretari and wife (as well as
half-sister) of Tuthmosis II. During the years of Tuthmosis
II, Hatshepsut was content to reign as his queen, even to the
point of having her tomb excavated for queenly burial. Yet,
as Redford points out, Hatshepsut was of the same fiber as her
grandmother, and Tuthmosis II, perhaps realizing the ambition

of his wife, contrived before his premature death to have his
son (by a slave girl) appointed King Tuthmosis III. [48] Upon
the death of her husband, Hatshepsut began to assert her ambition and in the second regnal year of the child-king Tuthmosis
III, with the backing of several powerful political officials,
had herself declared king, with full pharaonic power and title,
calling herself "the Female Horus Wosretkau, the King of Upper
and Lower Egypt Makare, the Daughter of Re, Khnemetamun Hatshepsut."[49]

Upon seizing power, Hatshepsut sought to solidify her position as king. She built a temple at Deir el-Bahri and in the
reliefs and inscriptions there sought to justify her take-over
of the throne through scenes of her divine birth as the daughter of Amun and of a fictitious appointment and coronation as
king by Tuthmosis I.[50] While Hatshepsut did make a supreme effort to modify the basis of Egyptian kingship and thereby even
designated her own daughter, Neferure, as her successor, giving
her the title, "lady of the two lands, mistress of Upper and
Lower Egypt," (see Harris, 8/1) Redford notes that "her person-
ality was not sufficient" to force a change and "her assumption
of *kingly* attributes was, in fact, a concession to patriar-
chy."[51] There is no evidence regarding the fate of Hatshepsut,
but in the twenty-second regnal year of Tuthmosis III, she
passes from the scene.

Hatshepsut's reign underscored the rising position of wom-
en in Egyptian society, a characteristic of Egyptian culture
which was to continue throughout the period of the New Kingdom.
The role of the queen in the 18th Dynasty achieved an unparal-
leled status in relation to prior Egyptian history. Queen
Teye, wife of Amenophis III, is frequently represented in statuary and is included in royal inscriptions from the reign of
her husband. On one particular memorial scarab, Teye and Amenophis III are pictured together and the inscription is reminiscent of the language of love poetry: "The great divine consort
and sovereign Teye has made this as her monument for her beloved *brother*" (that is, the deceased Amenophis).[52] Likewise,
Nefertiti, the wife of Akhenaten, is often pictured with her
husband in pictorial art (e.g., the famous *Wagenfahrt* relief
from Amarna) and with the king and their children. As many as

six daughters appear in temple and tomb reliefs in what seems
to be an attempt to show the domestication of the Pharaoh's
life and the royal family as a unit. This view contrasts with
the earlier privacy that was usually maintained by other
kings.[53]

There is a growing emphasis upon the depiction of nature
in pictorial reliefs in the 18th Dynasty. From the reign of
Hatshepsut, the famous journey to Punt is captured by artists
who portray the characteristic scenery of the tropical land:
the thatch houses of the Puntites, palm groves, incense trees,
and a variety of local fauna.[54] By the Amarna period, especially in the reliefs of the successors of Akhenaten, there appear scenes characterized by vivid gardens and natural imagery.
The "lovers' walk" in the garden and the pastoral scenes of
trees and flowers are favorite features of Amarana art. These
same scenes appear in the love poetry (see, e.g., the walk of
the lovers hand in hand [Harris, 14/9]; the imagery of the
flowers [Harris, 14/3-14/12]; and the garden scenes [Harris,
6/10-6/13 and Turin, 15/1-15/4]).[55]

The period of the New Kingdom in Egypt saw a new social
freedom taking place in which the role of the common man began
to emerge from political and economic obscurity. Although the
obstacle of class barrier was a hindrance, the social strata
were not determined and a person could change his status in
life. Even the freed slave, with industry and ambition, could
become part of the growing class of skilled workers.[56] Valuable resources in the determination of Egyptian cultural and
social development have been found at the workmen's village,
Deir el-Medineh, which dates from the 18th Dynasty. In ostraca from Deir el-Medineh, there are fragments of love lyrics
preserved as well as pictorial art showing various themes of
the love poetry.[57]

During the reign of Tuthmosis III, the successor to Hatshepsut, notable advances were made in Egyptian art. The
spirit of his reign was vigorous, and he was able to organize
the internal administration of the country so that his regime
was able to develop Egypt's natural resources and undertake
a large-scale building program (especially at Karnak and
Thebes). The Tuthmoside period, moreover, is well-known for a

series of military victories which expanded and consolidated
Egypt's domain. These victories were often celebrated in relief which reflected a feeling for the enjoyment of life and
the success of human endeavor.[58]

The emphasis upon the pursuit of worldly pleasures reached
a high point in the reign of Amenophis III at Thebes. Amenophis III was a builder and patron of the arts who taxed the
resources of the country to search for building materials. He
even ordered the dismantling of earlier monuments in order to
use the stone for his own creations. Amenophis' reign can only
be described in superlatives. The architecture of the day was
equaled by the furnishings of the court--all characterizing
an atmosphere of luxury and gracious living.[59] The reliefs of
this period show a society enjoying the luxury of the times.
It is to the period of Amenophis III that one may trace certain
themes which are graphically portrayed in Egyptian love poetry
(notably bird-snaring [Harris, 4/1 and 8/3] and detailed pictures of dancing girls and female musicians [having detail reminiscent of the $waṣf$, e.g., in Beatty, $C^1/2-C^1/6$]).[60] This
same attitude toward pleasure and the enjoyment of life was
carried over to Amarna (see above, p. 78).

In contrast to the vital spirit which characterized art in
the 18th Dynasty, languor and lack of vigor is frequently noted
in the artistic decline of the 19th Dynasty.[61] Although building continued, the atmosphere in art became more and more ethe-
real. In royal tombs, much of the space in relief appears to
be given over to scenes of the afterlife and of voyages through
the Netherworld. The excitement and the joy of this-worldly
activities that were particularly characteristic of the 18th
Dynasty art passed from the scene. The 19th Dynasty is, however, a time of great literary production. The love poetry
which is written down in the time of the 19th Dynasty is reminiscent of the atmosphere which typified the worldly pleasures
of an earlier time.

"POPULAR" OR "ARTISTIC" POETRY?

The background material of Egyptian love poetry is drawn
largely from, if not exclusively, a royal, certainly upperclass
style of life. The motifs depicted in the love poetry (e.g.,

fine oils, royal attire, servants, etc.) appear to be characteristic of a life-style which had time for leisure and could
afford and appreciate a finer quality of life. Is it possible,
then, to conclude that the love songs represent a literary
tradition produced by the elite?

The individual poems which are contained in larger collections are sophisticated compositions written by anonymous poets
who were skilled in a variety of literary techniques (e.g.,
paronomasia [Harris, 14/3; 14/7; 14/11]; repetition of syntax
[Harris, 14/10-11; 4/4]; and inclusio [Beatty, $c^2/9-c^3/4$]).[62]
Further support for the high cultural background of the love
lyrics is the use of literary fictions, forms, and topoi which
are characteristic of an "artistic" style and which evidence
knowledge of a wide range of literary traditions.[63] The literary quality of these lyrics has persuaded Schott to conclude
that the love poetry is the product of *einer dichterischen
Kunst.*"[64]

Although some of the collections bear evidence of units
which form short cycles of previously unified poems, the Egyptian poetry appears to be a loose unity of disparate poems
linked together by means of catchword association. There is no
evidence that any one collection derives from one hand. In the
Harris 500 collection, for example, the word [hieroglyphs] (*pẖrt*,
"prescription" or "perfume") plays an important role as a
catchword in Poems Two, Three, and Five (see Harris, 2/7,11 and
4/9). These independent units are connected by the recurrence
of this word. Likewise, Poem Three contains the word "love"
([hieroglyphs]), and a form of this word is repeated in Poem Four
([hieroglyphs] , "loving"), linking these poems together (see
Harris, 2/9 and 4/2). The repetition of this key word is made
even more pronounced by the occurrence of the word play in Poem
Three (Harris, 2/12) involving the name of a particular type
of wood in the description of the beloved's forehead: [hieroglyphs]
wood ("love"? wood).

The use of the word [hieroglyphs] ("love") in the Egyptian
poetry is again employed as a catchword in Poems Nine and Ten
of the Harris collection and in each independent unit, the word
functions as an inclusio. For example, in Poem Nine, the word
"beloved" ([hieroglyphs]) occurs twice at the beginning of the

poem as well as the appearance of "your love" (⸢𓄿𓆓𓏤𓃀⸣)
in the first lines. This root is repeated, then, in the final
line of Poem Nine, "one who is loved" (𓄿𓏤𓆑𓃀). Similarly, in the following poem (Harris, 8/7-9), the word "your
love" (𓄿𓆑𓃀) appears at the beginning and at the end,
serving both to unify the poem and to connect it with the preceding poem (Harris, 8/1-7).

The Egyptian poetry is also composed of short cycles which
appear to possess inner unity apart from their inclusion into a
larger collection of material. At the end of the Harris collection, there appears a cycle containing three flower poems
introduced by the following rubric: "The beginning of the
praise of pleasures" (Harris, 14/3). Characteristic of the
three poems in this cycle is an interesting word play on the
name of each flower. Hence, *Mekhmekh* flowers play on the word
𓏇𓏤𓅱𓏥𓏦 (*mḫȝ*), "to incline" (Harris, 14/3); *Sa^cam* plants
play on the word 𓊃𓂝𓅓𓏛 (*s^cm*), "to raise" (Harris,
14/7); and *Titi* flowers play on the word 𓍿𓏤𓏭𓇯𓏤 (*tȝy*),
"to snatch" (Harris, 14/11). Similar word plays may be noted
in the seven stanza cycle of the Beatty collection (Beatty,
$c^1/1-c^5/2$).

A setting of these poems in the literary, scribal circles
of Egypt appears to be certain, given the design, geographical
allusions, and varied motifs in the love lyrics.[65] The occurrence of a Harper Song between the second and third sections of
the Harris 500 manuscript may not, then, be as incongruous as
it might appear. The Harper Song is not love poetry, but rather is akin to the wisdom literature of ancient Egypt, at home
in the court-school. One may suppose that, in one early life-
setting of the Harris 500 text, there was no incongruity noted
in the Harper Song's proximity to love songs. For the wise man
who sought the proper balance to life's activities, yet, at the
same time, sought to achieve pleasure and happiness (Harris,
12/11), interest in the power and celebration of human love
would *not* be unexpected. It is not, therefore, unlikely that
the love poetry of ancient Egypt was *preserved* by those circles
of men who were interested in cataloging the whole of human
experience.[66]

One must, however, be cautious in limiting the life-setting of these love lyrics as well as denying that the imagery
contained in them is common to the experience of the *Volk*. The
possession and appreciation of the love songs by the workers at
Deir el-Medineh indicate that the life-setting of the poems
cannot be confined to a particular sphere. The celebration of
human love was not the sole possession of the elite in Egyptian
society. Moreover, the topoi of the love lyrics are universal
and perennial: descriptions of the beloved; a garden walk;
love-sickness; etc. The origin of these poems, then, cuts
across the strata of Egyptian society. The motifs contained
in the love poems not only reflect the quality of life attain-
able by the elite, but also describe the romance and fiction
which might characterize the fantasies of the *Volk*. Ancient
Egyptian love poetry is a collection of material which is at
the same time both "artistic" and "popular," a fact which
points out the inadequacy of such terms in describing the love
literature of the ancient Near East (see above, p. 54).

[1]See, for example, Gaston C. C. Maspero, "Les chants d'amour du papyrus de Turin et du papyrus Harris," *JA* ns (1883) 47. Maspero notes that "l'Hébreu et l'Egyptien avaient à peu pres la même conception de l'amour." Cf., however, W. Max Müller, *Die Liebespoesie der alten Ägypter* (Leipzig: J. C. Hinrichs, 1899) 8.

[2]Adolf Erman, *The Literature of the Ancient Egyptians* (trans. A. M. Blackman; London: Methuen, 1927) 242-43. Alan H. Gardiner has noted that the designations "sister" and "brother" for the man and woman in Egyptian love poetry follow "the regular Egyptian custom"; see Gardiner, *The Library of A. Chester Beatty: Description of a Hieratic Papyrus with a Mythological Story, Love Songs, and Other Miscellaneous Texts* (London: Oxford University, 1931) 28. In Cant 4:9-12 and 5:1-2, the woman is designated "sister." Yet, the word "brother" is not used in the Song to denote the man; rather the Hebrew דוד signifies the more general designation: "lover." See also Müller, *Liebespoesie*, 8 and F. Dornseiff, "Ägyptische Liebeslieder, Hoheslied, Sappho, Theodrit," *ZDMG* 90 (1931) 592. Dornseiff's work is among the first to recognize the close parallels which appear to exist between the Song and ancient Egyptian love poetry. His understanding of the Song, however, is influenced by a dramatic interpretation which discerns three scenes in the book (see p. 594).

[3]T. E. Peet, *A Comparative Study of the Literatures of Egypt, Palestine, and Mesopotamia* (London: Oxford University, 1931) 96. Peet's study is dated. Regarding the Egyptian love songs, he notes that from Babylon "literally nothing of this kind has come down to us" (p. 96). The published works of Held and Cooper have recently shown that noncultic love songs were known in the Assyro-Babylonian culture (see above, p. 23 n. 22).

[4]Pierre Gilbert, "La composition des recueils de poèmes amoreux égyptiens et celle du Cantique des Cantiques," *CE* 45 (1948) 22-23. See Gilbert's earlier translation of a selection of the Egyptian love lyrics in his *La poésie égyptienne* (Brussels: P. F. Merckx, 1943) 33-82, passim.

[5]F. R. Schröder, "Sakrale Grundlagen der altägyptischen Lyrik," *DtVi* 25 (1951) 273-93.

[6]Ibid., 275-77. The image of the goddess who gives suck comes from the Pyramid Texts. Erman translates as follows: "She hath compassion on him, she giveth him her breast, that he may suck it: 'My son, O king, take to thee this my breast and suck it, O king'"; see Erman, *The Literature*, 9. See also Raymond O. Faulkner, trans., *The Ancient Egyptian Pyramid Texts* (Oxford: Clarendon, 1969) 183 (Utterance 508). In the city of Apis where the chief divinity was Hathor, the high priestess

bore the title ᵚᵚ⊴ ⑂ (snḳyt), "she who gives suck." The high priestess was perhaps identified with Hathor, who is frequently pictured in Egyptian iconography suckling the Pharaoh. See Blackman, "On the Position of Woman in the Egyptian Hierarchy," *JEA* 7 (1921) 12. Blackman's "Figure 2" depicts Hathor suckling Sethos I.

[7]Schröder, "Grundlagen," 292-93.

[8]See Alfred Hermann, "Beiträge zur Erklärung der ägyptischen Liebesdichtung," *Ägyptologischen Studien* (ed. O. Firchow; DAWBIO 29; Berlin: Akademie-Verlag, 1955) 138-39.

[9]Müller's *Die Liebespoesie der alten Ägypter* contains hieroglyphic transcriptions of Papyrus Harris 500 (also known as the London Papyrus 10060) and a facsimile of Cairo Ostracon 25218 (in hieratic). There are also translations of this material as well as the Turin love songs. Maspero's "Les chants d'amour du papyrus de Turin et du papyrus Harris" contains hieroglyphic transcriptions and translations of both the Harris songs and the Turin material. Wilhelm Spiegelberg's "Eine neue Sammlung von Liebesliedern," in *Aegyptiaca*, Festschrift for G. Ebers (Leipzig: Wilhelm Engelmann, 1897) 117-21, contains a hieroglyphic transcription of the Cairo 25218 (with critical notes, but no translation). Finally, the Beatty love songs have been published by Gardiner, *Chester Beatty*, and include transcription, notes, and translation.

[10]These fragments include the following: Papyrus Anastasi II, verso, published by Adolf Erman, "Bruchstuck eines Liebesliedes," *ZÄS* 39 (1902) 147; Ostracon Deir el-Medineh 1038, verso; 1040; 1078, verso; 1078, recto; and 1079 published by Georges Posener, *Catalogue des ostraca hiératiques littéraires de Deir el Mêdineh*, Vol. I (Cairo: L'institut français d'archéologie orientale, 1938); Ostracon Érémitage no. 1125, a translation by B. van de Walle, review of *Altägyptische Liebeslieder* by Siegfried Schott in *BO* 9 (1952) 104-108. The translation of one important fragment has been included in the Appendix of this study, the Louvre C 100, published by Müller and subsequently by H. Page Hurd, *The World's Oldest Love Poem: Louvre C 100* (Newark: n.p., 1954).

[11]See Erman, *The Literature*, 242-51; Siegfried Schott, *Altägyptische Liebeslieder* (Zürich: Artemis Verlag, 1950); John A. Wilson, trans., "Egyptian Secular Songs and Poems," in *ANET*, 467-71; and William K. Simpson, *The Literature of Ancient Egypt* (New Haven: Yale University, 1972) 297-325. See also the section in Robert et al. entitled "Les parallèles non bibliques," *Cantique*, 340-52.

[12]Alfred Hermann, *Altägyptische Liebesdichtung* (Wiesbaden: Otto Harrassowitz, 1959) 138. This date is a consensus. See Schott, *Liebeslieder*, 34-35; Erman, *The Literature*, 244; Müller, *Liebespoesie*, 13; and W. Wolf, *Kulturgeschichte des alten Ägypten* (Stuttgart: A. Kröner Verlag, 1962) 402-403. Although agreeing with this dating, Gardiner points out that some of

these songs may date from the Middle Kingdom; see *Egyptian Grammar* (3d rev. ed.; London: Oxford University, 1973) §15.

[13]See M. Wegner, "Die Stilentwicklung der thebanischen Beamtengräber," *MDAI* 4 (1933) 56-57.

[14]See G. Grdseloff, "Zum Vogelfang," *ZÄS* 74 (1938) 52-55 and 136-39.

[15]Hermann, *Altägyptische Liebesdichtung*, 141-43.

[16]Ibid., Tafel Xa.

[17]Georges Posener, *Catalogue des ostraca hiératiques littéraires de Deir el Médineh*, Vol. II/3 (Cairo: L'institut français d'archéologie orientale, 1972) pls. 75-79.

[18]See John L. Foster, *Love Songs of the New Kingdom* (New York: Scribner's Sons, 1974). All of Foster's translations are quite free, almost to the point that some of the lines are unrecognizable when compared with a more literal rendering. Yet, Foster's purpose is to convey the "spirit" of the love poems and in order to do this, he has been quite imaginative in filling lacunae and expanding lines. On the contrary, the translation of these lines in the Appendix of this study attempts to be quite literal. One may find it beneficial to compare the translations. Foster's book has been illustrated with Egyptian tomb paintings from the 18th Dynasty which depict various themes found in the love songs: bird-snaring, flowers, fruit, figs, the marshes, fishing, etc. This artwork is taken from Nina M. Davies and Alan H. Gardiner, *Ancient Egyptian Painting* (3 vols; Chicago: University of Chicago, 1936).

[19]Hermann, *Altägyptische Liebesdichtung*, 145. Also, Müller, *Liebespoesie*, 38.

[20]See William C. Hayes, "Egypt: Internal Affairs from Tuthmosis I to the Death of Amenophis III," *CAH* 2/1, 329.

[21]Hermann, *Altägyptische Liebesdichtung*, 147 and 102. Speaking of Turin 12/1-13/5, Hermann notes the following: "Der Überbietungstopos ist hier mit dem 'Rangstreit der Bäume' verbunden, der in der altorientalischen, hebräischen und klassischen Dichtung häufig auftritt" (p. 102).

[22]Gardiner, *Chester Beatty*, recto 16, line 8 (see p. 26 n. 4).

[23]Cf. Pierre Gilbert, "Le grand poème d'amour du papyrus Chester Beatty I," *CE* 34 (1943) 186-87. Gilbert contends that linguistic indications, other similar love poems, and the descriptive elements in the Beatty songs point toward a date at the end of the 18th Dynasty or the beginning of the 19th Dynasty (p. 187). Although literary allusions may date from earlier periods, Hermann has correctly noted the cultural setting of the Ramesside period as a proper backdrop for this collection (see Hermann, *Altägyptische Liebesdichtung*, 156-57, passim).

[24]Aylward M. Blackman, "The Use of the Egyptian Word $ḥ \cdot t$ 'House' in the Sense of 'Stanza,'" *Or* 7 (1938) 64-67.

[25]Gardiner, *Chester Beatty*, 1. For a recent article concerning the title of this third section of the Beatty songs along with similar introductory titles in the Ramesside period, see Ulrich Luft, "Zur Einleitung der Liebesgedicht auf Papyrus Chester Beatty I r° XVI 9ff.," *ZÄS* 99 (1973) 108-16.

[26]Hermann, *Altägyptische Liebesdichtung*, 160-63. The explicit language of the Nakht-Sobek cycle of the Beatty love songs should lay to rest the following characterization of the love songs: "The theme is romantic, rather than erotic love..."; see John A. Wilson, *The Burden of Egypt* (Chicago: University of Chicago, 1951) 264. Hermann notes that the so-called "bed-motif," referring to the lovers' night of love that they share, is a common theme of the Ramesside period (Hermann, *Altägyptische Liebesdichtung*, 162-63). This motif, however, can be noted in earlier love lyrics (see Harris, 14/12 and Cairo, X/12). Schott notices a reaction to the sensual direction of art in the latter part of the New Kingdom. From Grave 45 at Thebes, Schott points out that servants and musicians are clothed. Yet, the tomb relief evidences an apparent repainting (*Übermalung*) which has provided once naked figures with proper attire! See Schott, "Ein Fall von Pruderie aus der Ramessiden-zeit," *ZÄS* 75 (1935) 100-106.

[27]Hermann, *Altägyptische Liebesdichtung*, 10. See P. G. Smither, "The Report Concerning the Slave Girl Senket," *JEA* 34 (1948) 31-34.

[28]K. Pflüger, "The Private Funerary Stelae of the Middle Kingdom and their Importance for the Study of Ancient Egyptian History," *JAOS* 67 (1947) 127-35, esp. p. 128. See also Hermann, *Altägyptische Liebesdichtung*, 12-13.

[29]See Hermann, *Altägyptische Liebesdichtung*, 10-14; also see Schott, *Liebeslieder*, 24-29.

[30]For the text used in this translation, see Kurt Sethe, ed., *Ägyptische Lesestücke* (Darmstadt: Wissenschaftliche Buchgesellschaft, 1959) 40. Also see Sethe's *Erläuterungen zu den ägyptischen Lesestücken* (Hildesheim: Georg Olms, 1960) 53-54; see *ANET*, 413.

[31]An outstanding example of sculpture in the 18th Dynasty is a sandstone figure of the cow of Hathor carved by the sculptors of Amenophis II at the Hathor shrine at Deir el-Bahri. See Hayes, "Egypt," *CAH* 2/1, 409 and Bertha Porter and Rosalind L. B. Moss, *Topographical Bibliography of Ancient Egyptian Hieroglyphic Texts, Reliefs, and Paintings* (Oxford: Clarendon, 1927) 2. 93.

[32]See Blackman, "On the Position of Women," 22. Also see Hermann, *Altägyptische Liebesdichtung*, Abbildungen 2 and 3 (pp. 19 and 21). Claas J. Bleeker has recently summarized characteristics of several Hathor festivals in his *Hathor and Thoth* (Leiden: E. J. Brill, 1973) 84-101.

[33] Claas J. Bleeker, "Der religiöse Gehalt einiger Hathor-Lieder," *ZÄS* 99 (1973) 82-88. A case is made below that these petitions are ironic; see p. 98.

[34] Hermann, *Altägyptische Liebesdichtung*, 17-18.

[35] Ibid., Abbildung 1, p. 17.

[36] Erman, *The Literature*, 35 and Schott, *Liebeslieder*, 169.

[37] Hermann, *Altägyptische Liebesdichtung*, 36.

[38] Ibid., 33.

[39] See P. C. Smither, "A Ramesside Love Charm," *JEA* 27 (1941) 131-32.

[40] Hellmut Brunner, *Grundzüge einer Geschichte der altägyptische Literatur* (Darmstadt: Wissenschaftliche Buchgesellschaft, 1966) 105-106. See Hermann, *Altägyptische Liebesdichtung*, 36.

[41] William W. Hallo and William K. Simpson, *The Ancient Near East: A History* (New York: Harcourt Brace Jovanovich, 1971) 257.

[42] The chronology which is followed in this study is that of Donald B. Redford, "On the Chronology of the Egyptian Eighteenth Dynasty," *JNES* 25 (1966) 113-24. Cf. the work of Erik Hornung, *Untersuchen zur Chronologie und Geschichte des Neuen Reiches* (Wiesbaden: Otto Harrassowitz, 1964) 108-109. Egyptian chronology is hampered by the problem of coregencies in which one king began to reign during the lifetime of his predecessor (e.g., the alleged coregency of Amenophis III and Akhenaten) and the difficulties of relative chronology with Syria-Palestine and Mesopotamia. See W. C. Hayes, "Chronology: I. Egypt--To the End of the Twentieth Dynasty," *CAH* 1/1, 173-92, and M. B. Rowton, "Chronology: II. Ancient Western Asia," *CAH* 1/1, 193-238.

[43] See Hayes, "Egypt," *CAH* 2/1, 327.

[44] Among the Hebrews, see Julian Morgenstern, "Beena Marriage (Matriarchat) in Ancient Israel and its Historical Implications," *ZAW* 6 (1929) 91-110 and *ZAW* 8 (1931) 46-58; and "David and Jonathan," *JBL* 78 (1959) 322-25. Morgenstern's views are refined in his *Rites of Birth, Marriage, Death, and Kindred Occasions among the Semites* (Cincinnati: Hebrew Union College, 1966). In Western Asia, see Rivkah Harris, "Woman in the Ancient Near East," *Interpreter's Dictionary of the Bible, Supplement* (eds. L. R. Bailey, K. Crim, and V. Furnish; Nashville: Abingdon, 1976) 960-963; and "The Case of Three Babylonian Marriage Contracts," *JNES* 33 (1974) 363-69.

[45] Donald B. Redford, *History and Chronology of the Eighteenth Dynasty* (Toronto: University of Toronto, 1967) 66.

[46]See T. G. H. James's discussion of the roles of these important women vis-à-vis the newly unified Egyptian state in "Egypt: From the Expulsion of the Hyksos to Amenophis I," *CAH* 2/1, 305-7. One may compare the status of these women with those of the court of Zimri-Lim of Mari; see Bernard F. Batto, *Studies on Women at Mari* (Baltimore: Johns Hopkins University, 1974) 9-11. See also Willem H. Ph. Römer, *Frauenbriefe über Religion, Politik und Privatleben in Mari* (AOAT 12; Neukirchen-Vluyn: Neukirchener Verlag, 1971) and Jack M. Sasson, "Biographical Notices on Some Royal Ladies from Mari," *JCS* 25 (1973) 59-78.

[47]Redford, *History*, 71-72.

[48]Ibid., 73.

[49]See the historical summary in James, "Egypt," *CAH* 2/1, 316-17. Redford, among others, has postulated that Hatshepsut had early on declared her intentions to Tuthmosis II regarding the assertion of female power and had worked out an agreement whereby their only child, the young daughter Neferure, would succeed to the throne. According to Redford, this agreement was broken by Tuthmosis II who arranged the succession of his own son (Tuthmosis III). The outraged Hatshepsut immediately sought to consolidate her power and place Neferure in a prominent role; see Redford, *History*, 74 n. 85.

[50]See James, "Egypt," *CAH* 2/1, 317.

[51]Redford, *History*, 85.

[52]Italics mine. Hermann, *Altägyptische Liebesdichtung*, 59 and Tafel VIa.

[53]See Hallo-Simpson, *History*, 270. The important role played by women continues through the 21st Dynasty. At the time of Psusennes I, two women play central roles at Thebes: Henttowy and her daughter Makare; see Jaroslav Černý, "Egypt: From the Death of Ramesses III to the End of the Twenty-first Dynasty," *CAH*, 2/2, 27 (Cambridge: Cambridge University, 1975) 650.

[54]See W. S. Smith, "The Land of Punt," *JARC* 1 (1962) 59-61 and Nicholas B. Millet, "A Fragment of the Hatshepsut Punt Relief," *JARC* 1 (1962) 55-57.

[55]See Hermann, *Altägyptische Liebesdichtung*, 63-64 and Tafel XI.

[56]Hayes, "Egypt," *CAH* 2/1, 380-81.

[57]See Posener, *Catalogue*, Vol. I, Ostraca 1038, verso; 1040; 1078, verso; 1078, recto; and 1079. See also Černý, "Egypt," 17-21 and Hermann, *Altägyptische Liebesdichtung*, Tafeln Xa and Xb.

[58]Hermann, *Altägyptische Liebesdichtung*, 50-52.

[59] Hayes, "Egypt," *CAH* 2/1, 340-42. For an extensive study of Egyptian art, including an emphasis upon the technique and ideals of given periods, see H. Schäfer, *Von ägyptischer Kunst* (Wiesbaden: Otto Harrassowitz, 1963); regarding the contribution of Amenophis III, see pp. 21 and 67-69.

[60] I. Woldering, *The Art of Egypt* (trans. A. E. Keep; New York: Crown, 1963) 144-49; see also Hermann, *Altägyptische Liebesdichtung*, Tafeln VII and IX.

[61] Raymond O. Faulkner, "Egypt: From the Inception of the Nineteenth Dynasty to the Death of Ramesses III," *CAH*, 2/2 (Cambridge: Cambridge University, 1975) 250.

[62] An analysis of the linguistic features of ancient Egyptian love poetry awaits scholarly investigation. One can conceive of such a study on analogy with similar work undertaken on narrative material from the New Kingdom; see Fritz Hintze, *Untersuchungen zu Stil und Sprache neuägyptischer Erzählungen* (DAWBIO 2; Berlin: Akademie-Verlag, 1950). Similarly, an analysis of Middle Egyptian literature has been undertaken by Siegfried Herrmann in *Untersuchungen zur Überlieferungsgestalt Mittelägyptischer Literaturwerke* (DAWBIO 33; Berlin: Akademie-Verlag, 1957).

[63] See Chapter III for an extensive study of the variety of literary forms and themes in the Egyptian poetry.

[64] Schott, *Liebeslieder*, 8.

[65] Hellmut Brunner, *Altägyptische Erziehung* (Wiesbaden: Otto Harrassowitz, 1957) 109.

[66] A brief survey of Egyptian wisdom can be found in Hans H. Schmid's *Wesen und Geschichte der Weisheit* (BZAW 101; Berlin: Töpelmann, 1966) 8-84.

CHAPTER III

EGYPTIAN LOVE SONGS:
AN ANALYSIS OF THEME, FICTIONS, AND *GATTUNGEN*

THE PROBLEM OF LYRIC POETRY

The corpus of literature known as Egyptian love poetry
has developed from the cultural-historical circumstances in
which the human expression of love and mutual affection between
a man and woman was realized. While several cultural developments from earlier periods serve as important presuppositions
for understanding the variety of motifs in the love poetry, it
is against the background of the 18th Dynasty that the embodiment of feeling regarding love and its expression is best
viewed.

Egyptian love lyrics contain verbal formulations (*Sprach-
gebärden*) of the growing consciousness of human love taking
place in ancient Egyptian society. This awareness of love,
as it is appropriated in structural patterns, themes, and
usage, reflects what A. Jolles has called a "basic mental concern" (*Geistesbeschäftigung*) which preoccupies humankind.[1] For
Jolles, the human mind is faced with a variety of psychological
and ontological matters which exist independently of verbal
expression. The literary expression of these concerns is to be
found in a variety of *einfache Formen*: saga, myth, riddle,
proverb, etc.[2]

Regarding Egyptian literature, A. Hermann has appropriated
Jolles' archetypal approach to literary criticism and notes
that the forms of ancient literature develop from basic psychological needs or tensions (*Spannung*).[3] Lyric poetry, then, is
the "linguistic resolution of a human tension" through the me-
dium of a literary form.[4] A variety of forms (or kinds) of
lyric poetry can be noted, each arising out of a human experience. A "magical saying" attempts to resolve the fear of the
unknown, which is characteristic of the human plight, by an
attempt to control reality through the spoken word. Hunger,
sickness, and death are elements of the human experience with
which magic seeks to deal and, thereby, control. The lyric of

ritual addresses the human questions arising out of an experience and preoccupation with the holy. The work song, hymn, and
prayer, likewise, attempt to resolve some of the concerns which
are accumulated in mankind's everyday life.[5]

These various literary forms have been preserved because
they are understood to represent clearly man's ontological
possibilities.[6] This archetypal approach to the explanation
of literary forms states, moreover, that human "tensions" are
universal and that the ontological concern that is embodied in
a given literary expression is not subject to cultural relativ-
ism and societal differences. Given such a theory of literary
development, lyric will change very little from century to century. Stories, for example, about saintly people will follow
similar patterns in all ages, whether the legend concerns medieval stories about saints or stories about contemporary folk-
heroes.[7]

The ancient Egyptian love lyrics are linguistic expressions of humankind's growing enchantment with the power and desire of love, reflected in the growing awareness of the love-
experience in the individual consciousness. The songs are not
only romantic and idyllic, expressing the tenderness and beauty
of love, but also they may be intensely passionate and erotic,
expressing the strong desire of one loving partner for the
other. These songs depict the joy that the lovers feel when
together as well as the pain of separation and the hurt of
jealousy. Because the moods and the situations of the love
lyrics are perennial, the ancient Egyptian songs reflect a form
of literary expression that should be classified as archetypal.[8] Hence, the variety of images and atmosphere of love-
making in that ancient society do not differ significantly from
the contemporary concern of humankind, reflecting on the power,
the dangers, and the celebration of love.

THE DESIGN OF EGYPTIAN LOVE POETRY[9]

1. The Poet as Speaker. In the anonymous collection of
love lyrics from Egypt, the verbal formulations celebrating
love are transmitted by a single individual, the poet.[10] One
must, however, distinguish between the poet's speech as an

assumption of the role of a third party (*der Dichter als Dritter*) and as one of the loving partners.

The speech of the poet, reflecting the point of view of a third person, is noted in several of the love songs. The poet speaks as a friend of the man and as an admirer of the woman in the Beatty Cycle of Three Songs ($G^1/1-G^2/5$), beseeching the man to "come to the sister quickly." In the first lines of the three poems, introduced by the wish particle (see above, p. 69), the man is addressed by the second person, "you." In the final lines of two of the songs, however, the poet addresses the man in the third person. Note the following:

> When he reached the house of the sister,
> his heart made exultations.
>   (Beatty, $G^1/4$)

> O how the heart of the sister knows
> that he is not far from the sister.
>   (Beatty, $G^1/6-G^2/1$)

The last line of the third poem of the cycle, however, reverts to using the second person form, "you," for the man, but speaks of the woman in the third person: "You shall have reached her den until kissing your hand four times as you pursue the love of the sister (Beatty, $G^2/4-5$). The rapid change of person in Egyptian love lyrics is a common occurrence (see, for example, Harris, 4/11-13). The first two stanzas of the Nakht-Sobek Cycle of the Beatty love songs display a similar address in which the poet (as a third person) speaks of the man as "you," while the woman is referred to in the third person. Again, the characteristic change in agreement is to be noted. In this case, the third person reappears in the final line of the poem, interrupting a series of second person references to the man. Note the following from Beatty, $R^{16}/12$:

> You can accomplish your desire in her thicket,
> The halls shall be whirling (?).
> The heavens pant with storms.
> *He* does not remove it.

The poet in these love lyrics also assumes the identity of the loving partners and speaks in the first person. At least three different variations of this speech occur in the love poetry, however. First of all, the poet (as the man) refers to the woman in the third person. Note the following from Harris, 4/9-11:

> I will lie down inside;
> [I] will be ill falsely.
> My neighbors will come in to behold me,
> and the sister will come with them.
> She will make the doctors unnecessary
> because she knows my sickness.

This characteristic speech of the poet can be noted in a variety of examples among the love songs. One may cite the following: Harris, 2/11-4/1; 4/6-9; 4/12-13; Beatty, C^1/1-8; and Cairo, X/7-18.

Secondly, the converse situation is also a frequent occurrence: the "I" of the poet refers to the woman and the man is spoken of in the third person. This type of discourse may be noted in Harris, 10/9-12. The following is an excerpt:

> I will set my face upon the outer door.
> Behold my brother is coming to me....
> Because of what he has, my heart is not silent....
> He is stunning before me.

Other examples of the woman speaking in the first person, referring to the man in the third can be noted in the following poems: Beatty, C^1/8-C^2/4; C^2/5-9; C^2/10-C^3/4.

Thirdly, an interesting phenomenon occurs when only the first and second persons are used in a given poem. In such songs, the poet assumes the "I" of the woman, exclusively, and the man is designated by the second person "you." These poems are the closest approximation to dialogue in the Egyptian love poems. Yet, in the poems that have been preserved, the woman speaks to the man. There are no examples of the converse. Although, in Egyptian, the first person suffixes can be easily confused (α [𓏭]; α [𓏤]), one can *generally* be accurate in the designation of the second person by the clarity of the suffixes ⲉ̄ 𓎡 (masculine) and 𓏏 (feminine).[11] Exemplary of the "I-you" discourse is the following:

> ...(my) heart inclines to you [masculine]
> I [feminine] shall do for you what it seeks,
> (when) I am in your embrace.
>   (Harris, 14/3-6)

Other examples of the woman speaking in the "I" form of the man in the second person are Harris, 2/1-6; 8/1; 8/2-7; and Beatty, R[17]/4.[12]

The Turin Papyrus is unique among the Egyptian love texts in that the speaker in each of the three poems is a different type of tree. It would appear, however, that the trees are analogous to the figure who speaks in the third person (i.e., the poet). In Poem Three, the "little sycamore" conveys a message to the woman, uniting "her," a reference to the beloved in the third person, and "her friend" (see Turin, 16/5) to share their love under the tree's branches. The first and second tree poems in the Turin cycle, while not speaking directly to either love partner, refer to each in the third person. An exception is to be found in Poem One of the Turin songs in which the woman is referred to as "she" and on one occasion the man as "you." Note the following: "She caused you to pass the day pleasantly" (Turin, 11/2).[13]

2. The Brother-Sister Speech. One of the most characteristic features of the Egyptian love lyrics is the employment of the designations "sister" (𓋴𓈖𓏏) and "brother" (𓋴𓈖) as epithets of the loving partners. A. Hermann notes that it is unlikely that the use of these terms originates in the incestuous marriage practices of the Egyptian court.[14] Although the evidence is scant, the use of "sister" and "brother" as general designations for people in love appear to have their origin in the *Volksprache* of the early 18th Dynasty, characterized by greater affection being expressed between a man and woman.

Against the wider background of the ancient Near East, sister-brother terminology is noted in texts from Western Asia. The terms were used in the ancient Mesopotamian ritual of sacred marriage to designate the divine pair, Inanna and Dumuzi (Tammuz/Ishtar) as well as in the Ugaritic literature. In 3 *Aqht* (rev) 24, the goddess ^cAnat speaks the following to Aqht: "You are my brother and I am [your sister]."[15] From Hurrian texts, however, the term "sistership" *may* designate a certain legal right and social status, and a wife could simultaneously have the status of sister. E. A. Speiser has utilized this alleged Hurrian social structure as a means of interpreting Abraham's attempt to pass Sarah off as his sister in Gen 12:10-20 (see Gen 20:1-18).[16] It would appear, however, that neither the designation "sister-brother" for the divine consorts nor the alleged use of sister in Hurrian culture is the correct *Vorlage* for the use of the word "sister" in the Song of Songs (Cant 4:9, 10, 12). Its use here most accurately assumes the similar function in the Egyptian love lyrics: a term of affection for the beloved.[17]

3. The Expression of Partnership. A thread which runs through the Egyptian love poems is the expression of mutual desire and admiration that the lovers convey to one another. Admiration is often displayed in the statements which note one lover's characterization of the unique qualities of the other. The woman describes the man as "the grandest in my heart" (Harris, 14/5). Similarly, the man portrays his beloved as one "without her duplicate, more beautiful than any woman" (Beatty, C^1/1).

The lovers express their mutual commitment through a desire to exclude others and share only the presence of one another. While bird-snaring, the woman desires that they go into the fields together, for "(then) I am alone with you" (Harris, 8/5). The desire to be alone with the beloved evidences the woman's devotion to the brother, for he is her "only concern" (Harris, 10/10). Likewise, the lovers appear to demand exclusivity in their love. In what purports to be a description of the night of love, the passion of love-making is only for the beloved:

> May you bring it (into) the hall of the sister,
> You alone, without another.
> You can accomplish your desire in her thicket.
> (Beatty, R[16]/11-12)

The desire that the lovers manifest in their relationship seeks a proper balance and order ($m\mathrm{\it ^{3}\it ^{c}t}$]) between the lovers and with the whole of creation.[18] This proper balance demands that passion be controlled, especially in public. Yet with discipline, their hearts can reach the proper attunement. Note the following from Harris, 8/10-11:

> ...I must control myself.
> (But) I serve my love
> when I am alone.

> When my heart is in accord with your heart,
> I cannot be far from all happiness.

This balancing of the heart appears to be an ideal in the love life of Egypt. The same idea is expressed in another Harris poem in which the woman seeks the embrace of her lover. Her heart "inclines" ($mḥ3$) toward the lover, for it is only when the two are in each other's presence that the heart can be properly aligned. Note the play on words as the woman longs for the arms of her lover:

> *Mekhmekh* flowers.
> (My) heart inclines ($mḥ3$) to you.
> I shall do for you what it seeks,
> (when) I am in your embrace.
>   (Harris, 14/3-4)

The longing that the man or woman feels for the other when they must be separated is reflected in a number of poems which describe the joy that is experienced when they are able to return or "come" to one another. The Beatty Cycle of Three Songs expresses this desire in the form of the wish: "Would that you might come to the sister quickly" (Beatty, G^1/1, 5; G^2/1). The adjuration that is expressed in the beloved's coming is noted in the following:

> I am seeking the sister as she returns.
> My heart is exulting;
> my arms separate to embrace her.
> My heart is joyful upon its proper station
> as...eternity,
> after the lady comes to me.
>   (Cairo, X/9-10)

One may note the same theme in the following from Beatty, C^3/6-7 as the woman returns to the man:

> She has come back of her own accord to see me.
> Something very great is happening to me.
> I rejoice, I am glad, I am great,
> ever since one said, "Hey, she is here!"

A similar joy on the part of the lovers is shared when they are able to "see" one another.[19] The woman invites the man to watch her swim: "Come, that you might see me" (Cairo, X/6). The sight of the beloved is a pleasurable experience. Hence, the brother longs to be the woman's Nubian maid, for, then he would see "the hue of every limb" (Cairo, X/13-14).

The woman also enjoys the pleasures of the voyeur and enjoys both seeing the lover and being seen by him. Note the following:

> My prayer is that my eyes may be painted,
> for my seeing you is the brightening of my eyes.
> I am one drawn to the sight of your love.
> (Harris, 14/4-5)

> He kept watching me when I walked by.
> I alone shout for joy.
> How glad is a heart in exaltation,
> O brother, because of my being seen.
> (Beatty, C^4/2-3)

4. The Lovers and Divinity. Although the mention of the divinity is not uncommon in Egyptian love poetry, references to the gods do underscore a characteristic nonchalance on the part of the lovers regarding the role played by the pantheon in human love. This attitude toward the gods borders on irony. For example, the petition of the man concerning the return of his beloved to him appears to be a tongue-in-cheek statement. At one time he says the following: "May the mistress (i.e., Hathor) entrust her to me" (Beatty, C^3/6). Ironically, the next line appears almost irreverent: "She (i.e., the beloved) has come back of her own accord to see me."[20]

In Poem Eight of the Harris collection, the woman travels down to Re's Heliopolis; yet the text is clear that the trip is not entirely for religious reasons! Her voyage gives her an opportunity to see the lover and the religious motivation is only a pretext. Note the following:

> I will rise up to hasten, without ceasing.
> My heart remembers Re.
> I will watch the arrival of my brother
> when he arrives at the garden house.
> (Harris, 6/4-6)

Likewise, the religious value of the various petitions made to the divinity may be of specious quality (so Hermann).[21] Compare the following:

> When I have found (you),
> may Amun give (you) to me,
> forever and ever.
> (Harris, 10/2-3)

As Amun lives, I shall come to you,
my loin cloth upon my shoulder.
          (Beatty, R^{17}/4)

Even Ptah of Memphis is summoned to aid the lover as he seeks
his beloved:

I will be in Ankh-towy,
and say to Ptah, Lord of Truth,
"Give to me my sister tonight!"
          (Harris, 4/6-7)

The relatively insignificant role played by divinity in
the Egyptian love texts only serves to underscore a characteristic aspect of these lyrics: the celebration of the lovers'
desire for one another. The atmosphere, the scenes, and the
variety of themes present enhance this desire. Religion and
the various deities are subordinated to the personal experience
and the individual expression of love, and therefore, play
relatively insignificant roles.[22]

THE TOPOI OF EGYPTIAN LOVE POETRY

W. Wolf has pointed out that Egyptian art and literature
reflect an attempt to mirror reality as "concrete realism."[23]
This realistic presentation of life is also illustrative of the
variety of topics or themes (topoi) which are found in Egyptian
love poetry.[24] The experience of love was a physical one for
the ancient Egyptians. The effects of love upon the partici-
pants were manifested in physical occurrences: seeing, hearing,
tasting, bodily sickness, etc. A. Hermann is, therefore, quite
accurate in his observation regarding the topoi of love poetry
when he states as follows: "...the Egyptian approach is not
abstract, but fully objective."[25] There appears below a representative list and analysis of many of these topoi which may
be found in the ancient Egyptian love lyrics.

1. Seeing. The sighting of the love partner and the subsequent pleasure that such perception brings to the eye of the
beholder is a familiar topos of the love songs. Not only is
the loved one merely observed, but the visual encounter stimu-
lates and confirms the love between a man and woman.[26] The be-
holding of the lover is said to brighten the eye of the beloved
so that she is able to make the following confession: "(You

are) the grandest in my heart" (Harris, 14/5). When the loved
one is observed, moreover, the beloved receives strength and
sustenance. Regarding her observation of the man, the woman
says the following:

> Whenever you are seen in every glance,
> it is more splendid for me than eating and drinking.
> (Harris, 14/10-11)

Likewise, when the woman has seen the man, she is made happy
because he also has seen her! Note the following:

> He kept watching me when I walked by.
> I alone shout for joy.
> How glad is a heart in exaltation,
> O brother, because of my being seen.
> (Beatty, C^4/2-3)

Finally, the great beauty of the beloved often causes others to
catch a second glance. Hence, in Beatty, C^1/6, one notes the
following:

> She causes that the necks of all men
> turn back at the sight of her.

2. Hearing. The voice of the lover brings pleasure and
provides a reason for the beloved's life in the following from
Harris, 14/10:

> Pomegranate-wine is my hearing your voice.
> I live because I hear.

This same life-giving force associated with the sense of hearing can heal the lover of disease (love-sickness). Although
his sickness cannot be diagnosed and the master physicians provide no cure, the voice of the beloved possesses great healing
power--greater than "the Compendium (of medicine)." Only when
he *hears* that she has come to him can he be revived. Likewise,
"when she speaks, (then) I will be strong" (Beatty, C^4/9;
C^5/2).

3. Touching. Along with the desire of the lovers to see
and be seen and to hear one another comes the theme of touching. This topos, while not extensive in the love lyrics and
often appearing in fragmentary lines, further underscores the
lovers' desire to be in one another's presence.

The kiss appears in three forms in the Egyptian love lyrics: the hand kiss, the mouth kiss, and the nose kiss.[27]

There is a single reference to the hand kiss in Beatty, $G^2/4$:
"You shall have reached her den in order to kiss your hand four
times as you pursue the love of the sister." Although the precise meaning of the line is obscure, one may assume that the
kiss has erotic overtones.[28] The "den" of the sister certainly
possesses sexual *double entendre*, and the hand kiss may refer
to the kissing of the genitals. The mouth kiss (Cairo, X/11)
is characterized by the open lips of the beloved: "I kiss her.
Her lips open." The man receives a kiss from the beloved in
Beatty, $C^4/4$:

> O Golden One, place it in his heart,
> (and then) I will go speedily to the brother,
> (and then) kiss him in front of his companions.

Unfortunately, several allusions to body-contact in the
love lyrics are only found in places of textual fragmentation.
At the end of the Harris 500 collection, one notes the following lines:

> I will snatch your wreaths,
> when you come intoxicated
> (and) sleep upon your bed.
> I will touch your feet.[29]

In the first lines of the Harris collection, the woman questions the man about touching her, but the state of the text ob-
scures the meaning. Compare the following:

> If you seek to handle
> my thighs together with my breasts...
> would you leave when you remember food?
> (Harris, 2/2-3)

Likewise, in the same poem, the woman invites the man to touch
her breasts:

> Take my breasts.
> Abundant for you is their offering.
> (Harris, 2/5)

The topos of touching is also noted in the "hand-in-hand"
motif, mentioned earlier as a frequent theme in the art work of
the Amarna period (see above, p. 78). Hermann points out that
this topos evidences both the affection between the love partners and the sense of equality in their relationship.[30] When
the voice of the turtledove sounds the break of day and the

parting of the lovers from their night of love, the lovers promise the following:[31]

> I shall not be far [from you]
> for my hand is in your hand.
> I shall walk about when I am with you
> in every pleasant place.
> (Harris, 10/7-8)

This theme is repeated as the lovers desire to share a walk in the garden:

> Your hand is in my hand.
> My body is at ease.
> My heart is joyful because of our journeying together.
> (Harris, 14/9-10)

Finally, a slight variation of this theme is noted in Poem Thirteen of the Harris 500 collection:

> O beautiful (one), I have a good desire
> for (my caring for) your things
> as your housemaid.
> Your arm lies upon my arm.
> (Harris, 10/3)

4. Smelling, Breathing, Tasting. These senses enable one to experience the variety of ointments and scents which are referred to in the love language of Egypt. In one instance, the woman prepares to meet her lover. As she takes branches from a garden tree, she approaches her beloved stating the following:

> My face faces the cottage;
> my arms are filled with Persea (branches);
> my hair is heavy with resin.
> I am like the Lady of the Two Lands.
> I am with you.
> (Harris, 6/12-8/1)

While bird-snaring, the woman notices that the birds from the spice land of Punt are anointed with myrrh. She, then, appears to identify her beloved and his scent with that of the snared bird whose "odor is brought from Punt" and "whose claws are filled with resin" (Harris, 8/4-5). The man also wishes to catch the scent of his beloved. The royal sheets of her bed are said to be "moistened with moringa oil" (Cairo, X/13). Moreover, the man longs to be the washerman of his beloved so that he can catch the scent of the moringa oil that is said to be in her kerchief (Cairo, X/15). Finally, in the Nakht-Sobek

Cycle of the Beatty collection, the intoxicating fragrance of
love-making is mentioned. Note the following:

> The heavens pant with storms.
> He does not remove it.
> That she may bring you her fragrance,
> an odor which overflows to cause
> those who are present to become intoxicated.
>   (Beatty, R16/12-R17/1)

Poem Twelve of the Harris 500 songs refers to the sense of
taste in the following lines:

> I see sweet cakes
> (but) [they appear to be] salt.
> (As for) pomegranate wine, the sweetness in my mouth
> is like the gall of birds.

This imagery may be related to the lines which follow that appear to refer to the nose kiss. This kiss may represent the
breathing or sniffing of one partner around the nose area of
the other. The kiss is known in Egyptian iconography from the
18th Dynasty.[32] In the love poetry, moreover, the kiss is said
to impart life to the recipient. Note the following:

> The breath of your nose alone
> is what enlivens my heart.

5. The Heart. The human heart held a place of special
significance for the ancient Egyptians. Hermann notes that it
serves not only as the "locale of personal experience," but
also functions as a "second being" with which a person may converse.[33] Each of these characteristics is documented in the
love poetry. First of all, "the breath" of the lover's nose
(the nose kiss) "enlivens" the heart, i.e., quickens the entire
person (see Harris, 10/2). The heart also functions as an
alter ego to which conversation is addressed. In the following
prayer from the Harris 500 collection, the lover confides to
his heart:

> I speak to my heart, within me, this prayer:
> "My great one is afar from me tonight,
> (and) I am like one in my grave."
>   (Harris, 10/4)

Likewise, in the Beatty songs, the woman speaks to her heart as
follows: "Do not act for me as a fool, O my heart!" (Beatty,
C3/2). Conversation with the heart is implied in the following

question from the Nakht-Sobek Cycle of the Beatty songs: "When do you talk with your heart?" (Beatty, $R^{17}/4$).

A variety of *activities* are attributed to the heart in ancient Egyptian love lyrics. The heart has the function of cognition and is said to "know" (see Beatty, $G^1/8$). This ability for discernment gives rise to the admonitions in the Harper Song contained in Harris 500 to *follow* one's heart. Note the following:

(What is) beneficial for you is
to follow your heart as long as you live.
.(Harris, 12/9)

Increase your beauty,
(and) do not let your mind languish.
Follow your heart and your happiness.
(Harris, 12/11)

Consequently, the heart should not be upset or disobeyed (Harris, 10/8). The attraction of the love partner can "disturb" the heart (Beatty, $C^1/8$).

It is the celebration of the heart that characterizes the lovers' experience of one another. Usually, it is the occasion of their presence that causes the heart to be "pleasing in excess" (Harris, 10/7), "joyful" (Harris, 14/10 and Cairo, X/9), "glad" (Beatty, $C^4/2$), and "exulting" (Cairo, X/9). In such circumstances, the heart is said to be "seized" (Beatty, $C^1/5$ and $C^4/1$) by love and is "raised up" (Harris, 14/6) when in the presence of the beloved and "springs to come forth" (Beatty, $C^4/5$) when the lover is seen. The heart, moreover, can both remember love (Harris, 10/12) as well as be caused to forget (Harris, 12/9) and can "go after" love (Harris, 8/2).

6. Love-sickness. Given the emphasis upon the heart in Egyptian lyrics, especially the state of joy and happiness caused by the proper attunement of one lover's heart with another, the well-being of bodily functions rests upon the maintenance of order ($m\mathbf{\mathfrak{z}}^{c}t$). When order is disturbed and the proper balance is upset, physical illness can ensue. The following portion of a Beatty love song describes this imbalance:

The brother disturbs my heart with his voice.
He causes a sickness to seize me.
(Beatty, $C^1/8$)

From the love texts, the disease of love-sickness appears to affect the whole body and can be potentially lethal to the victim.[34] Even though the lover feigns his sickness, Poem Six of the Harris collection evidences the potential danger of such an illness: the doctors and neighbors come to his aid. Note the following:

> I will lie down inside;
> [I] will be ill falsely.
> My neighbors will come in to behold me
> and the sister will come with them.
> (Harris, 4/9-10)

Consequently, when one is struck down with this illness, the physical suffering is great. The man overcome by love-sickness confesses as follows, "I am like one in my grave" (Harris, 10/4). The flesh of the afflicted becomes "heavy" and the body is so weakened that it is "ignored" (see Beatty, $C^4/7$).

The cure for this dread disease does not lie in the entire Compendium of medicine nor in the rites of the lector priests. The love-sick partner laments that if even the "master physicians" were to minister to him "my heart will not be satisfied with their remedies" (Beatty, $C^4/8$). The specialists are unable even to diagnose the disease (see Beatty, $C^4/8$); yet, the beloved appears to possess both the power of diagnosis and cure. Note the following from Harris, 4/11:

> She will make the doctors unnecessary
> because she knows my sickness.

Likewise, the presence of the sister "is more beneficial...than all remedies" (Beatty, $C^4/10$). The knowledge that the sister is in the vicinity clearly revives the patient. *She* is the only cure as the following indicates:

> My salvation is her coming in from outside.
> When I see her, (then) I will be healthy.
> When she opens her eye, my body is young.
> When she speaks, (then) I will be strong.
> When I embrace her, she exorcises evil from me.
> (Beatty, $C^5/1-2$)

7. The Friends and Enemies of the Lovers. A number of figures are portrayed in the love songs who in some way (for ill or good) affect the love relationship between the lover and the beloved. In the poems dealing with love-sickness, for example, a number of people play minor, and in this case, helpful

roles: the lector priests, master physicians, neighbors, etc. In Poem Three of the Turin cycle, the "little sycamore" plays an accommodative role in the love relationship between the man and woman. The tree sends a message to the beloved which "makes (her) hurry to the lover" (Turin, 15/1 and other references to "messages" in Harris, 10/10 and Beatty, G^1/1-2). The message is followed by an invitation to pass the day in pleasure beneath the tree's shade. Yet, the tree not only invites the lovers to make love there, but also assures them that it will be "discreet" and will not divulge their amorous activities (see Turin, 16/3-16/1).

A. Hermann notes that the figure of "servant" should also be included among the friends (or helpers) of the lovers by appearing, like the little sycamore, as an accomplice to their love-making.[35] One role of the servant is the preparation of the bed used for sexual play. Note the following:

> O servant, there I say to you.
> Place fine linen between (?) her limbs,
> as a bed for her, with royal sheets.
> (Cairo, X/12)

The voice of the sycamore fig alludes to its desire to play the role of a servant and thus be enslaved (and in close proximity) to the beloved:

> ...if there are no maidservants,
> I (will be) the slave
> [who is brought from the land of Khor]
> as plunder for my love.
> (Turin, 12/4-5)

Hathor, the divine patroness of love, is called upon by the lovers to provide aid in their love relationship. The love lyrics allude to thanksgiving that is made to Hathor because she hears the petitions that the lovers make (see Beatty, C^3/5-6) and because she entrusts one lover to the other (see Beatty, C^2/3 and C^4/4).[36]

In other poems, figures appear whose roles regarding the lovers remain ambiguous. Often the characters such as the mother, the door-keeper, and Mehy are not congenial to the couple.

The image that is represented by the mother (both of the man and of the woman) is particularly elusive. In one instance, the woman's mother prevents the lovers' meeting even though the man appears as "a neighbor of my mother's house." As the following indicates, the mother is quite resolute in her desire that the pair no longer see one another:

> He is a neighbor of my mother's house,
> (but) I do not know how to go to him.
> Is my mother good in charging him thus:
> "Abandon seeing her!"
> (Beatty, $C^1/9-C^2/1$)

Likewise, the woman agonizes over what excuse she will give her mother when, instead of tending her traps, she allowed herself to be "entrapped" by the love of the brother. The sister, therefore, asks the following question:

> What shall I (say) to my mother
> to whom (I) return daily
> when I am loaded down with catch?
> I did not set the trap today.
> Your love has seized me.
> (Harris, 8/8-9)

In other instances, however, the figure of the mother appears to support the love affair. The woman bemoans on one occasion that her lover does not know of her desire to embrace him nor does he solicit the aid of the mother so that she may assume the role of Cupid (see Beatty, $C^2/2$). Similarly, while passing by the house of her lover, the sister sees him along with *his* mother and brothers and sisters. The beloved is spotted by the man and his watching her prompts her to exclaim, "How glad is a heart in exaltation, O brother, because of my being seen." Immediately thereafter the sister laments that her love for the brother is unknown not only to him, but also to her own mother. She states the following: "Oh, that Mother might know my desire" (Beatty, $C^4/3$).

The figure of Mehy is equally elusive.[37] Although he appears to be a rival to the man and, therefore, an enemy of their love, it is clear that the woman cannot help her desire for him and his "lusty lovers." She realizes the danger that is involved in her "passing before him." If she should, then, she could not resist his delights (see Beatty, $C^2/8$). The ambiguity regarding the figure of Mehy is discernible in the last lines of the Third Stanza of the "Beginning of the Pleasures" in the Beatty collection. These lines are particularly difficult to interpret. If the woman should go with Mehy, he will

"boast" of her name and will place her in his "chief harem."
It is unclear whether or not such a happening would be (or
should be) considered an honor or humiliation for the beloved
(Beatty, C^2/9).[38]

Other rivals do appear (or are alluded to) in the text.
For the man, the door-keeper who has such easy access to the
beloved is one of whom he is jealous. Upon passing by the beloved's house and finding the door locked, the lover laments
that tonight must be "a good night for our door-keeper!"
(Beatty, R^{17}/8). For the sister, the danger that another woman
may come upon the scene and be her rival for the attention of
the brother is mentioned in Harris, 10/11-12. The woman asks,
"Shall the annoyances of another estrange me?"

Finally, the love text from Cairo Ostracon 25218 describes
enemies of the lovers in the forms of the crocodile and the
dangerous waters through which the lover must pass to reach his
lady (Cairo, X/7-8). These enemies, however, are not able to
keep the lovers separated, for the man is so strengthened by
the love of the sister that "the waves are like land to my
feet." With the help of a "water-spell," given by his beloved,
the lover is able to overcome these dangers and to finally embrace his lady love.

8. Animals and Plants. The variety of flora and fauna
which appears in the Egyptian love lyrics is striking in its
number and contributes to the idyllic atmosphere of the poems.

Not only does the garden setting of the Turin love songs
reflect the widespread use of plant imagery, but filtered
throughout the corpus of Egyptian love lyrics is mention of
flowers, trees and fruits. The Harris 500 collection contains
a three-song cycle of poems which utilize three different types
of flowers as literary catchwords, the names of which provide
subtle word-play in the contexts of the individual poems.[39]
Also in the Harris poetry, the sister is described as having
physical features which are detailed in the imagery of plants
and fruits: "vine-like"; "berries"(?); and "*mry*-wood" (Harris,
2/12). Upon her arrival at the "garden house" of her lover,
the sister says she will gather branches from the trees and
make a fan and, then, move toward his "cottage" with her arms
"filled with Persea (branches)."

The imagery of plants is occasionally used in instances in which sexual *double entendre* may be present. A possible reference to the female genital area is mentioned in Harris, 2/10-11: "Distracting are the plants of her rush." A similar reference is made in the Nakht-Sobek Cycle of the Beatty collection (R^{16}/11): "You can accomplish your desire 𓂝𓏤𓇋𓇋𓊪 𓇾𓏏𓈖 ('in her thicket')."

The frequent use of animal imagery is characteristic of this poetry. Often animals provide a descriptive technique by which the lover is portrayed. His scent is like that of a bird from Punt (Harris, 8/5; other allusions to birds may be found in Harris, 8/3; 8/10; and 10/2); his uniqueness and speed are like the king's horse (Beatty, G^1/6); and his desire for the beloved is like a hunted gazelle seeking escape (Beatty, G^2/2). The man, moreover, is portrayed hastening to glimpse his beloved "like a stallion on the field" (Harris, 2/8), and he is entrapped by her love like "a wild goose" in the snare (Harris, 4/1). The woman describes him by a pet name, "O jackal pup" (Harris, 4/2). In the love poetry, mention is also made of the turtledove (Harris, 10/6); hounds (Beatty, G^2/3); the ox (Beatty, R^{17}/9 and R^{17}/11); goats (Beatty, R^{17}/10); a "strong goose" (Beatty, R^{17}/10) and a "red *wt* fish" (Cairo, X/5).

THE LITERARY FICTIONS

Relying on the literary-critical work of Jolles, the study of A. Hermann, *Altägyptische Liebesdichtung*, has described the literary fictions or travesties that are characteristic of love literature in the ancient and modern world. Working primarily with the literature of modern Europe, Jolles has described the categories of literary *Travestien* which portray the human desire to occupy a different station and status in life, while at the same time remaining one's self. Such alterations may include attempts by characters to clothe themselves in the garments of a higher social class (*"Ritter"-Travestie*), in the humble garments of the shepherd (*"Hirten"-Travestie*), or in garments of one who seeks to flee society and play the role of the rogue or rascal (*"Schelm"-Travestie*).[40] Hermann has noted that literary fictions are to be found in the ancient Egyptian love lyrics. He classifies them as follows: 1) "royal"-fiction; 2) "servant"-fiction; and 3) "shepherd"-fiction.[41]

1. "Royal"-Fiction. Although the king himself is not a character in the Egyptian love lyrics, a variety of royal allusions are present. The lover is urged to "come to the sister quickly" like a *messenger* of the king who is rushing to his lord so that the message can be received (see Beatty, G^1/1). Likewise, in the same Beatty Cycle of Three Songs, the lover is implored to approach his beloved quickly "like a horse of the king" (Beatty, G^1/5). To underscore the priority of his haste, this horse is described as the choicest of the king's stables. The steed is further characterized as follows:

> It is distinguished in its feed,
> (and) its master knows its paces.
> If it hears the sound of a whip,
> it knows no holding back.
> There is not a chief in the chariotry
> who can overtake it.
> (Beatty, G^1/6-7)

The imagery of royalty is preserved in descriptions of the beloved as well as the lover. In the Cairo poems, the servant is asked to prepare the woman's bed with the finest linen characteristic of "royal sheets" (see Cairo, X/12). In the Louvre C 100 poem, Mutiridis, the priestess of Hathor, is described as "the lovable *princess*, fairest of women" (Louvre, 16/2). In an obvious reference to the make-believe feeling of royalty which the beloved has felt when in the presence of her lover, Harris 8/1 refers to an epithet of the queen: "I am like the Lady of the Two Lands."[42] Similarly, one should consider Hermann's proposal that the phrase "the first of the beautiful ones" (Harris, 10/8) is reminiscent of a similar epithet of Queen Hatshepsut.[43]

The "royal"-fiction (or *"Ritter"-Travestie*, to use Hermann's designation adapted from Jolles) also describes another facet of the ancient Egyptian love poetry: the hunt scene. In the Third Song of the Beatty Cycle of Three Songs, there is an allusion to the gazelle hunt. The hunt is a characteristic theme of the iconography of the New Kingdom and hunting scenes are prevalent in Theban mortuary art. Such a scene may depict a peculiarly aristocratic pastime. The

hunting exploits of Amenophis II and Tuthmosis IV are recorded
on their monuments, and Amenophis III publicized his big game
hunting from his chariot on two series of commemorative
scarabs.[44] In the Egyptian love poetry, however, the hunting
of the gazelle appears to be but a subtle allusion to an aristocratic life-style, for the emphasis in the following poem
appears to be upon the frantic escape of the gazelle being like
the desire of the lover for his beloved:

> Terror has entered into its (the gazelle's) limbs.
> Hunters are after it.
> Hounds are with them,
> (but) they do not see his dust.
> It sees a resting place like a mirage (?).
> It takes a river as a road.
>   (Beatty, G^2/2-4)

Finally, the fragmentary Poem Two of the Harris 500 collection
may reflect a royal allusion in the form of a comparison characterizing the lover. He is depicted as a circling falcon.
The royal image of the falcon is well-known from the titulary
assumed by the Pharaoh on the day of his accession. The so-
called "Horus name," partially depicted by the hieroglyphic
sign of the falcon, represents the role of the king as the embodiment of the falcon-god, Horus.[45]

2. "Servant"-Fiction. According to Hermann, the "servant"-fiction corresponds to the shepherd figure in Western
literature.[46] Regarding the Egyptian love lyrics, however, the
servant role is reflected in that figure who assumes a role below the social class to which he normally belongs and _willingly_
accepts such a position. As a result, the "servant"-fiction is
often introduced by the wish particle, 𓄿 "would
that."

In Poem Seven of the Harris 500 collection, the man desires to be near his beloved. In his longing, he notes that he
would even be willing to become her door-keeper: "Would that
one would make me her door-keeper" (Harris, 4/12). Such a desire is not purely altruistic, however. If the lover had such
a job, he, then, would be in close proximity to his beloved "so
that I would hear her voice when she is angry (and be) a child
in dread of her" (Harris, 4/13). In Harris, 10/3, it is the
beloved who expresses a desire to be a servant of the lover.
Note the following:

O beautiful (one), I have a good desire
for (my caring for) your things
as your housemaid.

The "servant"-fiction is noted in a three poem cycle at
the end of the Cairo Ostracon text, bound together by the re-
occurring wish particle (see above, p. 71). The desire that is
expressed in each of the poems is the longing of the lover to
clothe himself in a different role in order to gain access to
his beloved.[47] Such hoped-for proximity can enable the lover
to have pleasurable experiences. Note the following from
Cairo, X/13-14:

Would that I were her Nubian (maid)
who is her personal servant.
Then I would see the skin of all her body.

Likewise, if the lover could become the beloved's washerman,
even "for a single month," he could not only enjoy her scent
but might be in a position to win her favor (see Cairo, X/14-
15). Unfortunately, the fragmentary state of the ostracon prevents a full assessment of the lover's desire to be "her seal
ring," but the close proximity of the ring to her finger indicates his desire for intimate contact with his beloved (see
Cairo, X/17-18).[48]

    3. "Shepherd"-Fiction. Hermann notes that this fiction
is a universal theme in literature which, in terms of Egyptian
love poetry, does not reflect an attempt to demean one's self,
but rather to cast off the weight of *Stadtkultur* and to flee
civilization.[49] The role that is assumed is one which reflects
a movement "back to nature."

A rustic atmosphere is well depicted in the Turin cycle in
which the beloved is pictured as a gardener who plants "the
little sycamore" (Turin, 13/5). The beauty of the garden and
the variety of natural images provide the setting for love-
making. In that idyllic setting, the lovers can "pass the day
in pleasure" (Turin, 16/3). The woman is also pictured as a
rustic gardener in the Harris collection. She speaks the
following lines:

(As for) me, behold I am like the Crown Lands
which I planted
with flowers and with all fragrant *ḥꜣwt* plants.
    (Harris, 14/7-8)

One again notes that it is the pastoral setting which provides
a place for the lovers to enjoy one another. She continues as
follows:

> A good place for my walking (is) there.
> Your hand is in my hand.
> My body is at ease.
> My heart is joyful because of our journeying together.
>   (Harris, 14/9-10)

The beloved appears in another guise which may be termed
an aspect of the "shepherd"-fiction: the bird-snarer.[50] The
woman describes herself as a bird-snarer who goes out and comes
in from snaring with her traps, cage, and hunting instrument.[51]
Yet, the love poetry expresses that snaring is particularly
enjoyable for her because her lover accompanies her:

> You are there with me,
> when I set a snare.
> The happiness (is) the going to the fields
> of the one who is loved.
>   (Harris, 8/6-7)

Because of her fantasies about love, the woman is unable to
snare successfully. She bemoans that she must return home to
her mother with empty traps:

> I did not set the trap today.
> Your love has seized me.
>   (Harris, 8/9)

In at least one instance, the lover assumes the role of
the farmer. Such a guise is a continuation of the pastoral
imagery noted above, associated with the beloved. The man is
seen traveling down the Nile loaded with reeds. Consider the
following:

> I travel downstream in the ferry-boat
> by the stroke of the command;
> my bundle of reeds upon my shoulder.
>   (Harris, 14/6)

This rustic image of the lover is closely followed by the trav-
eler's longing to be with his beloved. As he travels, he im-
plores Ptah, "Give to me my sister tonight!" (Harris, 14/7).

The "shepherd"-fiction can also be detected in a variety
of images which are taken from the *Hirtenwelt*.[52] Illustrative
of such imagery are the various elements in the *waṣf* in Poem
Three of the Harris collection. The sister is compared with

features taken from nature. She is a lotus bud; her eyes are
like berries; her head is described as a snare of "*mry*-wood"
(an image taken from the fictional role of bird-snaring).
Similarly, the man is given the pet name "jackal pup," a word
which might reflect the experience of the shepherd in driving
away wolves and jackals from the flock by beating them with
clubs, palm branches, etc. (see Harris, 4/2-5).

GATTUNGEN OF LOVE POETRY

Hermann has isolated three distinct literary *Gattungen* in
the Egyptian love poems which he notes carry a *sustained* theme
through an entire poem in contrast to a topos which appears
sporadically.[53] The designations of *Gattungen* may be listed as
follows: 1) the descriptive song; 2) the day song; and 3) the
lament at the door.

1. The Descriptive Song (*Beschreibungslied*). This literary form is the poetic description of the physical charms of
one of the love partners using imagery common to the ancient
Egyptian culture. The name, "descriptive song," reflects the
use of a similar literary form in Arabic literature, the *waṣf*.
The history of this form, however, is extensive, for *waṣf*-like
material is noted in the divine love lyrics of ancient Mesopotamia, in Egyptian love poetry, in the description of Sara in
the so-called Genesis Apocryphon from Cave I at Qumran, and in
modern Syrian wedding ritual.[54]

While the descriptive song in modern Syrian literature may
have a definite life-setting in the marriage feast, Hermann
notes that there is no one life-setting for this type of song
in ancient Egypt. Poem Three of the Harris collection appears
to be set against the background of a rustic scene, for the
elements of the comparison are rural. Note the following
description of the woman by her lover:

> Distracting are the plants of her rush.
> The sister is a lotus bud.
> Her breasts are of perfume.
> Her arms...[vine-like],
> [her eyes] are fixed berries (?).
> Her forehead is the snare of *mry*-wood,
> and I am a wild goose!
> (Harris, 2/10-4/1)

The motif of the "shepherd"-fiction may provide this poem with its rustic imagery. The movement of this description, moreover, appears to describe first the woman's lower regions ("plants of her rush" being a euphemism for genitals) and, then, to depict her body in an *upward* order: breasts, arms, eyes, and forehead.

A second descriptive song in the Egyptian love lyrics describes the beloved in a reverse order from that given in the Harris poem above. Note the following from Beatty, $C^1/2$-5:

> ...who is beautiful of eyes which stare.
> Her lips, which speak, are sweet.
> She has not a word too much.
> One high of neck, one bright of nipples,
> real lapis-lazuli is her hair.
> Her arms excel gold;
> her fingers are like lotus flowers.
> One drooping of buttocks, one tight of inmost parts,
> her thighs extend her perfection.
> Her step is pleasing when she treads upon the earth.

Only the phrase, "real lapis-lazuli is her hair," appears to disturb what otherwise is a *downward* sequence to this descriptive song: eyes, lips, neck, arms, fingers, buttocks, feet. The imagery of the poem is varied and does not betray a life-setting. The mention of "gold" and "lapis-lazuli" may allude to statuary and "lotus flowers" to the delta region, but the images are too general to conclude that the description of the woman is based upon any one facet of Egyptian culture. Parenthetically, one may note that the woman not only has ideal physical attributes, but also maintains the Egyptian ideal of silence: ⌐ 〰 ⊘ 〰 ઠ e ⅄ ꞉ 𓅱𓋴𓏏 e 𓏤𓏤𓏤 ("she has not a word too much"). The ideal of silence and the virtue associated with proper speech is a frequent topos of Egyptian wisdom texts, for the proper balance of the tongue sustains the cosmic order ($m3^ct$) of life.[55]

Another descriptive song is preserved in the Louvre C 100 text. Here the Hathor-priestess, Mutiridis, is described as "fairest of women," one "whose likeness has not been seen" (Louvre, 16/3). Following this general description, the following physical attributes are noted: hair, "blacker...than the blackness of the night"; teeth, "whiter...than flakes of (white) stone at cutting"; and breasts, like "(two) wreaths... settled at her arm" (Louvre, 16/3-4).

116

Finally, in the Turin cycle of tree poems, there are descriptive songs which utilize garden imagery to describe beauty. In the first of the Turin poems, the tree describes the young woman, comparing her charms with that of the tree which is "foremost in the orchard" (Turin, 9/2 and 10/1). Note the following:

> It [says]:
> My seeds (are) like her teeth;
> my fruit like her breasts.
> ...[I am foremost] in the orchard.
> I am established in every season,
> which the sister passes with her brother.
> (Turin, 8/1-9/3)

In the third Turin poem, moreover, "the little sycamore" attempts a *self-description*. Note the following:

> It is beautiful; its branches are lovely,
> greener than [the grass].
> It is loaded with the abundance of notched sycamore
> figs.
> It is redder than red jasper.
> Its leaves...a hue of green feldspar.
> Sap like *bsbs* oil.
> (Turin, 14/1-5)

2. The Day Song (*Tagelied*). This designation of *Gattung* reflects the theme of separation (*Liebestrennung*) which the loving partners experience.[56] In particular, it is the arrival of the morning which forces the lovers to part company after their night of love-making. A classic example of this form is found in Poem Fourteen of the Harris collection. Here, one encounters the role of the turtledove, the harbinger of the morning. It is his cry that announces the end of their night of love. Note the following:

> The voice of the turtledove speaks. It says:
> "The day breaks, what is your way?"
> Quiet, O bird,
> must you scold me so?
> I found my brother on his bed.
> My heart is pleasing in excess.
> We said:
> "I shall not be far [from you]
> for my hand is in your hand.
> I shall walk about when I am with you
> in every pleasant place."
> He makes me the first of the beautiful ones.
> He has not upset my heart.
> (Harris, 10/6-8)

The day song may be represented in the fragmentary first
poem of the Harris 500 collection. There, the lover appears
to be leaving his beloved, and the reason may be that the day
has come and the lover must depart. His beloved is not content
with his leaving and seeks his explanation for his departure.
Note the following questions that she asks her lover:

> ...where will you set your heart?
> ...(would) you leave when you remember food?
> Are you a gluttonous man?
> (would) you...[go] because of clothes?
> ...(Would) you go because of hunger?
> (Harris, 2/1-4)

The passion of the night which is reflected in the Nakht-
Sobek Cycle of the Beatty collection is described by the poet
to the lover. The inviting scene of the night of love is depicted to the man and he will "bring her to an end in her
night" (the consummation of the love affair, Beatty, R^{16}/11).
Yet, the passion of the night is so great that it will continue
until the morning breaks. Note the following:

> Thus she will tell you:
> "Take me in your embrace.
> When the day dawns, we will be likewise."
> (Beatty, R^{16}/11)

3. The Lament at the Door (*Türklage*). This literary form
is attested in Greco-Roman literature as the *Paraklausithyron*
which has been defined by F. O. Copley as follows: "...the
song sung by the lover at his mistress's door, after he has
been refused admission to her house...it is usually a lament,
a song of disappointment and sorrow."[57]

An instance of the lover's disappointment and frustration
upon his not being allowed entry into the house of his beloved
is noted in the following:

> (As for) that which the sister did to me,
> shall I keep silent from her
> letting me stand in the door of her house
> while she went inside?
> She does not speak to me of a good release
> while she shared in my night.
> (Beatty, R^{17}/6-7)

The lover laments that the beloved's door prevents the culmination of their love, and (if one may freely exegete) he

ironically notes that she cannot speak of *his* good sexual relief because it failed to happen.

The Seventh Stanza of the Nakht-Sobek Cycle provides a
particularly interesting example of this literary form. The
lover passes by the door of his beloved, knocks, but the door
does not open. The lover is hindered not only by the sleeping
door-keeper who fails to answer the door, but also by the door
itself, which he appears to address as a personified spirit:[58]

> Door, you are my fate.
> Are you my spirit?
> Our ox will be slaughtered inside.
> Door, do not use your might!
> (Beatty, R[17]/9)

The poem then continues the lament, citing the brother's desire
that the door be accessible to him. He envisions a door of
grass and a door-bolt of reeds that will allow continual entry
into the sister's house. Yet, even this fantasy ends with a
touch of irony, for upon gaining entry into the house and upon
finding his beloved in the midst of a linen-laid bed, the maid
announces to him that he is not welcome. Hence, the following
discovery is made:

> The maid will say to me:
> "This place belongs to the son
> of the mayor of the village."
> (Beatty, R[17]/13)

THE ATMOSPHERE OF THE EGYPTIAN LOVE LYRICS

There is an unmistakable pastoral, idyllic quality about
the love-language of the ancient Egyptian love poetry. The
expressions of mutual desire and longing are accomplished
through the use of natural imagery (trees, the delta, plants,
animals, etc.), and the setting of love's enjoyment is equally
rustic (the garden house, under the trees, etc.). At the same
time, there is a "make-believe" quality to the expression of
love, characterized most clearly by the use of the literary
fictions. Hence, the lovers are transformed into guises that
are playful and elusive.

It is the thesis of this study that from the Egyptian love
poetry one learns something about the nature of love-language
current in the ancient Near East. The commonality of topoi,

genres, and literary style provide one with valuable insights
into the language, themes, and style of the Hebrew Song of
Songs. One would not wish to go so far as Gerleman and state
that Egyptian influence on the Song is so far-reaching that the
descriptive songs in Canticles reflect Egyptian pictorial
art.[59] It would not, however, be an exaggeration to assume
that the earlier love poetry of Egypt did exert influence on
the love songs that came to be collected as the Song of Songs.
Certainly, the love poetry of Israel participates in the same
atmosphere and shares in the love-language of the Egyptian
lyrics.

NOTES

[1] See André Jolles, *Einfache Formen* (3d ed.; Tübingen: Max Niemeyer, 1965) 36, 39, and 45.

[2] Jolles's work has been particularly important for Old Testament study as well as recent literary criticism in general. For analyses of Jolles's work see the following: Robert Petsch, "Die Lehre von den 'Einfache Formen,'" *DtVi* 10 (1932) 335-69; Hermann Bausinger, *Formen der "Volkspoesie,"* (Berlin: E. Schmidt, 1958) 51-64. In terms of Old Testament study, see especially Hans-Jürgen Hermisson, *Studien zur israelitischen Spruchweisheit* (WMANT 28; Neukirchen-Vlvyn: Neukirchener Verlag, 1968) and M. Buss, "The Study of Forms," in *Old Testament Form Criticism* (Trinity University Monograph Series in Religion 2; ed. John H. Hayes; San Antonio: Trinity University, 1974) 38.

[3] Hermann, *Altägyptische Liebesdichtung*, 66.

[4] Ibid., 71.

[5] Ibid., 66-70.

[6] W. Kayser supports a similar view. He notes that the various concepts such as lyric, epic, and dramatic are as E. Staiger has noted "...scientific literary names for fundamental possibilities of human existence as a whole"; see Kayser, *Das sprachliche Kunstwerk* (12th printing; Bern: Francke Verlag, 1967) 333.

[7] For a survey of the various details and practice of archetypal criticism, see Northrop Frye, *Anatomy of Criticism* (Princeton: Princeton University, 1957).

[8] Jolles's correlation between literary form and human concerns is a classic presentation in literary criticism. Recently, however, critics have noted deficiencies in such a psychological-ontological approach to literature. Dan Ben-Amos has recently outlined the nature of "native taxonomy" in characterizing literary genre; cf. Ben-Amos, "Analytical Categories and Ethnic Genres," *Genre* 2 (1969) 275-301. In terms of biblical studies, cf. William G. Doty, "The Concept of Genre in Literary Analysis," *Proceedings* (ed. L. C. McGaughy; Society of Biblical Literature, 1972) 413-48. Doty notes that, while he is sympathetic to the correlation of literary genres and "particular human interests," these correlations are difficult to specify (441). Consequently, Doty calls for a careful analysis of the *use* of literary patterns and their *function* vis-à-vis original author and audience.

[9] Hermann uses as structural principles several characteristics which appear throughout the corpus of Egyptian love literature, e.g., the brother-sister speech, the speech of the poet, etc. Hermann's use of "structure" connotes a general

reference to pervasive literary characteristics which provide a framework to the love poetry. The designation "topos" is used interchangeably with the word "theme" and has no structural connotation for Hermann. In the jargon of recent literary criticism, this designation is often understood as a rhetorical device denoting a structural principle: the logical or recurring elements of thought. See Frye, *Anatomy*, p. 103 and Buss, "The Study of Forms,"6. For the sake of organization, Hermann's literary designations will be followed, but the reader should be aware of the fluid state of literary designations and the variety of definitions given for certain technical terms (topos, genre, literary travesty, etc.).

[10]See Hermann, *Altägyptische Liebesdichtung*, 72.

[11]See Adolf Erman, *Neuägyptische Grammatik* (Hildesheim: Georg Olms, 1933) §§60, 65, and 68.

[12]See Gardiner, *Chester Beatty*, 37 n. 3. A curious parallel to this address is noted in the ŠA.ZI.GA. (potency) incantations from Mesopotamian literature. These incantations are usually recited by a woman, addressing the man who is sexually impotent. Such address is in the second person. See Robert D. Biggs, *ŠA.ZI.GA. Ancient Mesopotamian Potency Incantations* (Locust Valley, NY: J. J. Augustin, 1967) 2.

[13]See Hermann, *Altägyptische Liebesdichtung*, 73 n. 21.

[14]Ibid., 76. J. Černý has shown that *Geschwisterede* was not widely practiced outside the context of the court, and we may assume that the sister-brother terminology has nothing to do with the practice of incest; see his "Consanguineous Marriages in Pharaonic Egypt," *JEA* 40 (1954) 23-29.

[15]See Dahood, review of *Seven Books of Wisdom*, by R. E. Murphy, *Bib* 42 (1961) 235-37.

[16]For a discussion of the Hurrian family practices, see P. Koschaker, "Fratriarchat, Hausgemeinschaft und Mutterrecht in Keilschrifttexten," *ZA* (1933) 1-89. For these practices in relation to the Old Testament, see E. A. Speiser, "The Wife-Sister Motif in the Patriarchal Narratives," *Biblical and Other Studies* (ST 1; ed. A. Altmann; Cambridge: Harvard University, 1963) 15-28. There is little evidence to assume that the Egyptian "sister-brother" terminology is presupposed in understanding Gen 12:10-20. Although the beauty of Sarah is noted, reminiscent of the description of the beauty of the woman in Egyptian love lyrics, one may suppose that the Yahwist has a fraternal relationship in mind. Kinship is certainly to be noted in the Elohist's presentation of this tradition, for he attempts to justify Abraham's "white lie" by noting that Sarah was, in fact, Abraham's half-sister (Gen 20:12).

[17]See Gerleman, *Das Hohelied*, 155; Rudolph,*Das Hohelied*, 150; Würthwein, *Die Fünf Megilloth*, 53. William K. Simpson has noted that, because the sister-brother address in the Egyptian lyrics designates the lady and her lover, one may render the terms "lady" or "lady love" and "love" or "boy," respectively;

see Simpson, *The Literature*, 297. In the Appendix, *sn*
("brother") and *snt* ("sister") have been translated literally
and the modern reader should take note that these terms describe the customary Egyptian designations for lovers.

[18]Hermann, *Altägyptische Liebesdichtung*, 79. The concepts
of balance, order, and truth in Egypt are concerned with the
maintenance of *mꜣ*꜡*t*, "the innermost part of the Egyptian ethic;
see Siegfried Morenz, *Egyptian Religion* (trans. A. E. Keep;
Ithaca: Cornell University, 1973) 121-22. For a discussion of
the origins of the concept *mꜣ*꜡*t*, see Hellmut Brunner, "Gerechtigkeit als Fundament des Thrones," *VT* 8 (1958) 426-28 and
Morenz, 120. For the significance of this concept vis-à-vis
Egyptian wisdom literature, see Schmid, *Wesen und Geschichte*,
23-26 and A. Volten, "Der Begriff der Maat in den ägyptischen
Weisheitstexten," *Les sagesses du Proche-Orient Ancien* (Paris:
Presses Universitaires de France, 1963).

[19]"Seeing" is a familiar topos of Egyptian love poetry;
see below, pp. 99 and 134-35.

[20]See Foster's free translation of Beatty, C^3/5-7 in which
the young man's prayer is an attempt to "butter up" Hathor!
(54).

[21]Hermann, *Altägyptische Liebesdichtung*, 84-86.

[22]In spite of the rather insignificant role of "established religion," another manifestation of the numinous does
appear: magic. At least two examples of magical overtones appear in the love songs. In Cairo, X/8, there is mention of a
"waterspell" which is used to protect the lover from the crocodile. In Beatty, R^{17}/9, the object of the door appears to
possess magical power and is personified. Note the following:
"Door, you are my fate. Are you my spirit?" See Hermann,
Altägyptische Liebesdichtung, 86.

[23]W. Wolf, "Über die Gegenstandsbezogenheit des ägyptischen Denkens," *Ägyptologische Studien* (ed. O. Firchow; DAWBIO
29; Berlin: Akademie-Verlag, 1955) 407-408.

[24]An analysis of recent advances of recent advances in the
use of "topoi" in literary criticism may be found in W. Veit,
"Toposforschung: Ein Forschungsbericht," *DtVi* 37 (1963) 120-63;
see above, n. 9.

[25]Hermann, *Altägyptische Liebesdichtung*, 89.

[26]Ibid., 90.

[27]The hand kiss and mouth kiss employ the sense of touch
and are discussed here. The nose kiss may best be described
as "breathing" and is discussed below, pp. 102-03.

[28]The hypothesis of E. Suys that the number "four" refers
to the administration of a religious rite is unlikely; see E.
Suys, "Les chants d'amour du Papyrus Chester Beatty I," *Bib*
13 (1932) 227.

[29] "Feet" may be employed as a euphemism for the genitals; compare the Hebrew use of רגל.

[30] Hermann, *Altägyptische Liebesdichtung*, 93.

[31] For the genre designation *Tagelied*, see below, p. 149.

[32] The pose that is struck by Akhenaten and his wife Nefertiti in the famous *Wagenfahrt* scene represents the nose kiss; see Hermann, *Altägyptische Liebesdichtung*, Abbildung 5, p. 61.

[33] Ibid., 95. See H. Brunner, "Das Herz als Sitz des Lebensgeheimnisses," *AO* 17 (1954/55) 140-41; "Das hörende Herz," *TLZ* 79 (1954) 697-700.

[34] Hermann, *Altägyptische Liebesdichtung*, 99. A curious parallel in the Mesopotamian literature may allude to "love-sickness." From the so-called "Inanna Dialogue," Thorkild Jacobsen has recently translated a fragmented line to read as follows: "I shall grow paler and paler." Jacobsen's interpretation of this line is that it reflects the love pangs which Dumuzi feels for Inanna; see his "The Sister's Message," *JANESCU* 5 (1973) 199.

[35] Hermann, *Altägyptische Liebesdichtung*, 102.

[36] See above, Chapter II, p. 73.

[37] See P. C. Smither, "The Prince Mehy of the Love Songs," *JEA* 34 (1948) 116.

[38] Hermann, *Altägyptische Liebesdichtung*, 107.

[39] This word play, mentioned above, p. 81, is illustrated as follows in Harris, 14/7 (note the repeated hieroglyphic figures): ⌒ "s3ᶜm plants"; ⌒ "one is s3ᶜmed (elevated)."

[40] Jolles's categories and discussion may be found in his "Die literarischen Travestien," *BdP* 6 (1932) 281-94; also see Hermann, *Altägyptische Liebesdichtung*, 111.

[41] Hermann's use of *Travestie* closely follows the pioneering work of Jolles. His application of the word "travesty," however, does not possess the connotation of a literary motif which ridicules a subject or treats a serious subject frivolously--a nuance which is frequently used in contemporary literary criticism. See, for example, W. F. Thrall, A. Hibbard, and C. H. Holman, *A Handbook to Literature* (New York: Odyssey Press, 1960) 494. For purposes of clarity, this study will use the term "fiction" to denote that type of literature which presents a subject in a different context from that inherently held by the subject; see Hermann, *Altägyptische Liebesdichtung*, 111-24. In using the term "fiction," this study follows similar use by R. E. Murphy, "Form-Critical Studies," 414.

[42]See the use of this epithet by Queens Henttowy and Makare in Černý, "Egypt," 650; also see Simpson, *The Literature*, 301 n. 9.

[43]Hermann, "Beiträge," 119 and *Altägyptische Liebesdichtung*, 113 n. 66.

[44]See further discussion regarding the sport of hunting in James, "Egypt," 337.

[45]Gardiner, *Grammar*, 71. For example, the first of the five "great names" (𓏏𓅓 *rn wr*) for Sesostris I of the 12th Dynasty is 𓂋𓏏𓇳𓎛𓏏 (*Ḥr ʿnḫ mswt*, "Horus, 'Life-of-births'").

[46]Hermann, *Altägyptische Liebesdichtung* 116. Another literary fiction (the "shepherd"-fiction) supplies a more exact designation of this role in ancient Egyptian literature, according to Hermann.

[47]Ibid.

[48]There is no support for Schott's reconstruction of the last lines of the Cairo 25218 to read as follows: "(Ach, wäre ich) ein altes (Kleid) der Geliebten. (Dann...)"; see Schott, *Liebeslieder*, 67. The Spiegelberg hieroglyphic text does not reproduce such lines in transcription and the hieratic facsimile edited by M. Georges Daressy cannot substantiate further textual reconstruction than that provided in Appendix I of this study; see Daressy, ed., *Catalogue général des antiquités égyptiennes du musée du Caire* (Cairo: De l'institut français d'archéologie orientale, 1901) pls. XLII; XLIV; and XLV.

[49]Hermann, *Altägyptische Liebesdichtung*, 116 and 119.

[50]Hermann, *Altägyptische Liebesdichtung*, 120. Hermann also alludes to the role of the woman as fish catcher which he interprets as a part of the "shepherd"-fiction. However, in context, it would appear that this particular image in the extant love poetry is ambiguous. The woman is described as having gone down into the water with her lover "in a tunic of fine, royal linen" (Cairo, X/4). It would appear that this reference to "royal linen" could well allude to the "royal"-fiction in describing the swimsuit of the beloved. Nevertheless, a picture of a woman capturing a fish is preserved from Deir el-Medineh and the scene in the love poetry may reflect a rustic picture of the beloved; see Hermann, *Altägyptische Liebesdichtung*, Tafel Xa.

[51]See the iconographic evidence of a woman bird-snaring, ibid., Tafel Xb.

[52]Ibid., 122-23.

[53]Ibid., 124.

[54]See Wilhelm Hermann, "Geschichte des altorientalischen Beschreibungsliedes," for a summary of the lines of historical tradition embodied in this literary form. For Mesopotamian

evidence, see *ANET*, 496 and for modern Syrian parallels, see the work of Wetzstein (see above, p. 59, n. 25). The most recent commentary on the Genesis Apocryphon is that of J. Fitzmyer, *The Genesis Apocryphon of Qumran Cave I* (BibOr 18a; Rome: Pontifical Biblical Institute, 1971).

[55] See, e.g., "The Teaching of Merikare," and "The Teaching of Vizier Kagemni," in Simpson, *The Literature*, 177-178 and 181.

[56] Hermann, *Altägyptische Liebesdichtung*, 130.

[57] F. O. Copley, *Exclusus Amator*: A study in Latin Love Poetry, American Philological Association, *Monograph* 17 (1956) 22; quoted in Hermann, *Altägyptische Liebesdichtung*, 132. See also A. T. Hatto, "Das Tagelied in der Weltliteratur," *DtVi* 36 (1962) 489-506.

[58] Hermann notes that the *Türgespräch* which is found in the 125th chapter of the Book of the Dead may lie behind the lover's address to the door (*Altägyptische Liebesdichtung*, 134).

[59] Gerleman, *Das Hohelied*, 69-71.

CHAPTER IV

THE SONG OF SONGS:
AN ANALYSIS OF LOVE-LANGUAGE

The publications of S. Schott's translations of ancient
Egyptian love poetry, *Altägyptische Liebeslieder* (1950), and of
A. Hermann's analysis of the topoi of this literature, *Alt-*
ägyptische Liebesdichtung (1959), were quite influential in
European scholarship on the Song of Songs during the last decade. To varying degrees, the following commentaries show an
acquaintance with the alleged Egyptian parallels to the Song
and an appreciation of their value (particularly in terms of
imagery and motifs): Rudolph (1962); Krinetzki (1964); Gerleman (1965); Würthwein (1969); and Loretz (1971). Along with
Gerleman's commentary, the analysis of the Egyptian material
vis-à-vis the Song by R. Tournay in the commentary of Robert,
Tournay, and Feuillet (1963) stands as an important attempt to
delineate the relationship between these two collections of
love songs.[1]

This chapter shall attempt to outline a variety of themes
which the Song of Songs shares with the Egyptian love lyrics.
As is so often the case in Old Testament study, a recourse to
an ancient Near Eastern corpus of literature can provide illu-
mination of the literary forms which are found in a biblical
book. Because in each instance one is dealing with the expression of human love, the similarities of motifs and themes
across the cultural continuum of the ancient world give us some
understanding of the way ancient humankind expressed their
feelings of love.

THE DESIGN OF THE SONG

1. The Title. The superlative title שִׁיר הַשִּׁירִים and the
ascription of the work to Solomon forms a title which most
scholars discern to be editorial. Whether one works with the
editorial superscription in 1:1 or with an hypothesized title
to the Song as proposed by J.-P. Audet ("A Kissing Song of the
Betrothed"),[2] it should be noted that many of the anonymous
Egyptian love poems have also been provided titles which appear
to introduce specific collections.

Poems Nine and Eighteen of the Harris 500 collection begin
with what the text itself denotes as a brief introduction to
the poems which follow. The scribe sets the following apart by
drawing the signs in red in the manuscript: [hieroglyphs]
[hieroglyphs] ("The Beginning of the Praise of Pleasures").
In Harris, 8/1-2, the title, often called a "rubric,"[3] introduces eight love poems which form a small collection and in
Harris, 14/3, the same title introduces the three-poem cycle
about flowers. Other titles are noted in the Beatty love
songs. The first cycle of seven songs is introduced by the
following: "The Beginning of the Utterances of the Great Pleasure" (Beatty, C^1/1). Likewise, in Beatty, R^{16}/9, the following introduction precedes a seven-stanza cycle:[4]

> The beginning of the sweet sayings found
> while holding a scroll composed by the writer
> Nakht-Sobek of the necropolis.

2. The Dialogue of the Lovers. The speakers in the Song
of Songs may be classified as follows: the man; the woman; the
poet; the Daughters of Jerusalem; and the brothers (8:8-9). In
the Song, moreover, the second person form of address appears
to predominate, giving the impression that the Song is an or-
chestrated dialogue between the lover and his beloved. In the
unit 7:7-11, one notes an especially interesting example of dialogue in which the lover speaks a "song of admiration" (*Bewunderungslied*) to his lady love. There, he affirms her
beauty (v. 7) and compares her figure and breasts (v. 8) to the
palm tree and its "clusters" (אשכלות).[5] He, then, expresses
his desire--a yearning to possess the beloved (vv. 9-10a).
In the MT there is a sudden transition and, then, the *beloved*
now speaks (v. 10b), noting that the wine of which the lover
spoke in his comparison of her mouth, now flows for him.[6] She
concludes the unit with a statement of possession: "I belong
to my lover" (v. 11a).

The second person form of address is noted in the Egyptian
material; yet, as pointed out above, p. 94, this speech is exclusively placed in the mouth of the woman (speaking in the
first person) who addresses the man as the second person "you."
In the majority of instances, however, the man or woman speaks
in the first person about his or her love partner who is

referred to *in the third person* (see Harris, 4/9-11; 4/12-13; 10/9-12; Beatty, C^1/1-8; and C^1/8-c^2/4).

Yet, the love partner being referred to in the third person is also characteristic of the Song. In 2:3, for example, the beloved expresses to the Daughters the delight which she feels in the presence of her lover: "I delight to dwell in his shadow, and his fruit is sweet to my palate." She, then, describes an encounter with her lover and her subsequent love-sickness. Note the following:

> He brings me into the "banqueting house";
> his banner over me is love....
> His left hand is under my head,
> his right hand embraces me.
>   (Cant 2:4, 6)

Similarly, as an address to the Daughters (3:1-4) or in what appears to be a response to a question of the Daughters (5:10-16), the woman speaks of the lover in the third person.

Another facet of the Egyptian poetry is the role of the poet who speaks as a neutral, third person (*der Dichter als Dritter*) in the poems. Gerleman has championed an attempt to see the elusive figure of the poet in the Song. Often his designation of the "poet" as speaker occurs in instances in which the address could be that of the Daughters. His attempt to see the poet speaking in parts of the very difficult unit 1:2-4 is hypothetical and does not clarify who is speaking in these lines.[7] He, likewise, sees the poet speaking in 7:1, inviting the onlookers to gaze upon the Shulammite who is dancing and in 5:1, inviting the "friends" (i.e., the couple) to enjoy love.[8] In each of these instances, one can argue that the Daughters or even the lover himself could be making the invitation. Gerleman's proposal that the poet responds to the beloved's questions regarding the whereabouts of her lover in the *Scherzgespräch* of 1:7-8 fails to appreciate the light dialogue that is characteristic of this unit. It is the lover, not the poet (Gerleman) or his companions (Krinetzki),[9] who responds to the beloved's inquiry. In this instance, then, there is no need to postulate a third party, for the lover is present!

Although one would not wish to add a speaker to the already complex problem in the Song regarding the identity of the speaker, a third party does appear in at least one unit in the

130

Song. Gerleman, concurring with Rudolph, notes that the poet
is speaking in 3:6-8 (the procession of the princess) and in
3:9-11 (the mention of the king).[10] Given the invitation *to*
the Daughters in v. 11 to "come forth and look upon King
Solomon," it is, therefore, difficult to designate the Daughters as the speaker in the unit 3:6-11. The figure of the poet
may take the position of a spectator as he views the grand
procession.

3. The Designation of the Beloved as "Sister." Approx-
imating the use of the term "sister" in the ancient Egyptian
love songs, the term אחתי ("my sister") denotes the beloved.
This connotation of אחתי is best illustrated in Cant 5:2 in
which אחתי is paralleled with רעיתי ("my beloved"), a distinctive name for the woman (see also 4:9; 4:10; 4:12; and
5:1).

In the Song, the term "brother" does not appear denoting
the lover. Yet, like the Egyptian poems, the family connotation of sister/brother appears along with (in the case of the
Song) "sister" used as a synonym for the beloved. In 8:1, the
woman longs that her lover would be her brother, the family
connection determined by the following description: "Suckled
at my mother's breasts." Likewise, the beloved's brothers
address her as "our sister" in 8:8.[11] In Beatty, $C^3/10-C^3/2$,
the beloved passes the house of her lover and finds him there
with "all his brothers and sisters."

4. Expressions of Mutuality and Uniqueness. One of the
characteristic repetitions in the Song is a phrase depicting
the relationship between the loving pair. The phrase is spoken
by the beloved and in 2:16 and 6:3, describes their mutual possession as follows: דודי לי ואני לו ("My lover belongs to me
and I to him"). In 7:11, the following variation of the repetition occurs, underscoring the sexual desire that the lover
has for the beloved: אני לדודי ועלי תשוקתו ("I belong to my
lover and for me he is yearning").

A further example of commitment and exclusivity in their
love relationship is sounded by the lover when he describes his
beloved as a גן נעול מעין חתום ("an enclosed garden, a fountain sealed" [4:12]). The theme of the garden appears to be
part of a larger unit (4:9-5:1) in which the lover expresses
his admiration for the beloved (*Bewunderungslied*).[13] Part of

this admiration includes her fidelity to the man--she is "enclosed" and "sealed" and, thus, remains his *exclusive* possession.

Such statements of mutual possession recall similar expressions of partnership in the Egyptian poems. The woman desires to "set the love of my brother as my only concern" (Harris, 10/10). Likewise, the lovers desire to be alone, thus, exluding others from their relationship and sharing only in one another's presence (see Harris, 8/5). As noted above, p. 96, this desire for exclusivity is characteristic of their love-making (see Beatty, R[16]/11-12), a theme which parallels the exclusive character of the faithful lovers in the Song (Cant 4:9-5:1).

Closely related to the expressions of mutual desire in the Egyptian poems are the statements of admiration in which one of the lovers describes the uniqueness of the other partner. The woman, thus, describes the man as "the grandest in my heart" (Harris, 14/5) while the man notes that his beloved is one "without her duplicate, more beautiful than any woman" (Beatty, C[1]/1).

In the Song, the woman is often characterized as one of unique beauty. In 1:8, the lover sounds a theme which is subsequently reiterated by the Daughters (6:1; 5:9). The beloved is addressed as follows: הַיָּפָה בַּנָּשִׁים ("O most beautiful among women"). Likewise, in 2:1, there is an example of *Selbstschilderung* in which the beloved describes herself as unique by the use of flower metaphors: "I am a flower of Sharon, a lily of the valley." Yet, her short self-description appears to be part of a larger unit (2:1-3) that Horst and other commentators describe as a song of admiration in the form of a dialogue.[14] In the following verse, then, the *lover* takes up the beloved's use of metaphor and further describes her uniqueness--"a lily among thorns" (2:2). In 2:3a, the *beloved* again speaks, returning the compliment to him. She states that he too is unique--"as an apple tree among the trees of the forest." The woman, consequently, states the delight which she feels when she can be present with him (2:3b).[15]

In the unit 6:8-10, the lover again describes the uniqueness of his beloved. He compares her to the royal harem and

finds her distinctive among all the others. She is "one alone,
my dove, my perfect one" (6:9a). The response of the harem to
the beauty of the beloved is reminiscent of the acknowledgment
that the garden trees in the Turin love songs make of the beloved's beauty. She is compared with the trees' own beauty and
is like them, both "foremost in the orchard" (Turin 9/2 and
10/1) and "noble" (Turin, 12/3). Also in the Egyptian poems,
onlookers and bystanders respond to the beauty of the beloved.
Note the following:

> I rejoice, I am glad, I am great,
> ever since one said, "Hey, she is here!"
> Behold, she came and the lovers are bowing down
> to the greatness of her love.
>   (Beatty, C^3/7-8)
>
> She causes that the necks of all men
> turn back at the sight of her.
>   (Beatty, C^1/6)

Finally, the words of praise which are uttered by the
women of the harem (6:10) concerning the appearance of the beloved recall similar astral imagery used in the Egyptian
poetry.[16] In Beatty, C^1/1-2, the beloved is said to be like
the Star Goddess (Sothis) "rising at the beginning of a favor-
able year." In the Song, the harem describes the woman as "one
coming forth like the dawn" (6:10a).

5. The Lovers and Divinity. As noted above, (p. 98), in
the ancient Egyptian love lyrics, when divinities are mentioned, references display a characteristic nonchalance and, at
times, almost irreverence regarding the pantheon (see Beatty,
C^3/6). The deities that are mentioned are often presented in
enigmatic ways, subordinated to the expressions and experiences
of love, characteristic aspects of these lyrics.

In the Song of Songs, there is no explicit mention of the
deity. Does this feature of the love poems mean that the collection is radically "secular" (reflecting an even stronger
attitude of nonchalance about the deity) or that the community
which preserved these songs had no interest in theological
questions?

Although the questions raised concerning the "theology" of
the Song are too broad to be fully considered in the scope of
this study, one may propose that the theological view presented

in the ancient Egyptian poems cannot be said to describe the
outlook held by those who preserved love songs in Israel. For
the Israelite sages, Yahweh was the creator, and the created
order and man's role in it were aspects of the sages' interest.
These wise men reflected on the beauty and goodness of that
creation and sought to understand the seemingly impenetrable
mysteries:

> Three things are too wonderful for me,
> and four I cannot understand:
> the way of an eagle in the air;
> the way of a serpent upon a rock;
> the way of a ship on the high seas;
> and the way of a man with a maiden.
>   (Prov 30:18-19)

Yet, even in their concern for *this* world, the sages never lost
sight of the creator. Essential, then, to their world-view was
the theological affirmation: "The fear of Yahweh is the
beginning of wisdom" (Prov 9:10).

The sages were "open" to investigate the empirical world
because it was divinely created.[17] Human sexual love, portrayed in the Song of Songs, was a crucial, strategic aspect
of creation with which humankind must deal responsibly. The
"theology" of the Song reflects the human attempt to deal responsibly with the male-female relationship as a gift of the
created order. For the sages, the Song displayed a lesson in
mutual love and expressed the importance of fidelity. Even the
language of the Song is reminiscent of the following lines from
Prov 5:18-19:

> And have joy in the wife of your youth,
> your lovely hind, your graceful doe.
> Her love will invigorate you always,
> through her love you will flourish continually.

The Song, moreover, appears to make its own comment about
the proper balance in the human love relationship, within the
context of fidelity and mutuality. The role of the woman who
both desires and is desirable (see Cant 2:1-3) serves as a cor-
rective to the male-oriented perspective which narrowly per-
ceived the woman's value vis-à-vis her ability to provide for
her husband and children (cf. Proverbs 31). Likewise, the Song
discloses that within the God-given male-female relationship,

sensual love and sexual pleasure need not be restrained (see Cant 7:9-13).

The mere absence of God's name in the Song does not denote the work as "non-theistic" literature. On the contrary, the Song was appropriated, or even edited, by the wise men of Israel who sought to understand and celebrate the male-female relationship as a part of God's creative domain. The Song, therefore, celebrates the human capacity to love as ordered by the creator. To this extent, the Song of Songs describes the human attempt to come to terms with sexual love--part of the natural and social world. The "theology" of the Song participates in the broader scope of wisdom theology: that which participates within the framework of God's creation.[18]

THE TOPOI OF THE SONG OF SONGS

There follows a representative list and analysis of topoi which appear in the Song. In striking similarity with the Egyptian love lyrics, the Hebrew love songs present the experience of love in terms of physical occurrences. The atmosphere which is established in the Song shares in common the sights, sounds, tastes, fears, and joys of human love with similar language to that of the Egyptian lyrics.

1. Seeing. The sight of one's love partner is an appealing experience in the Song. In the tease of 2:14-15, the lover speaks to his beloved who appears to be hidden or inaccessible to him ("in the clefts of the rock"). He states the following: "Let me see your face" (2:14). Likewise, as she searches for her lover at night, longing to see him, she asks the watchmen of the city the following question: "Have you seen him whom my heart loves?" (3:3).

The descriptive song in 6:4-7 includes a reference to the awesome power and mystery of the beloved: "Turn your eyes away from me, for they torment me" (6:5). Würthwein proposes that this reference is a "playful" (*spielerisch*) one.[19] Yet, the potential danger of the woman, especially in terms of her ability to entrap a man, appears to be a universal theme of literature and can be noted in the Egyptian love lyrics. In the following, note the reference to the eyes:

> She casts the noose at me with her hair.
> With her eyes she catches me,
> (and) with her necklace she causes me to bow down.
> With her seal (ring), she brands me.
>   (Beatty, R17/2-3)

The theme of entrapment, parenthetically, can also be seen in
the capture of the lover in the hair of his beloved (see Cant
7:6). Moreover, in 4:9, the glance of the beloved is said to
disturb "the heart" of the lover, a reference to the physically
disconcerting aspects of the lover's being seen by the beloved.

The Daughters of Jerusalem, in 7:1, speak to the
Shulammite and invite her to dance. Their invitation involves
their desire to see the beauty of the woman, as the following
indicates: "Turn, turn, O Shulammite, turn, turn, in order
that we may gaze upon you!"[20] The Shulammite accepts their invitation, and there follows a description of the woman's beauty
(7:2-6). The lover also enjoys viewing his beloved and is
described in 2:9 as a gazelle or stag who gazes (שׁגח) and
peers (צוץ).

Finally, the sense of sight is not only important for the
recognition of the beauty of the love partner, but also for the
appreciation of the locale of love. In 6:11, the beloved describes her visit to the nut garden.[21] She notes that her
visit there affords her an opportunity "to look at (לראות) the
shoots of the valley; to see if the vine is in bloom."

2. Hearing. In the Egyptian poetry, the voice of the
lover, when heard by the beloved, brings about life-giving
sustenance. Note the following from Harris, 14/10:

> Pomegranate-wine is my hearing your voice.
> I live because I hear.

In the Song, the voice of the beloved is the object of the
man's desire. In 2:14, he speaks to his inaccessible partner
as follows:

> Let me hear your voice,
> for your voice is sweet
> and your face lovely.

Likewise, in 8:13, the lover again longs to hear the voice of
his beloved.

O garden dweller,
my friends listen for your voice.
Let me hear it!

An interesting contrast is presented in the Song between instances in which the voice of the lover is heard by the beloved and, later, not heard. In 2:8, the beloved perceives the
approach of the man when she exclaims: קוֹל דּוֹדִי הִנֵּה-זֶה בָּא ("The
voice of my lover! Here he comes!"). The arrival of the lover
brings about his invitation to her to enjoy one another's presence: "Arise my beloved, my beautiful one, and come!" (2:10).
When the beloved could not hear the voice of the lover, however, the situation of joy turns into tragedy. In 5:6, the
beloved calls out to him, but "he did not answer me." She
seeks to find him, but he does not hear her call. The following verse adds a touch of irony. While seeking *to find* her
lover, she herself *is found* by the watchmen of the city who
subsequently assault her.[22]

   3. Touching. The topos of touching in the Song is noted
in the lovers' allusions to kissing and embracing. The Song of
Songs begins with the beloved's yearning to receive the kisses
of her lover. In 1:2, this desire is expressed as follows:
"Let him kiss me with the kisses of his mouth." A similar
yearning is expressed in 8:1 where the beloved longs to kiss
her lover in public. Such a desire is similar to that expressed by the woman in the ancient Egyptian poetry who longs
to kiss her lover "in front of his companions" (Beatty, C[4]/4).
In the Song, the Beloved covets the presence of her lover and
states the following: "If I should meet you outside, I would
kiss you, and none would show contempt for me" (8:1).

   The unit 8:1-4 is termed a "song of yearning" by Horst.[23]
The beloved desires that her lover were her brother. If that
were so, then she could kiss him in public without contempt and
could take him to her mother's house (8:2a). If such a yearning were to come into reality, then the lovers could intimately
share one another's presence. The opportunity would, then, be
afforded them to share in an embrace. The following description is the fulfillment of the beloved's wish: "His left hand
is under my head, and his right hand embraces me" (8:3). This
refrain also appears in 2:6, immediately following the

beloved's mentioning of her love-sickness. The embrace of the lover appears to cure her illness.

Another allusion to touching is noted in 3:4, in the context of the beloved's search for her lover (3:1-5). When she finally discovers him, she states the following: "I laid hold of him and I would not let him go until I should bring him unto the house of my mother, unto the room of my parent." Such a physical seizure of the lover denotes the strong desire of the woman to possess the lover and share in his presence.[24]

4. Smelling, Breathing, Tasting. A perusal of the Song indicates that the idyllic atmosphere which is portrayed is quite reminiscent of the atmosphere in the ancient Egyptian lyrics. The imagery of the Song describes the setting of love as lovely gardens and rustic spots where the love partners may meet for rendezvous (see 1:15-17; 4:12-5:1; 6:1-3; 6:11-12; etc.).

The pastoral setting described in the Song is particularly pleasing to the senses. The fragrances that are associated with love are a dominant topos in the Song.[25] In 1:12-14, the beloved is expressing her admiration of her lover. She begins (1:12) by pointing out that *her* scent ("my nard") is pervasive when she is in the presence of her lover ("When the king is round about me" [see above, p. 45]). The woman, then, proceeds to describe the scent of her lover. He is as fragrant as a "sachet of myrrh" which rests between her breasts (1:13) and as a "cluster of henna" which has been brought from the "vineyards of En-gaddi" (1:14).

In the extensive unit 4:9-5:1, which should properly be designated a "song of admiration," the lover now expresses his delight with frequent references to her pleasing scent. Her own fragrance (that given off by her "oils") is said to exceed "all spices" (4:10). In striking similarity to an allusion in the Egyptian love poetry, the lover mentions the scent that is given off by the garments of his beloved. This fragrance is "of Lebanon."[26] One may recall the lover's desire in the Egyptian lyrics to become his beloved's washerman in order to catch the scent of the moringa oil in her kerchief (Cairo, X/15). In this same unit in the Song, the garden (a symbol for the beloved?) is described as a fragrant place, filled with

aromatic plants: nard, cinnamon, incense, myrrh, the finest
spices, etc., (4:14). The lover, then, summons the wind (4:16)
to blow upon his garden "that its perfumes may distill outward"
(נזל).

The exotic aroma of plants is a frequent image in the
Song. In describing the beauty of spring, the lover mentions
the fragrance of vines which are in bloom (2:13). Likewise, in
4:6, the lover notes his intention to flee "to the mountain of
myrrh, to the hill of incense." A similar mention of fragrant
plant-life is made by the beloved who describes the cheeks of
her lover as "beds of spice with ripening aromatic herbs"
(5:13; see also 6:2 and 7:14).

In speaking the name of her lover, the beloved again alludes to the sense of smell. In 1:2, she characterizes the
qualities of his name as follows: "Your name spoken is a
spreading perfume" (שֶׁמֶן).[27] One may also take note of the
description of the litter of Solomon which is depicted in 3:6
in the following manner:

> Laden with myrrh and incense,
> with all the exotic dust of a merchant.

The topos of breathing, observed in the Egyptian lyrics in
relation to the "nose kiss," appears in Cant 7:9 (see Harris,
10/2). It is uncertain whether or not the Song discloses in
this verse the existence of the nose kiss in Israel, but the
quality of the "breath of your nose" was particularly appealing
to the lover. Its fragrance was "like apples."[28]

The tasting of food and drink was a pleasurable experience
for the lovers in the Song. After being invited by the beloved
to enjoy his garden (i.e., the beloved herself?), the man announces that he is ready to accept the invitation and to possess his garden (5:1). In a passage which certainly contains
double entendre, the lover states that he will eat his "honey
and syrup" (יַעְרִי עִם-דִּבְשִׁי) and will drink his "wine and milk."
Similar imagery is used in 4:11 in the lover's admiration of
his beloved. Note the following:

> Your lips drip domesticated honey (נפֶת), my bride,
> and syrup and milk are under your tongue.

Images of eating and drinking are preserved elsewhere in the
Song. In 8:2, the woman desires to drink "spiced wine" and

"pomegranate juice." Likewise, in 2:5, she asks the Daughters
to strengthen her with "raisin cakes" and "apples."

Specific references to taste are observed in descriptions
of the mouth of a love partner. The woman, in 5:16, notes
that the mouth of her lover is "the essence of sweetness"
(מַמְתַקִּים). In describing her mouth, the lover points out
that it is "like a good wine" (7:10).

5. The Heart. Mention of the heart in the Song does not
occur as frequently as in the ancient Egyptian poems. Yet,
mention of the heart as the seat of the emotions, reason, and
will is noted.[29] Before describing the qualities that he admires in his beloved (4:10-15), the lover describes the following effect that his lady love has on him (4:9): "You have
ravished my heart (לִבַּבְתִּנִי), my sister, my bride." Such a description of the disconcerting effects of one love partner on
the other is also noted in the Egyptian lyrics: "The brother
disturbs my heart with his voice" (Beatty, C[1]/8). Canticles
5:2 is also reminiscent of the Egyptian poems wherein the presence of the lover causes the heart to be "roused up" (עֵר).
Compare the following from Harris, 14/6:

> Since I have spent the night with you,
> you have raised up my heart.
> I am sad, when he is far from me.

6. Love-sickness. Two poems in the Song reflect the beloved's physical illness which she attributes to "love-sickness" (חוֹלַת אַהֲבָה). In 2:4-5, after mentioning a rendezvous
which she has with her lover at the בֵּית הַיָּיִן ("banquet house"),
the woman calls out for sustenance.[30] Note the following from
Cant 2:5:

> Strengthen me with raisin cakes,
> refresh me with apples,
> for I am love-sick.

It is, however, the presence and embrace of the lover which is
able to sustain her in her illness. Similarly, the presence of
the love partner as the only medicine for love-sickness is
noted in the Egyptian poems. Note the following from Beatty,
C[4]/10-C[5]/2:

> The sister is more beneficial to me than all remedies.
> She is greater to me than the Compendium (of medicine).
> My salvation is her coming in from outside.

When I see her, (then) I will be healthy.
When she opens her eye, my body is young.
When she speaks, (then) I will be strong.
When I embrace her, she exorcises evil from me.

In the beloved's description of her dream (?)-experience
(5:2-8), she relates her reaction upon opening her door and
finding her lover gone (5:6b):

I sought him, but did not find him:
I called him, but he did not answer me.

The absence of her lover (plus her discovery by the city watchmen) leads her to make the following adjuration to the Daughters (5:8):

I adjure you, Daughters of Jerusalem
if you find my lover--
What will you reveal to him?--
that I am love-sick!

Nevertheless, earlier in the same unit, the beloved evidences
physical anxiety because she believes her lover to be *present*!
In 5:4, as the lover places his hands on the lock of the door
(euphemism?), the beloved states the following:

My inward parts became restless;
I lost my wits when he spoke.[31]

7. The Friends and Enemies of the Lovers. As in the
Egyptian poetry, a number of figures pass on and off the stage
of action in the Song. Their roles affect the lovers' relationship for either ill or good. The figure of the mother is
one which is found in both Hebrew and Egyptian love lyrics. In
the Song, the mother is a friend of the couple. The lover de-
clares his delight in the uniqueness of his beloved and points
out that she is her mother's choicest (אַחַת הִיא לְאִמָּהּ [6:9]).

The mother, and specifically the mother's house, provides
a haven for the loving pair. In the description of the love
experience given in 3:1-5, the beloved, upon finding her lover,
returns with him to her mother's house (אֶל-בֵּית אִמִּי).[32] The
unit itself functions to portray the intense devotion which the
woman has for the man. Upon finding him, she takes him to a
place of security. A similar yearning for security is expressed in 8:1-4, where the beloved longs that her lover might
be her brother (8:1). The advantages of such a relationship
would be that the lovers could then maintain closer intimacy

and have a haven for the celebration of their love. Note the
following:

> I would lead you;
> I would bring you unto the house of my mother.
>> (Cant 8:2)

Another mention of "mother" is found in 8:5, an independent unit which appears to be connected to the preceding verses
by the catchwords אִמֶּ֫ךָ / אִמִּי ("your mother" [v. 5] / "my mother"
[vv. 1 and 2]). The meaning and structure of the verse is
puzzling, and Würthwein concludes that the verse contains two
fragments of separate poems.[33] In 8:5b, the lover appears to
be addressing his beloved, perhaps recalling their earlier intimacy "under the apple tree" (תַּחַת הַתַּפּ֫וּחַ). The setting of this
affair may have been near the house of the mother, for the
lover continues: שָׁ֫מָּה חִבְּלַ֫תְךָ אִמֶּ֫ךָ ("there your mother conceived
you").

The figures of the בנות ירושלם ("Daughters of Jerusalem")
also appear as friends of the loving pair in the Song. In
three instances, the Daughters are observed in the following
refrain of adjuration (see 2:7; 3:5; and 8:4; also above, p.
29):

> I adjure you, O daughters of Jerusalem,
> by the gazelles and hinds of the field.
> Do not arouse, do not stir up love
> before its own time.
>> (*NAB*)

This frequent repetition comments on the nature of love itself:
it is a delight that must happen in its own time and should not
be prodded unnecessarily.

In the construction 5:2-6:3, the Daughters play a helpful
role in the beloved's search for her lover. An adjuration is
made in 5:8 that the Daughters aid the beloved in seeking the
man. Distressed and wounded, she asks them to pass on the following message to her lover if they should find him: "that I
am love-sick." The topos of the message passed to the love
partner is reminiscent of the role played by the friendly tree
in the Turin love songs. It is the tree which sends a message
to the beloved which "makes (her) hurry to the lover" (Turin,
15/1). It is interesting to note that in 5:9, the Daughters,
then, take up the adjuration of v. 8 and ask for a *description*
of the lover (which follows in 5:9-16). Upon concluding her

description of her lover, the Daughters ask a further question:

> Where has your lover gone,
> O most beautiful among women?
> Where has your lover gone,
> that we may seek him with you?
>   (Cant 6:1)

To these questions, the beloved replies that her lover is in
his garden, i.e., he was never lost at all (6:2).

Just as the figures of the Daughters play an important
role in the movement of the dialogue in the unit 5:2-6:3, they
serve as a foil to the beloved's speech in 1:5-6. The beloved
not only describes herself in these verses, but also appears to
defend herself before the Daughters. Note the following addressed to them:

> Do not stare at me because I am black.
> for the sun has burned me.
>   (Cant 1:6)

In this instance, the role of the Daughters may be a bit ambiguous vis-à-vis their stance as friend or foe (see similar features in the roles of the mother, the door-keeper, and Prince
Mehy in the Egyptian poems, above, pp. 106-107).[34] Rudolph has
observed that vv. 5 and 6 form a conflict taking place between
the rural, peasant girl and the city maids over the issue of
color.[35] Yet, Gerleman has perhaps most accurately characterized the setting of this unit as playful and coquettish, reminiscent of what he terms "the Cinderella motif" (*Aschenbrödel-
motiv*).[36]

Several obstacles to the love of the man and woman are
mentioned in the text. Paralleling the dangerous waters which
threaten love in Cairo, X/7-8 is the following allusion to
chaotic waters which, according to the Song, cannot hinder the
power of love:

> Deep waters are not able to quench love,
> nor floods sweep it away.
>   (Cant 8:7)

Similarly, the watchmen of the city appear as enemies of the
lovers, but even they are not able to overcome love's power.
Hence, in 3:6, even though the watchmen cannot help her in her
search for the lover, immediately upon leaving them, the beloved does find "the one whom my *nefeš* loves" (3:4). Even

though the beloved is attacked and beaten by the watchmen in
5:7, they are not able to destroy her love for the man. She,
therefore, asks the Daughters to tell him that she remains
love-sick for him (5:8).

Finally, the brothers of the beloved are antagonists in
the Song. They are introduced in 1:6 and are described by the
beloved as being angry with her. She has been charged with the
duty of caretaker of the vineyards; yet she has neglected her
own vineyard (herself?). The brothers' reappearance in 8:8
forms an inclusion to the entire work. In the unit 8:8-10, a
statement by the brothers regarding the youth of their sister
("Our sister is little, and she does not yet have breasts"
[v. 8a]) and their proposed handling of her future courtship
(v. 8b-9) introduces the sister's boastful self-description in
8:10: "I am a wall, and my breasts are like towers."[37] The
section contrasts the brothers' "paternalism" regarding their
sister (and their possible considerations of the bride price!)
with her independence and single-minded motivation: love for
the man.[38] Once again, the "enemies" of love are not able to
overcome the power of love. In 8:10b, the beloved announces
that she has found her own "place in the sun" (שלום), and will
not be deterred by her brothers' designs.

8. Animals and Plants. The animals and plants which are
described in the Song of Songs portray a similar idyllic atmosphere to that in the ancient Egyptian love poems (compare the
theme of "love under the trees" in the Turin poems and in Cant
1:15-16).

The use of "garden" (גן [4:12, 16; 5:1; 6:2]) and "vineyard" (כרם [1:6, 14; 2:15; 7:13; 8:11-12]) in the Song provides
a rustic setting for many of the love poems and evidences a
subtle *double entendre* also characteristic of the plant-imagery
in the ancient Egyptian lyrics (see, e.g., Beatty, R[16]/11 and
Harris, 2/10-11). A variety of trees (fig [2:13]; apple [2:3;
8:5]; palm [7:9]) and flowers (2:1, 2; 4:5; 7:3; 8:2). References to different types of wood appear (1:17; 8:9; 5:15).

Recalling a similar use in the ancient Egyptian lyrics,
the animal imagery is frequently employed to describe one or
the other of the love partners. The beloved's breasts are like
"twin fawns" (4:5; 7:4); her eyes are like doves (4:1; see

2:14); her teeth are "like a flock of ewes" (כְּעֵדֶר הַקְּצוּבוֹת
[4:2]; כְּעֵדֶר הָרְחֵלִים [6:6]); her hair "like a flock of goats"
(4:1; 6:5); and her adornment like that of one of Pharaoh's
mares (1:9). Likewise, the man is portrayed having hair black
as "a raven" (עֹרֵב [5:1]) and having strength and speed like
"a gazelle or a young stag" (2:9; 2:17; 8:14 [cf. the imagery
of speed associated with the king's horse in Beatty, G[1]/5]).
Animals are also mentioned in the beloved's adjuration:
בִּצְבָאוֹת אוֹ בְּאַיְלוֹת הַשָּׂדֶה ("by the gazelles and hinds of the field"
[2:7; 3:5; 8:4]).[39] Other references to animals may be found
in 2:15 (foxes, compare Harris, 4/2; 2:12 (the song of the
dove); and 4:8 (lions and leopards).

9. The Presence and Absence of the Lovers. The Song
shares with the Egyptian lyrics the topos of the enjoyment of
the presence and the anguish of separation experienced by the
lovers. In Harris, 10/3-6, the lover, desiring the presence of
his beloved, remarks that he would like to take care of her
things like a housemaid. Yet, unfortunately, he is separated
from his beloved and expresses his accompanying anguish in the
following prayer:

> "My great one is afar from me tonight,
> (and) I am like one in my grave."
> (Harris, 10/4)

In contrast to this experience of separation is the joy which
the woman expresses upon being "drawn near to the sight of" her
lover. She desires that the hours that they have together will
lengthen and not pass by quickly. Note the following from
Harris, 14/5-6:

> How lovely is my hour!
> May the hour stretch out for me as eternity.
> Since I have spent the night with you,
> you have raised up my heart.

Unfortunately, her joy is tempered by the realization that separation must come: "I am sad, when he is far from me" (Harris,
14/6).

In the Song, the topos of the desire for the presence of
the loved one is expressed in several units which depict a
"seek and find" theme. For example, in 1:7-8, the beloved
seeks her lover, wanting to know where he pastures his flock
(1:7). He responds (v. 8) with a teasing suggestion that she

follow her instincts! In 2:16-17, the beloved announces her
love for the man using a formula of mutual possession and,
then, invites him to share her presence עַל-הָרֵי בָתֶר ("upon the
mountain of Bether").[40] Similarly, in 8:13-14, the lover requests to hear the voice of the beloved (v. 13). She responds
by urging her lover to be swift in his seeking her:[41]

> Be swift, my lover,
> like a gazelle or a young stag
> on the mountains of spices.
>   (Cant 8:14)

In the units 3:1-5 and 5:2-6:3, the beloved is observed
searching (בקש) for her lover. In the former unit, she finds
him (מצא), seizes him, and takes him to the security of her
mother's house (3:4). In the latter pericope, however, after
seeking her lover, she only finds the city watchmen (5:7).
Yet, at the end of the unit (6:2), we discover that the lover
has not really been missing at all!

The theme of the inaccessibility of the lovers is related
to the seek and find theme and is found in both the Song and
in the Egyptian literature. In Cant 4:8, we discover that the
lover invites the beloved to come to him. She is to be found,
however, in places that are remote (the tops of mountains, the
dens of lions, and the mountains of leopards). Cairo, X/7 describes the beloved as inaccessible to her lover. In order to
reach her, he must cross dangerous waters and face the fierce
crocodile. On the other hand, the beloved, in Harris, 4/2-5,
states that she will not allow her lover to become inaccessible
to her. She will prevent his being driven away to remote
places.[42] Note the following:

> I will not allow him to receive a beating
> and to spend the day in the delta marshes,
> or [to be driven] to the land of Khor with clubs
>   and staves,
> to the land of Cush with palm branches,
> to the highland with switches,
> to the freshland with rushes.
> I will not obey their counsel
> to leave the desire.
>   (Beatty, 4/3-5)

THE LITERARY FICTIONS

An analysis of the ancient Egyptian love lyrics has shown that the use of various literary fictions provides a make-believe quality to many of the love poems. The lovers often occupy guises and portray themselves as royal figures who move in the social class of the elite or as pastoral figures whose rustic nature provides a sensuous atmosphere for the love poems. The portrayal of the man in the Song as king and as shepherd has intrigued interpreters over the centuries.[43] The analysis of the Egyptian love lyrics, however, has yielded an interesting interpretation of both royal and pastoral images in the Song of Songs. They are illustrative of the literary fictions common to the language and expression of love in the ancient world.

1. "Royal"-Fiction. Unlike the Egyptian lyrics where the figure of the king as the lover is absent, the king is frequently mentioned in the Song. A reference is made to the king in 1:4 when the beloved requests to be brought into the royal chambers. Likewise, the song of admiration spoken by the beloved in 1:12-14 is said to have its setting עַד־שֶׁהַמֶּלֶךְ בִּמְסִבִּי ("when the king is round about me"). Although observing the rustic imagery of 1:15-17, Gerleman contends that the lovers' trysting place appears to be constructed of "royal" timber: cedar and cypress.[44] Mention of the figure of the king is also made in 7:6 where the king is described as captured by the hair of the beloved.

The unit 3:6-11, described by most commentators as a wedding procession, is filled with royal imagery.[45] Foremost among the allusions is the frequent repetition of the name of Solomon (3:7, 9, 11). Mention of the גִּבֹּרִים ("mighty men") who are skilled swordsmen (3:7-8); the king's carriage (אַפִּרְיוֹן); and the description of the carriage (decorated with purple cloth, gold, silver, and ivory) add to the regal atmosphere of the procession.[46] Just as the wedding procession is compared to the royal caravan, so also is the uniqueness of the beloved compared with the royal harem in 6:8-9. She is praised even by the harem as unique in her beauty (6:9b).[47]

2. "Servant"-Fiction. In the Egyptian poetry, this fiction was reflected in the guise, willingly assumed by a love

partner, which was considered below the social class to which one normally belonged. An underlying aspect of this fiction was the desire of the lover to be in close proximity to his beloved while he fulfilled his servant role.

In the Song, there does not appear to be a figure which may be equated with a servant although there are two striking parallels with aspects of the "servant"-fiction found in the Egyptian love corpus. First of all, there is a desire expressed by the beloved that her lover be her brother (8:1). She, therefore, yearns that the lover assume a guise which would bring him into continually close proximity with her. The language which introduces the beloved's desire appears to be reminiscent of the wish particle (𓅓 𓏭 𓏥 𓏲 𓎡) frequently introducing this fiction in Egyptian: "Oh that you were my brother" (מִי יִתֶּנְךָ כְּאָח לִי [literally, "who might give you as a brother to me"]). Secondly, the beloved desires the presence of her lover and longs to be "as a seal upon your heart, as a seal upon your arm" (8:6). This desire closely parallels a similar request by the lover in the Egyptian poems to be the beloved's "seal ring" (see Cairo, X/16-18).[48]

3. "Shepherd"-Fiction. A variety of images appear in the Song from the rustic *Hirtenwelt*. Among these allusions are the following: the gazelles and hinds of the field (2:7; 3:5; 8:4); the young stag (2:9; 2:17; 8:14); and various elements which are used in descriptions of the lovers ("flock of ewes"; "flock of goats" [see 4:1; 4:5; 6:5; 7:4]); and the camp of the shepherds (1:8). The idyllic imagery which is common in the Song indicates that the description of love in the out-of-doors and back to nature motifs are as characteristic of the Hebrew love songs as of the Egyptian poems.

The lovers in the Song assume roles which should be characterized as examples of "shepherd"-fiction. The woman is seen as a caretaker of a vineyard and gardener (1:5-6). Likewise, the lover is portrayed as a shepherd who "wanders after the flocks" (1:7-8). These elements of poetic fiction are further developed in the Song by other rustic allusions. In 1:16-17, their place of love is described in idyllic imagery. Likewise, in 7:12-14, the beloved invites her lover to the fields and vineyards where she promises to give him her love: "There I

will give to you my love" (7:13). In 7:14, she appears as a
gardener who has stored up "fruits" for her lover (see Harris,
14/7-8). In 8:13, the lover addresses his lady love as "the
garden dweller" (הַיּוֹשֶׁבֶת בַּגַּנִּים).

The theme of love in the out-of-doors or "under the trees"
is a familiar topos of love literature. In 8:5, an allusion
is made to an earlier experience of love shared "under the
apple tree," a reference which is reminiscent of the Turin
love songs (see Turin, 16/3-17/1).

THE *GATTUNGEN* OF THE SONG IN LIGHT OF EGYPTIAN POETRY

In Chapter I of this study (see above, pp. 49-55) there is
a treatment of several problems associated with genre designations in the Song. The work of F. Horst (1935) remains singularly the most complete analysis of genre in the Song. The
ancient Egyptian love lyrics serve to confirm the work of Horst
by supplying extra-biblical evidence of his examples of genre.
In the Egyptian poetry, A. Hermann has delineated three primary
Gattungen: the descriptive song; the day song; and the lament
at the door. We shall first compare Hermann's categories of
genre (found in the Egyptian love corpus) with the Song and,
then, attempt to move beyond the designations of Hermann to
show how the ancient Egyptian love poetry confirms Horst's
designations of genre.

1. The Descriptive Song (*Beschreibungslied*). The use of
the descriptive song in the Song of Songs (4:1-7; 6:4-7;
5:10-16; and 7:1-6) functions in a similar manner to the
wasfs in the Egyptian poetry.[49]

Illustrative of the descriptions of the lovers' bodies in
the Song is language which is rustic and imagery which is related to the "shepherd"-fiction. Hence, the following images
are found: a flock of goats (4:1; 6:5); ewes with twins (4:2;
6:6); fawns (4:5; 7:4); young gazelles (4:5; 7:4); a heap of
wheat (7:3); etc. These rustic images are reminiscent of
similar bodily descriptions contained in the Egyptian lyrics
(see, e.g., Harris, 2/10-4/1).[50]

There is an order to the bodily description of the love
partner usually in ascending or descending steps (see Beatty,
C[1]/2-5 and Harris, 2/10-4/1). In 4:1-7 (see 5:10-16),

therefore, the beloved's body is described in a *downward* order beginning with the facial features (4:1-3) and descending to the breasts (4:4-5). On the other hand, the description of the dancing Shulammite is in an *upward* movement, first mentioning her feet and thighs (7:1-2) and, then, ascending to her facial features (7:5).

In the description of the beloved in Beatty, C^1/2-5, several allusions are made to metals (lapis-lazuli, gold), perhaps indicating that the woman is being compared with statuary. In Cant 5:10-16, the woman's description of her lover may also refer to his bodily appearance using iconographic imagery. His head is of "pure gold" (5:11); his arms are "rods of gold" covered with "chrysolite" (תַּרְשִׁישׁ [5:14a]); his body is a "work of ivory" covered with "lapis-lazuli" (סַפִּירִים [5:14b]). In 5:15, the phrase "his legs are columns of alabaster" (שׁוֹקָיו עַמּוּדֵי שֵׁשׁ) is interesting in that the Hebrew "alabaster" (שֵׁשׁ) may be an Egyptian loan word (*ꜣs*, 𓈙 𓏤 𓂝).[51]

2. The Day Song (*Tagelied*). This designation of *Gattung* describing the lovers' parting upon the coming of day-break, not wide-spread even in the Egyptian love poetry, appears in the Song only in an abbreviated form. There it may be designated as the topos of "disturbed love."

This theme is noted in what Gerleman calls "*die gefährdete Liebe*" represented in the adjuration neither "to arouse" (תָּעִירוּ) nor "disturb" (תְּעוֹרְרוּ) love (see Cant 2:7; 3:5; and 8:4).[52] In the Egyptian lyrics, the dove (𓅓𓈖𓏏𓏏 , *mnt*) emerges as one who disturbs the night of love shared by the man and woman (Harris, 10/6-8). There, the beloved admonishes the bird not to disturb their love. In the Song, however, the Daughters are pictured as the literary figures to whom the request is made that love not be disturbed.[53]

3. The Lament at the Door (*Türklage*). As in the case of the day song, the lament at the door does not appear as an adequate designation of genre in the Song of Songs. There are allusions, however, to activity which may have "the door" as its setting, and this evidence justifies "the door" as a topos in the Song. Gerleman attempts to make certain comparisons between Cant 2:8-14 and the *Paraklausithyron*; yet the allusions to a door are vague. Moreover, Gerleman is forced to admit that these verses contain no lament![54]

The setting of 5:2-6 is the beloved's door. Yet, these verses should be understood as part of a larger unit, 5:2-6:3, and can be most accurately described as a *dream experience* on the part of the beloved.[55] Whereas the *Türklage* is character- ized by a lament sung by the lover upon being refused admission to the beloved's house (see Beatty, R^{17}/6-7), in the Song, there is no lament spoken. Moreover, the reaction depicted is that of the *beloved*--her reaction to his knocking and her re- gret that he is not at the door when she finally opens it (see Cant 5:6).

4. Confirmation of Horst's Classifications. When Horst classified the *Gattungen* in the Song of Songs, his primary cri- terion was the *content* of the given units.[56] The designation "genre," however, usually refers to a "typical" unit of human expression (written or oral). "Typicality means that one would expect to find several examples of a similar genre in biblical and ancient Near Eastern literature."[57] Although Hermann's analysis of *Gattungen* in ancient Egyptian love lyrics takes a narrower stance in the designations of genre, these lyrics do evidence similarities of genre with the Song along the lines of the designations affirmed by Horst.

The song of admiration, according to Horst, usually has two aspects: the adornment of the individual (excluding physi- cal characteristics) and the effects that the admiration has upon the admirer (see Cant 1:9-11; 4:9-11; 1:15-17; etc.).[58] Both of these aspects are observed in the woman's admiration of the scent of the man in Harris, 8/4-7. The context of the ad- miration appears to be a description of a love related experi- ence: "I will tell you of a scene which happened" (Harris, 8/2). The scene is that of bird-catching, and upon snaring "the first (bird) to come" the woman describes him as follows:

> His odor is brought from Punt;
> his claws are filled with resin.

The scent of the bird (the lover?) quickens the beloved's de- sire for her lover's presence (see Cant 1:12-14). The effect, then, of the admiration is to be found in her desire to give up the pretext of bird-snaring:

> My desire (shall be) to you that we might release
> it together.

> (Then) I am alone with you....
> You are there with me,
> when I set a snare.
> The happiness (is) the going to the fields
> of the one who is loved.
>   (Harris, 8/5-7)

A similar admiration of the lover is spoken by the beloved
in Harris, 14/5-6. Here, the woman admires the uniqueness of
her lover:

> I am one drawn near to the sight of your love.
> (You are) the grandest in my heart.

The effect of her admiration culminates in her desire for their
night of love to continue for a longer duration. She states
the following:

> How lovely is my hour!
> May the hour stretch out for me as eternity.
> Since I have spent the night with you,
> you have raised up my heart.
> I am sad, when he is far from me.

The genre of self-description may be observed in both
the ancient Egyptian lyrics as well as in the Song (see Cant 1:
5-6; 8:8-10; and 2:1).[59] In Poem Eight of the Harris collection, the beloved has a meeting with her lover at "the garden
house." As she approaches the place of their rendezvous, she
describes herself as follows:

> My face faces the cottage;
> my arms are filled with Persea (branches);
> my hair is heavy with resin.
> I am like the Lady of the Two Lands.
> I am with you.
>   (Harris, 6/12-8/1)

Similarly, in Harris, 10/12-12/2, the beloved remembers the
love of the man and hastens to him. She describes her eager-
ness to find him as follows:

> I have been neglectful of my tresses
> ...that I may put on my braids.
> I am always ready!
>   (Harris, 12/1-2)

Although the first lines of the Ostracon 25218 are fragmentary, one can discern an example of a coquettish tease spoken by the beloved to her lover. She describes her swimsuit
("a tunic of fine, royal linen") and describes the fish she

has just caught with her fingers ("a red *wt* fish" [Cairo,
X/4-5]). She, then, invites her lover to come and see her
(Cairo, X/6). The unit represents the woman's desire for the
presence of her lover; yet, the language of her invitation
forms a teasing summons to her lover that he join her in a
swim. The tease in Cant 1:7-8, a light dialogue between the
man and woman, may reveal a similarly serious undertone: the
desire of the lovers for one another.

The song of yearning (see, e.g., Cant 1:2-4; 2:4-5; 2:10-
13; and 8:6) designates a unit in which the desire of one love
partner for the other is straightforwardly expressed. This
genre can be frequently observed in the Egyptian lyrics (see
the short cycle in Cairo, X/13-17). In Harris, 4/12-13, the
lover longs to be the door-keeper of his beloved so that he can
be near enough to "hear her voice when she is angry." Likewise, he longs to be her housemaid so that he may touch his
beloved. Thus, he may say the following: "Your arm lies upon
my arm," (Harris, 10/3-4). The first two stanzas of the Nakht-
Sobek Cycle of the Beatty songs expresses a yearning for sexual
fulfillment and the consummation of the lovers' relationship.
Note the following:

> You may bring it to the house of the sister
> when you pant after her cave....
> May you bring her to an end in her night....
> May you bring it (into) the hall of the sister,
> you alone, without another.
> (Beatty, R^{16}/11-R^{17}/1)

The recital of a love-related experience, noted in the
Song in 2:8-9 and 5:2-6, is characteristic of several songs
among the Egyptian collection of love poems. In Harris, 4/6-9,
the lover relates his voyage to Memphis; in Harris, 4/10-11, he
mentions his experience with love-sickness; and in Beatty,
C^2/5-9, the beloved mentions her experience passing by Prince
Mehy. Beatty, C^3/10-C^4/6 describes the beloved's experience
passing by the open door of her lover. Similarly, Cairo,
X/10-13 describes the lovers' embrace and kiss.

The designation *Prahllied* ("boasting song") may also be
found in the Egyptian love poetry and parallel Horst's designations of Cant 6:8-9 and 8:11-12 as boasting songs.[60] In
Beatty, C^1/6-8, the lover reports the effects that the beauty

of his beloved has upon him and upon others. Reminiscent of
the designation *Prahllied* in the Song, this unit boasts of the
uniqueness of the beloved recognized both by the lover and all
men who see her. Note the following:

> She seizes my heart with her embrace.
> She causes that the necks of all men
> turn back at the sight of her.
> Everyone who embraces her is happy.
> He is like the chief of the lovers.
> Her going forth is seen
> like that (one), a unique one.

Similarly, in Beatty, $C^2/3$-4, the "perfection" of the lover
is recognized not only by the beloved but also by the parents
of the woman. Even "all mankind" sings a song of praise for
the lover (Beatty, $C^2/4$).[61]

THE ATMOSPHERE OF THE SONG OF SONGS

The ways of speaking about love in the Song display a
striking correspondence to the language of the Egyptian lyrics
and illustrate a pastoral, make-believe world in which the
desires and fancies of lovers are expressed. The scenes themselves appear to be acquired from a kaleidoscope of love-language in the ancient world which depicted love's desires and
pleasures by means of language both pleasing to the senses and
characteristically playful.

The Song of Songs, then, unmistakably shares the topoi,
elements of design, and genre which are characteristic of the
ancient Egyptian corpus of material. It would be unwarranted
due to problems of chronology and cultural interchange to
propose that the Song of Songs is *literarily dependent* upon
the ancient Egyptian love lyrics. Nevertheless, because the
Song participates in the same atmosphere and shares in the
love-language of the Egyptian lyrics, an interpretation of
recent questions such as the meaning, structure, setting, and
genre of the Song may be illuminated by the Egyptian poetry.
Chapter V of this study will attempt a short retrospect of the
preceding chapters and will allude to the prospect that can be
derived from an analysis of the Song in light of ancient
Egyptian love poetry.

NOTES

[1]See Tournay, "Les parallèles non bibliques," in Robert et al., *Cantique*, 340-52. There has yet to appear a *complete* analysis of the similarities between the Egyptian and Hebrew love songs, although R. E. Murphy has recently noted the importance of the Egyptian material in a relevant article on the Song; See his "Form-Critical Studies," 414.

[2]Audet, "Love and Marriage," 82-83. See above, pp. 55-56 for a discussion of the title of the Song of Songs.

[3]See Foster, *Love Songs*, xvii.

[4]Recently, Ulrich Luft has analyzed this title and other introductory rubrics from Egyptian literature. See especially his translations of these titles in his "Zur Einleitung der Liebesgedichte," 108-116. Gerleman points to these introductions in Egyptian poetry in discussing the superscription of the Song (*Das Hohelied*, 93).

[5]Following the designation of Horst, "Formen," 177. Rudolph, *Das Hohe Lied*, 173-74 and Gerleman, *Das Hohelied*, 201-202 correctly establish the unit as 7:7-11.

[6]The beloved begins speaking in v. 10b, for the לדודי there can only be spoken *by* the woman. There is no need to emend the text so that all of v. 10 is spoken by the lover (cf. Rudolph, *Das Hohe Lied*, 174).

[7]See Gerleman, *Das Hohelied*, 95.

[8]Ibid., 193 and 162. In 5:1, Wurthwein (*Die Fünf Megilloth*, 54) follows Gerleman's position.

[9]See above, p. 52. Also Krinetzki, *Das Hohe Lied*, 95 and Gerleman, *Das Hohelied*, 102-3.

[10]Rudolph (*Das Hohe Lied*, 138-39) correctly establishes this unit as 3:6-11; also Würthwein, *Die Fünf Megilloth*, 48-49. The consensus of scholars see the unit as a wedding procession (Würthwein, *Die Fünf Megilloth*, 49; Rudolph, *Das Hohe Lied*, 140-41; Krinetzki, *Das Hohe Lied*, 147; Loretz, *Liebeslied*, 23-25; and Staerk, *Lyrik*, 294).

[11]Exum notes that the Daughters speak in 8:8-9 ("Analysis," 76).

[12]It is interesting to note here that sexual yearning which is characteristic of the *woman* in Gen 3:16 (ואל-אישׁך תשׁוקתך ["and your yearning shall be for your husband"]) is attributed to the *man* for the beloved; see Rudolph (*Das Hohe Lied*, 175) and Krinetzki (*Das Hohe Lied*, 225).

[13]Most commentators (Gerleman, Rudolph, Würthwein) follow Horst and separate 4:9-11 from 4:12-5:1 (Horst, "Formen," 178). It would appear, however, that the admiration of 4:9-11 continues in 4:12 and culminates in the invitation by the *beloved* in

4:16b (and subsequent acceptance in 5:1) that the lover explore his garden (i.e., the beloved).

[14]Horst, "Formen," p. 176; also Würthwein, *Die Fünf Megilloth*, 43 and Gerleman, *Das Hohelied*, 115-16.

[15]Krinetzki has noted a striking chiasmus in this unit: statement (2:1); comparison (2:2); comparison (2:3a); and statement (2:3b); see *Das Hohe Lied*, 114.

[16]That v. 10 reflects the response of the harem to the beauty of the beloved, see Würthwein, *Die Fünf Megilloth*, 61; Rudolph, *Das Hohe Lied*, 165; and Loretz, *Liebeslied*, 39-40. Regarding the astral imagery, see Gerleman, *Das Hohelied*, 187-88 and Tournay, "Les parallèles," 341.

[17]See Roland E. Murphy, "The Hebrew Sage and Openness to the World," in *Christian Action and Openness to the World* (The Villanova University Symposia Vols. II-III; ed. Joseph Papin; Villanova, PA: Villanova University, 1970) 219-44.

[18]One is reminded of Walther Zimmerli's statement regarding the connection between wisdom and creation: "Wisdom thinks resolutely within the framework of a theology of creation; see Zimmerli, "The Place and Limit of Wisdom in the Framework of Old Testament Theology," *SJT* 17 (1964) 148. Murphy has examined the Song in the context of the sages' view of the world in "The Hebrew Sage," 233-234; see also Audet, "Love and Marriage," 80.

[19]Würthwein, *Die Fünf Megilloth*, 60.

[20]The invitation to dance (7:1) appears to introduce a *waṣf* which most commentators take to be a song which accompanies the dance. However, many commentators have been too specific in their designation of the dance in the context of the wedding celebration. See Würthwein, *Die Fünf Megilloth*, 63; Krinetzki, *Das Hohe Lied*, 212; and Rudolph, *Das Hohe Lied*, 171.

[21]Horst, "Formen," 184 identifies the genre of the unit 6:11-12 as a "description of a love-related experience" (*Erlebnisschilderung*). Würthwein proposes that the elements of the garden really symbolize the beauties of the beloved; yet, he certainly goes too far when he proposes that the setting of the unit is the first night (that of consummation) of a week-long marriage celebration; see *Die Fünf Megilloth*, 61.

[22]The same point is made by Exum ("Analysis," 56) and Krinetzki (*Das Hohe Lied*, 143).

[23]Horst, "Formen," 186.

[24]The refrain to "not arouse nor disturb love" appears to follow the references to touching in 3:4 and 8:3. Such a repetition may underscore the beloved's desire for intimacy; see Gerleman, *Das Hohelied*, 213.

[25]See ibid., 109. He refers to the topos of the scent of the one loved as an important one in the ancient Egyptian love poems (see Harris, 8/4-5 and 6/12-8/1).

[26]The word-play in this entire unit is interesting ("Lebanon," [לְבָנוֹן]; "incense," [לְכוּנָה]; and "ravish the heart," [לִבַּבְתִּנִי]) as well as the key-word repetition (גַּן ["garden"]).

[27]The mentioning of the name of the love partner is also a topos of love literature. While in the Song, the mention of the name elicits a comparison to "spreading perfume," in the Egyptian lyrics, the name has a restorative function. Note the following from Beatty, C[4]/9-10:

Telling me, "Behold her," that is what will
    revive me.
Her name is that which will raise me up.
It is the coming and going of her messages
which bring life to my heart.

[28]See Gerleman, *Das Hohelied*, 203.

[29]For the use of לב in Hebrew thought, see von Rad, *Theology*, 1. 153 and Edmond Jacob, *Theology of the Old Testament* (trans. A. W. Heathcote and P. J. Allcock; New York: Harper & Row, 1958) 163-66.

[30]See Harris, 10/1 and Gerleman, *Das Hohelied*, 118.

[31]The phrase נַפְשִׁי יָצְאָה בְדַבְּרוֹ should be transposed from 5:6 to 5:4; see *BHK*. Holladay translates *yāṣe'â nafšô* as follows: "lose one's wits" (*Lexicon*, 139).

[32]An *Erlebnisschilderung*, Horst, "Formen," 184. Usually this unit is interpreted as a dream sequence; see, e.g., Würthwein, *Die Fünf Megilloth*, 47-48 where the unit is identified as a *Mädchentraum*.

[33]Würthwein, *Die Fünf Megilloth*, 67.

[34]Following the witness of the LXX, Gerleman (*Das Hohelied*) interprets the MT of 6:12--עַמִּי-נָדִיב (literally, "my noble people")--as a proper name: Amminadab. He, then, equates this figure with Prince Mehy of the Egyptian lyrics (188-93). See also R. Tournay, "Les chariots," 288-309, who interprets Cant 6:12 allegorically. Unfortunately, the textual uncertainty of this verse makes interpretation difficult. Who or what עמי-נדיב is remains uncertain, and the textual evidence cannot support Gerleman's hypothesis that the literary figure represented is a parallel figure to Mehy; see Würthwein, *Die Fünf Megilloth*, 62.

[35]Rudolph, *Das Hohe Lied*, 124.

[36]Gerleman, *Das Hohelied*, 99.

[37]See Horst, "Formen," 182-83. The unit appears to have a serious tone. Cf., however, Würthwein, *Die Fünf Megilloth*, 69 who sees this section as a "joking song."

[38]See Rudolph, *Das Hohe Lied*, 183 regarding the brothers' motivation for "capital gain" through the anticipated bride price.

[39]To read this phrase in 8:4, one must accept the witness of the Greek which supplies the line absent from MT. See *NAB*.

[40]See Gerleman, *Das Hohelied*, 129.

[41]Van den Oudenrijn has entitled the unit 8:13-14, *Verstoppertjesspel* ("hide and seek"); see *Het Hooglied*, 43.

[42]Gerleman, *Das Hohelied*, 151-52.

[43]See the works of Delitzsch and Pouget-Guitton; also see above, pp. 33-34.

[44]Gerleman's contention that the mention of these royal trees in 1:17 and the earlier mention of sweet fragrances in 1:12-14 provide evidence for the Song's being *Kunstdichtung*, the product of a high social sphere, is unfounded; see *Das Hohelied*, 115-16 and Hermann, *Altägyptische Liebesdichtung*, 54-56. Against Gerleman's position, see above, pp. 54-55.

[45]See Loretz, *Liebeslied*, 23-5; Rudolph, *Das Hohe Lied*, 138-52; Würthwein, *Die Fünf Megilloth*, 48-50; Krinetzki, *Das Hohe Lied*, 147; and Staerk, *Lyrik*, 294.

[46]See Gerleman, *Das Hohelied*, 137.

[47]Ibid., 185. Another allusion to royal fiction may be found in 7:2 where the beloved is addressed as בת-נדיב ("a prince's daughter").

[48]The similarity of the Egyptian poetry and the Song regarding the allusion to the longing of one of the lovers to be a "seal" is underscored by the close linguistic relationship between Hebrew חוֹתָם (8:6) and the Egyptian 𓆓𓂝𓏏𓊭 (Cairo, X/16). Thomas O. Lambdin has designated חוֹתָם as an Egyptian loan word, the root of which is found extensively in other Semitic languages; see his "Egyptian Loan Words in the Old Testament," *JAOS* 73 (1953) 151.

[49]The descriptive song or *waṣf* has been recognized by recent commentators on the Song as a motif shared with other literatures; see W. Hermann, "Geschichte," 176-97. Rudolph was among the first to recognize a parallel between the Egyptian *waṣf* and examples of the same form in the Song of Songs (see e.g., *Das Hohe Lied*, 99 and 169). See also Feuillet, "Les parallèles non bibliques," 341; Krinetzki, 77-79; Würthwein, *Die Fünf Megilloth*, 51-52; and Loretz, *Liebeslied*, 26-27.

[50]In Beatty, $C^1/4$, there appears the following description: "Her fingers are like lotus flowers." The image of

"lotus flowers" (⸻ ⸺ [*sšn*]) which is noted in
Egyptian love songs may be linguistically related to the Hebrew שׁוֹשָׁן ("lily"; see Cant 2:1).

[51]See Lambdin, "Loan Words," 155. An analysis of this
word is given in John R. Harris, *Lexicographical Studies in
Ancient Egyptian Minerals* (Berlin: Akademie-Verlag, 1961) 77-
78.

[52]Gerleman, *Das Hohelied*, 120.

[53]"The voice of the dove" (Egyptian, ⸻)
is a topos which also appears in the Song. See Cant 2:12.

[54]Gerleman, *Das Hohelied*, 123-25.

[55]With Würthwein, *Die Fünf Megilloth*, 57-58 and Rudolph,
Das Hohe Lied, 155-56. Against Gerleman, *Das Hohelied*, 165
and Loretz, *Liebeslied*, 34.

[56]See Horst, "Formen," 177-78. Recent commentators have
followed Horst's designations with few substantive changes (see
above, pp. 50 and 53-54).

[57]John B. White, "Conversing with the Text," *Duke Divinity
School Review* 39 (1974) 173. See also R. Knierim, "Form Criticism: The Present State of an Exegetical Discipline," paper
presented to the Form Criticism Seminar-Hebrew Scriptures,
Society of Biblical Literature Annual Meeting, New York, October 27, 1970 and "Old Testament Form," 460-61.

[58]See Horst, "Formen," 176-77.

[59]See above, pp. 50-51.

[60]Horst, "Formen," 183.

[61]The recognition of the beauty of the love partner and
the accompanying praise that is sung by the bystanders is a
theme of the Song (6:8-10). Würthwein designates this unit as
a *Preislied* ("song of praise"), *Die Fünf Megilloth*, 61 and 70.
Note the reaction of the "lovers" upon the entrance of the beloved in Beatty, C³/8.

CHAPTER V

CONCLUSION: RETROSPECT AND PROSPECT

RETROSPECT

This study has attempted to delineate the points of literary contact between the corpus of ancient Egyptian love poetry and the Song of Songs. In order to demonstrate the shared imagery and love-language, the reader was provided an adequately literal translation of this material (Appendix). In many ways, these translations are the heart of this dissertation. The hieroglyphs, themselves, provided the genesis point for the literary analysis which affirmed the close similarities between the Egyptian poems and the Song.

An historical survey traced the cultural background and origins of the Egyptian love literature to the period of the 18th Dynasty, the beginning of the New Kingdom, and an awakening of the Egyptian spirit reflected in art and literature. This period provides the most fertile ground for the development of love lyrics due to the rising social position of women and the secure political scene allowing time for the enjoyment of this-worldly pleasures. These factors, coupled with a new social freedom for the growing class of skilled workers, set the scene for the celebration and enjoyment of human love.

The expression of love, moreover, had a language all its own, and as a literary analysis of the Egyptian love poetry has shown, specific themes (topoi), genres, and literary fictions provide love's expression with a characteristic manner of speaking. There is an established design to the Egyptian love lyrics which distinguishes the role of the poet as a speaker; designates nomenclature for the lover and his beloved; affirms expressions of mutual admiration and desire on the part of the lovers; and characterizes the divinity in a most enigmatic way. The topoi of these songs make a strong appeal to the senses, and the atmosphere conveyed through the love-language is sensual and idyllic. The literary fictions that are preserved in several of the poems contribute to the playful world of make-believe in which elusive characters pass on and off the scene.

Finally, the genre designations, characterizing sustained
themes throughout the Egyptian lyrics depict typical scenes:
the description of the beloved's physical attractions; the
anguish of separation which the lovers feel upon parting; and
the exclusion from the continual presence of the love partner
which is typified by the closed door of the beloved.

The Hebrew Song of Songs shares in the design, language,
and literary genres expressing the human joy of love. An analysis of the Egyptian poems provides the interpreter of the Song
with what he may expect in terms of themes, literary fictions,
and atmosphere in Canticles. Not only does the Song's rustic
imagery betray a close association with the ways of expressing
love in Egypt, but the commonality of love-language denotes
archetypal vehicles through which human, sexual love was celebrated in the ancient world. Thus, it is not surprising that
specific topoi be common to both Hebrew and Egyptian love literature. The fragrances, sight of the love partners, embracing
and kissing, friends and enemies of the lovers, and even specific parallels (scent of garments, the mother figure, love
under the trees, gazelles, etc.) denote the Song's participation in the world of human love expression. Moreover, a study
of the genres in the Song can even illuminate appearances of
genre in the Egyptian love lyrics, broadening the terminology
heretofore used to characterize the *Gattungen* of the Egyptian
lyrics.

PROSPECT

While the delineation of the points of contact and similarities of love-language found in Egyptian love lyrics and the
Song allows one to affirm that the salient features of theme,
style, and literary genre are shared in the common milieu of
love expression, the value of such a study is incomplete without assaying its significance for the interpretation of the
Song. Chapter I of this study has provided the reader with a
survey of recent work on the Song. In light of the positions
presented there, does the existence of the Egyptian corpus of
love literature shed light on the Song's interpretation?

To paint with bold strokes and contend that the Song's
structure, setting, genre, and meaning coincide with that of
the Egyptian songs would be as unwarranted as a position which
would disregard the value of the Egyptian material altogether.
That there exists a body of love songs bearing such striking
similarities with the Song must, however, inform the literary
analysis of the Song.

1. Structure. Regarding the two major positions concerning the structure of the Song (a unity of several short
poems versus an anthology of disparate poems), the Egyptian
lyrics appear to support the claim that the Song is a collection of independent love songs which have been brought together. The Egyptian poems, themselves, are collections of independent poems linked by means of catchword association. Although some of the collections bear evidence of units which
form short cycles of previously unified poems, there is no evidence that an entire collection derives from one hand.

The Song is a collection of approximately thirty independent units linked together by means of catchwords. For example, the unit 2:4-7 appears to be linked to the preceding one
(2:1-3) by the occurrence of the catchword תפוח in 2:3 and
2:5. Similarly, a form of the root עור ("to stir up" [4:16 and
5:2]) and the word אחתי ("my sister" [5:1 and 5:2]) connect the
unit 4:9-5:1 with the construction which follows (5:2-6:3; see
also above, pp. 32-33).

The secondary composition 5:2-6:3, detailing the dream (?)
experience of the beloved, her lost lover, and his subsequent
appearance in his garden, is reminiscent of the cycle constructions in the Egyptian love corpus. In this unit, previously
independent pieces have been molded into a unified composition.
The questions which are asked by the Daughters in 5:9 and 6:1,
and the conclusion in 5:16b regarding the identity of the lover
add movement to the unit and the theme of the lover's absence
further adds to its continuity.

2. Setting. The life-setting of the Egyptian lyrics appears to be in the general celebration of human love which
takes place between a man and woman (see above, pp. 81-82 and
91-92). This fact alone, however, does not deny the possibility that marriage is a primary setting for the units in the

Song, but it does argue that a setting in marriage need not be
demanded nor contrived for the genres of the Song of Songs.
Like the Egyptian lyrics, one may argue that given genres in
the Song cannot be pinned down in terms of life-setting and
that, for the most part, the genres fit into the variety of
situations and emotions experienced by lovers.

Reference to the Egyptian lyrics could, on occasion, check
overzealousness on the part of a commentator in his attempt to
detail a life-setting for a given unit. For example, the topos
of love-sickness which appears in 2:4-7 is a far too universal
theme in love literature to be rigidly defined in terms of a
single setting. Würthwein proposes that the unit reflects the
bride's wedding day and indicates that v. 6 refers "clearly"
to the consummation of the marriage.[1] Such a claim goes beyond the textual evidence. Reference to the Egyptian material,
on the other hand, suggests that this unit has a setting in a
beloved's yearning for her lover and the subsequent effects
which love has upon her (see above, p. 104).

The preservation of love poetry in the wisdom circles of
Israel and Egypt provides an important setting for this type of
literature (see above, pp. 55-56 and 132-34). The appearance
of a Harper Song in the Harris 500 collection underscores the
thesis that the love poems found a *geistige Heimat* with the
sages who were interested in the phenomenon of human, sexual
love (see above, p. 81). In Israel, the preservation by the
sages may not only explain the Song's ascription to Solomon
but also may provide a rationale for the Song's inclusion
among other sacred literature: the lesson provided in the
fidelity of human love.

3. Genre. Earlier in this study (see above, pp. 49-55),
it was argued that the Song of Songs participates in the world
of love-language in which a variety of genres are used to convey typical expressions concerning human love. The genre
designations of Horst are, for the most part, confirmed by an
analysis of the Egyptian lyrics (see above, pp. 148-150).
Moreover, this study argued that the genre designations used
by Hermann were too narrow in categorizing the types of units
which appear in the Egyptian love poetry. We have shown above
(pp. 150-153) that a comparison with the Song of Songs actually

furthers the analysis of *Gattungen* made by Hermann.

4. Meaning. The ancient Egyptian love poems celebrate human, sexual love and the sensuous pleasures associated with the man-woman relationship. Similarly, the Song of Songs, participating in a common language of love, shares this celebration of the joys of human love. Although one would not wish to exclude marriage or betrothal as presuppositions to certain units in the Song, the Egyptian love corpus evidences that the Song should not be moralized to the point that sanctions diminish the erotic dimension of human love. The Egyptian love corpus also evidences that *human* love was celebrated in the ancient world and that references to an allegorical meaning or to a cultic drama to explain the Song are simply no longer convincing.

NOTE

[1] Würthwein, *Die Fünf Megilloth*, 44.

APPENDIX

A TRANSLATION OF EGYPTIAN LOVE POEMS

THE LOVE SONGS OF PAPYRUS HARRIS 500[1]

Poem One

    (2/1) I am with [you],
    where will you set your heart?
    Not do you embrace...
    time [you] arrive...the amusement (2/2).
    If you seek to handle
    my thighs together with my breasts[2]...(2/3),
    (would) you leave when you remember food?
    Are you a gluttonous man?
    (Would) (2/4) you...[go] because of clothes?
    I am a possessor of sheets.
    (Would) you go because of hunger?
    (2/5) Take my breasts.
    Abundant for you is their[3] offering.
    Glorious is the day of [your] embrace (2/6).
    ...an utterance, myriads and millions.[4]

Poem Two

    Your love is mixed with my body,
    like...(2/7)...with water,
    like a prescription joined with gum,
    like milk mixed with...(2/8) its $s\underline{h}\underline{3}$.[5]
    You hasten to look at your sister,
    like a stallion on the field,
    like...[on] (2/9) his papyrus marsh.
    Heaven gives up her love,
    as a flame falls...,
    (2/10) like a circling[6] falcon.

Poem Three

    Distracting are the plants of her rush.
    (2/11) The sister's [mouth(?)] is a lotus bud.

Her breasts are of perfume.
Her arms (2/12)...[vine-like],
[her eyes] are fixed berries (?).[7]
Her forehead is the snare of *mry*-wood,
(4/1) and I am a wild goose![8]
My feet[9] are in [her] hair
as bait for the snare.

Poem Four

(4/2) My heart is relaxed by your loving,
O jackal pup, your drunkenness arouses me.
I will not (4/3) allow him to receive a beating
and to spend the day in the delta marshes,
or [to be driven] to the land of Khor with clubs (4/4)
    and staves,
to the land of Cush with palm branches,[10]
to the highland with switches,
to the freshland (4/5) with rushes.
I will not obey their counsel
to leave the desire.[11]

Poem Five

I travel downstream in the ferry-boat
(4/6) by the stroke of the command,
my bundle of reeds upon my shoulder.
I will be in Ankh-towy,
and say to Ptah, Lord (4/7) of Truth,
"Give to me my[12] sister tonight!"
The river[13] is wine,
Ptah its reeds,
Sekhmet its (4/8) bloom,
the Dew Goddess[14] its lotus bud,
Nefertum its lotus flower.
[The Golden One][15] is joy.
(4/9) The land brightens through her beauty;
Memphis is a jar of perfume
placed before one beautiful of face.[16]

Poem Six

I will lie down inside;
(4/10) [I] will be ill falsely.[17]
My neighbors will come in to behold me,
and the sister will come with them.[18]
(4/11) She will make the doctors unnecessary
because she knows my sickness.

Poem Seven

At the country house of the sister,
his (4/12) entrance is in the middle of her house,
and her door is open.
Her doorbolt[19] is sprung.
The sister is angry.
Would that one would make me her door-keeper!
(4/13) I would make her angry at me
so that I would hear her voice when she is angry,
(and be) a child in dread of her.

Poem Eight

As I travel downstream (6/1) upon the canal of the
    ruler, lph,
as I enter into the (way) (6/2) of Re.[20]
My heart will go to prepare these (6/3) tents
at the top of the entrance of the lagoon.
(6/4) I will rise up to hasten, without ceasing;
my heart (6/5) remembers Re.
I will watch (6/6) the arrival of my brother
when he arrives at the garden house.
(6/7) I will stand with you at the entrance of the
    lagoon,
(and) you may take (6/8) my heart to Re's Heliopolis.
When I retire with you (6/9) to the trees of the garden
    house,
(6/10) I will snatch from the trees of the garden house
(6/11) arms full as[21] my fan,
(and) I will observe (6/12) as it is made.
My face faces the cottage;
(6/13) my arms are filled with Persea (branches);[22]

my hair is heavy with resin.
(8/1) I am like[23] the Lady of the Two Lands.
I am [with you].

Poem Nine

The beginning of the praise of fine pleasures for your
    sister.
The beloved (8/2) of your heart is one having come from
the fields.
My brother, my beloved,
my heart (goes) after your love.
All has been created for you,[24]
and I will tell you of a scene which happened.
I came from snaring,
(8/3) my traps (are) in my hand,
in my (other) hand, my cage[25]
(and) my hunting instrument (?).[26]
(As for) all the birds of Punt,
(8/4) they alight upon Egypt, anointed with myrrh.
The first to come seizes my bait.
His odor is brought[27] (8/5) from Punt;
his claws are filled with resin.
My desire (shall be) to you that we might release it
    together.
(Then) I am alone with you.
I cause you to hear my (8/6) shrill voice.
My ointment is good myrrh.
You are there with me,
when I set a snare.
The happiness (is) the going to the fields (8/7)
of the one who is loved.

Poem Ten

The voice of the goose cries out,
captured by his bait.
Your love (8/8) entraps me
(and) I do not know how to loosen it.
I shall take up[28] my nets.
What shall I (say) to my mother

to whom (I) return daily
(8/9) when I am loaded down with catch?
I did not set the trap today.
Your love has seized me.

Poem Eleven
The goose is flying and (8/10) alighting
(and afterwards) the net sank for him.
Many birds are circling;
I must control myself.
(But) I serve (8/11) my love
when I am alone.
When my heart is in accord with your heart,
I cannot be far from all happiness.

Poem Twelve
I will go out for the brother.
(10/1) [As for] your love,
my heart stops within me.
I see sweet cakes
(but) [they appear to be][29] salt.
(As for) pomegranate wine (10/2), the sweetness in my
    mouth
is like the gall of birds.
The breath of your nose alone
is what enlivens my heart.
When I have found (you),
may Amun give (you) to me,
forever (10/3) and ever.

Poem Thirteen
O beautiful (one), I have a good desire
for (my caring for) your things
as your mistress of the house.
Your arm lies upon my arm.[30]
Your love is (10/4) pervasive for you.
I speak to my heart, within me,[31] this prayer:
"My great one is afar from me tonight,
(and) I am like one in my grave (10/5).
But are you not health and life?

Rejoicing has met me through your health
because my heart is[32] (10/6) seeking you."

Poem Fourteen

The voice of the turtledove speaks. It says,
"The day breaks, what is your way?"
Quiet,[33] O bird,
must you scold me so?[34]
(10/7) I found my brother on his bed.
My heart is pleasing in excess.
We said:
"I shall not be far [from you][35]
for my hand is in your hand.
(10/8) I shall walk about when I am with you
in every pleasant place."[36]
He makes me the first of the beautiful ones.
He has not upset my heart.

Poem Fifteen

I will set my face upon the (10/9) outer door.
Behold my brother is coming to me.
My eyes are upon the road;
my ears hear
that I wait on[37] Pa-Mehy (10/10)
(and) set the love of my brother as my only concern.
Because of what he has, my heart is not silent.
He sent to me one message, which overtakes me,
feet (10/11), coming and going,
in order to tell me that he wronged me
thinking[38] that he has found[39] another (woman).
He is stunning before me.[40]
What about him?
Shall the annoyances of (10/12) another estrange me?

Poem Sixteen

My heart remembers your love.
Half of my temple was braided,
but I have come hastening to seek you.
(12/1) I have been neglectful of my tresses

...that I may put on
my braids,
(12/2) I am always ready!

Poem Seventeen: <u>The Song of the Harper</u>[41]
   The songs which are in the temple of Intwf, the
departed, which are in front of the (12/3) singer at
the harp.
This good noble is one who makes flourish
a good destiny.
Sick bodies go,
(while) others (12/4) remain,
since the time of the ancestors.
The gods who came into being before me
(and) who are resting in their pyramids,
the nobles and the beatified (ones) (12/5) likewise
   are buried in their pyramids.
Temples were built, but their places do not exist
so that (12/6) eye(s) might behold them.
I have heard sayings (of) Iymḥtp and Ḥardedef
which are frequently (12/7) quoted in their tales
   entirely.
What are the places thereof?
Their walls are ruined.
Their (offering) places do not exist,
as if they had never come into being (12/8).
There does not exist one who comes from there
that he may tell of their nature or quote their
   affairs[42]
(or) who will still our hearts
until we go speedily (12/9) to the place where they
   have gone.
May it please you,
to cause the heart to forget it.
(What is) beneficial for you is
to follow your heart as long as you live.
(12/10) Place myrrh upon your head,
(and) clothe yourself in fine linen,
it being anointed with true wonders

(12/11) of the things of god.
Increase your beauty,
(and) do not[43] let your mind languish.
Follow your heart and your happiness.
(12/12) Be about your business upon earth.
Do not disobey[44] your heart.
That day of crying will come to you.
The Weary-Hearted will not (14/1) hear their [crying].
Theirs cannot save the heart of a man from the
    netherworld.
Moral: (14/2) Make celebration!
Do not tire yourself[45] of it.
Behold, it is not given to man that man take his
    possessions with him.
Behold, there does not exist (one) (14/3) who goes away
    and forthwith returns.[46]

Poem Eighteen[47]

The beginning of the praise of pleasures.
Mekhmekh flowers,
(my) heart inclines to you.
I shall do for you what (14/4) it seeks,
(when) I am in your embrace.
My prayer is that my eyes may be painted,[48]
for my seeing you is the brightening (14/5) of my eye.
When I have drawn near to see your love,
grandest[49] of my heart,
how lovely is my[50] hour!
(14/6) May the hour stretch out for me as eternity.
Since I have spent the night with you,
you have raised up my heart.
I am sad, when he is far from me.

Poem Nineteen

(14/7) *Sa^{c}am* plants are in it,
by which one is elevated in their presence.
I am your best sister.
(As for) me, behold I am like the Crown Lands
which I planted

with flowers (14/8) and with all fragrant *ḫśwt* plants.
Lovely is the water canal in it,
which[51] your hand digs out
in order to refresh ourselves with the northwind.
(14/9) A good place for my walking (is) there.
Your hand is in my hand.
My body is at ease.
My heart is joyful because of our journeying (14/10)
    together.
Pomegranate-wine is my hearing your voice.
I live because I hear.[52]
If I am seen in every glance,
(14/11) it is more spendid for me than eating and
    drinking.

Poem Twenty
    Titi flowers (are) in it.
    I will snatch your wreaths,
    when you come (14/12) intoxicated
    (and) sleep upon your bed.[53]
    I will touch your feet.
    The children in your...
    because I rejoice in the morning....

THE CHESTER BEATTY LOVE SONGS[54]

(First Stanza)
    (C^1/1) The beginning of the utterances of the great
        pleasure.
    Unique is a sister, without her duplicate,
    (who is) more beautiful than any woman.
    See, she is like the Star Goddess (C^1/2) rising,
    at the beginning of a favorable year.
    (She is) an excellent one who is bright,
    who is shining of skin,
    who is beautiful of eyes which stare[55] (C^1/3).
    Her lips, which speak, are sweet.
    She has not a word too much.
    One high of neck, one bright of nipples (C^1/4),

real lapis-lazuli is her hair.
Her arms excel gold;
her fingers are like lotus flowers.
(C^1/5) One drooping of buttocks, one slim-waisted,
her thighs extend[56] her perfection.
Her step is pleasing when she treads upon the earth.
(C^1/6) She seizes my heart with her embrace.
She causes that the necks of all men
turn back at the sight of her.[57]
Everyone (C^1/7) who embraces her is happy.[58]
He is like the chief of the lovers.
Her going forth is seen
like that (one), (C^1/8) a unique one.[59]

Second Stanza

The brother disturbs[60] my heart with his voice.
He causes a sickness to seize me.
He is (C^1/9) a neighbor of my mother's house,
(but) I do not know how to go to him.
Is my mother good in charging him (C^2/1) thus:
"Abandon seeing her!"
Behold my heart is upset when he is remembered;
his love seizes me.
Behold, he (C^2/2) is foolish,[61]
(yet) I am like him.
He does not know my desire to embrace him,
(and) he does not send[62] for my mother (C^2/3).
Brother, would that I might be entrusted to you
by the Golden One of women.[63]
Come to me that I can see your perfection.
My father and mother (C^2/4) (are) rejoicing.
All mankind is rejoicing in one place for you.
They rejoice for you, brother.

Third Stanza

My heart planned to see (C^2/5) its perfection,
while I was sitting in the midst of it.
I found Mehy in a chariot on the road,
with his lusty lovers[64] C^2/6).

I do not know how to take myself from his presence.
Shall I pass by him unhindered?
See, the river (C^2/7) is like a road,
for the place of my feet is not known.
How very ignorant are you, my heart![65]
Why do you still stroll by Mehy?
See, if I pass (C^2/8) before him,
I will tell him my feelings.[66]
Behold, "I am yours," I will say[67] to him.
He will boast of my name.
(C^2/9) He will allot me to the chief harem
which is among his followers.

Fourth Stanza

Flees my heart quickly,[68]
(C^2/10) since I remembered the love for you.
He does not let me walk like (other) people,
(for) he leaps up (from) his proper station.
He does not cause me to don (C^3/1) a tunic,
nor to cover myself with a fan,
nor to put *sdm* on my eyes,
nor to anoint myself at all.[69]
(C^3/2) "Do not wait, go home!"
He says to me each time [I][70] remember him.
Do not act for me as a fool, O my heart!
Why are you acting (C^3/3) as a madman?
Sit still, be cool! The brother[71] comes to you.
My eye is blinded so.[72]
Don't let the people say concerning me,
"A woman (C^3/4) has given in[73] to love."
Be firm[74] each time that you think of him.
O my heart, do not flee!

Fifth Stanza

I praise (C^3/5) the Golden One.
I applaud her majesty;
I exalt the Lady of the Sky.
I make praises to Hathor,
thanksgiving (C^3/6) to the mistress.

I report to her in order that she may hear my
    petitions.
May the mistress entrust her to me.
She has come back of her own accord (C^3/7) to see me.
Something very great is happening to me.[75]
I rejoice, I am glad, I am great,
ever since one said, "Hey, she is here!"
(C^3/8) Behold, she came and the lovers are bowing
    down
to the greatness of her love.
I prayed[76] (C^3/9) to my goddess
that she give to me a sister as a gift.[77]
Three days have passed since my petitions.
In her name, may she come forth with me on the fifth
    day.

(C^3/10) Sixth Stanza

I passed[78] in the neighborhood of his house.
I found his door open,
the brother standing beside his mother.
All his brothers and sisters (C^4/1) were with him.
Love of him seizes the heart of all who tread upon
    the road.
An excellent youth, without equal,
a brother of choicest character.
(C^4/2) He kept watching me when I walked by.
I alone shout for joy.
How glad is a heart in exaltation,
O brother, (C^4/3) because of my being seen.
Oh, that Mother might know my desire!
(Yet) she entered it at the proper time.
O Golden One, place it (C^4/4) in his heart,
(and then) I will go speedily to the brother,
(and then) kiss him in front of his companions.
I will not weep because of the people,
(but) I will rejoice (C^4/5) because of their
    perception:
that you know me.[79]
I will make festivals for my goddess.

My heart springs to come forth,
(C^4/6) to let me look over the brother tonight.
How happy is the passing by.[80]

Seventh Stanza

Seven days till yesterday and I have not seen the
   sister
(C^4/7) An internal disease has crept into me.
I have become heavy in my flesh.
My own body is ignored.
If the master physicians come to me,
(C^4/8) my heart will not be satisfied with their
   remedies.
As for the lector-priests, there is no help through
   them.
My sickness will not be diagnosed.
(C^4/9) Telling me, "Behold her,"[81] that is what will
   revive me.[82]
Her name is that which will raise me up.
It is the coming and going of her messages
(C^4/10) which bring life to my heart.
The sister[83] is more beneficial to me than all
   remedies.
She is greater to me than the Compendium (of medicine).
My salvation (C^5/1) is her coming in from outside.
When I see her, (then) I will be healthy.[84]
When she opens her eye, my body is young.
(C^5/2) When she speaks, (then) I will be strong.
When I embrace her, she exorcises evil from me.
She has been gone from me for seven days.

The Chester Beatty Cycle of Three Songs

(First Song)
(G^1/1) Would that[85] you might come to the sister
   quickly,[86]
(as) a king's messenger whose[87] lord's heart
is impatient (G^1/2) after his message,
(and) his desire is in hearing them.

The stables are completely ready for him.
(G^1/3) He has horses at the resting place.
The chariot is yoked at its station (G^1/4).
He has no rest upon the road.
When he reached the house of the sister,
his heart made exultations.

(Second Song)
    (G^1/5) Would that you might come [to the sister
       quickly],[88]
like a horse of the king,
the choice of a thousand of steeds of (G^1/6) every
    kind,
the foremost of the stables.
It is distinguished in its feed,
(and) its master knows its paces.
(G^1/7) If it hears the sound of a whip,
it knows no holding back.
There is not a chief in the (G^1/8) chariotry
who can overtake it.
O how the heart of the sister knows
that he is not far from (G^2/1) the sister.[89]

(Third Song)
Would that you might come to the sister quickly,
as a gazelle
leaping across the desert.
(G^2/2) Its feet are lame (?).
Its body is weary.
Terror has entered into its limbs.
Hunters are after it.
Hounds are (G^2/3) with them,[90]
(but) they do not see his dust.
It sees a resting place like a mirage (?).[91]
It takes (G^2/4) a river as a road.
You shall have reached her den
until kissing[92] your hand four times
(G^2/5) as your pursue[93] the love of the sister.
It is the Golden One who has handed her over[94]

to you, my friend.

The Nakht-Sobek Cycle of P. Chester Beatty I

(First Stanza)

(R^{16}/9) The beginning of the sweet sayings found
while holding a scroll composed by the writer Nakht-
    Sobek of the necropolis.
You may bring it[95] to the house of the sister
when you pant (?) after her cave.
(R^{16}/10) It is made in the form of her *ḥrᶜ*.[96]
Her *nbt*, moreover, is a place of slaughter.[97]
She is provided with song and dance.
Wines and strong ale are her protection,[98]
that you may confound (R^{16}/11) her senses (?).[99]
May you bring her to an end[100] in her night.
Thus she will tell you:
"Take me in your embrace.
When the day dawns, we[101] will be likewise."

(Second Stanza)

May you bring it (into) the hall of the sister,
you alone, without another.
(R^{16}/12) You can accomplish your desire in her
    thicket.[102]
The halls shall be whirling (?).
The heavens pant with storms.
He does not remove it.
That she may bring you her fragrance,
an odor (R^{17}/1) which overflows to cause
those who are present to become intoxicated.
The Golden One has sent her to you[103] as a reward,
to let you bring to an end your time.

(Third Stanza)

(R^{17}/2) How well the sister knows the casting of the
    noose.[104]
Indeed she is not *$\overset{?}{irw}$*.[105]
She casts the noose at me with her hair.

$(R^{17}/3)$ With her eyes she catches me,
(and) with her necklace she causes me to bow down.
With her seal (ring), she brands me.

(Fourth Stanza)
When[106] do you argue with $(R^{17}/4)$ your heart?
After her! Embrace her!
As Amun lives, I shall come to you,
my loin cloth upon my shoulder.

(Fifth Stanza)
I found $(R^{17}/5)$ the brother at the irrigation canal,
his feet set down in the river.
He builds an altar of the day-time,
(and) honors (?)[107] (it) with beer.
He brought skin[108] to $(R^{17}/6)$ my thighs.
He is taller than he is broad.

(Sixth Stanza)
(As for) that which the sister did to me,
shall I keep silent from her
so that I am made to stand in the door of her house
while she $(R^{17}/7)$ went inside?
She does not speak to me of a good release[109]
while she shared in my night.

(Seventh Stanza)
I[110] passed by her house $(R^{17}/8)$ at night.
I knocked, but (it) did not open to me.
A good night for our door-keeper!
Door-bolts, I will open.
Door, you are $(R^{17}/9)$ my fate.
Are you my spirit?[111]
Our ox will be slaughtered inside.
Door, do not use your might!
$(R^{17}/10)$ An ox will be slaughtered for the door-bolt,
goats for the threshold,[112]
a strong goose for the door-post,
flesh (?) for the $^{c}\underline{dw}$.[113]

(R^{17}/11) All the choicest flesh of our ox
shall belong[114] to the carpenter's son.
He will make us a door-bolt of reeds,
a door of (R^{17}/12) grass. [115]
Anytime when the brother comes,
he will find her house open,
he will find a bed laid (R^{17}/13) with linens,
a lovely one in the midst of them.
The maid will say to me:[116]
"This place belongs to the son
of the mayor of the village."

THE TURIN LOVE SONGS[117]

(Poem One)
    (8/1) It [says]:
My seeds (are) like her teeth;
my fruit (are) (9/1) like her breasts.
...[I am foremost] in the orchard (9/2).
I am established[118] in every season,
which the sister passes with (9/3) her brother.[119]
...my....
They are (9/4) drunk with wine and juice,
(and) immersed [in] (9/5) moringa oils and resins.
...all (9/6) perish
except me in the field. I spend 12 months.
...as I stand. Last year's blossom (9/8)
falls from me.
I am foremost (10/1) [in the orchard].
Behold: I am for them[121] (as) a second.
(10/2) If it (is) to be done again,
I (will) not (be) silent for them.
...(10/3) her....
The liar will be seen.
(10/4) Discipline is made for the lover.
That she may not [drop] (10/5) her blossoms (?),[122]
of lotus flowers[123] (and) of (10/6) lotus-buds,
ointments...(11/1)...(and) costly (oil)[124] of all
    kinds.[125]

She caused you to pass the day pleasantly (11/2).
A house of reeds is in a guarded place....
(11/3) See, he is coming in truth.
Come,[126] let us flatter (11/4) him.
Let him pass the entire day
...(11/5) (where) he hides.

(Poem Two)

    (12/1) The sycamore fig sends forth its voice.
Its foliage (?) (12/2) speaks (thusly):
...do....
I come forth to the mistress.
(12/3) If[127] (she) is a noble like myself
(and) if there are no (12/4) maidservants,
I (will be) the slave
[who is brought from the land of (12/5) Khor]
as plunder for my love.
She caused (me) to be placed (13/1) in [her] orchard.
She did not permit[128] me...[to drink] (13/2) on the
   [day] of drinking.
Nor was my body filled[129] from the water of waterskins.
(13/3) I was found to be amusing (?)[130]
...(13/4) because of not drinking.
As my $k3$ endures, O beloved, [he] (13/5) will be
   brought into your presence.[131]

(Poem Three)

    The little sycamore
(that) she planted (13/6)[132] with her hand
sends forth its [voice] to speak:
The (13/7) flowers (?) [are like] liquid of honey.
(14/1) It is beautiful; its branches are lovely,
greener than [the grass] (14/2).
It is loaded with the abundance of notched sycamore-
   figs.
It is redder (14/3) than red jasper.[133]
Its leaves...a hue (14/4) like fayence.
Its bark like the hue of green feldspar.
(14/5) Sap like the *bsbs* oil.

It attracts him who is not beneath it.[134]
(14/6) Its shade causes the air to cool.
It gives[135] (14/7) a message by the hand of a girl,
the daughter of the chief- (15/1) caretaker.
It makes (her) hurry to the lover.
Come, (15/2) spend a moment with the girls.
The field (15/3) shall have[136] its day.
A festival (and) a tent (are) beneath me.
My foremen (?) (are) (15/4) joyful,
the children at seeing you.
(15/5) Let my servants be sent ahead of you,
equipped with their (15/6) utensils.
One is drunk when traveling to you,
(and) one has not yet taken a drink.[137]
(15/7) Your servants come
bearing their (16/1) possessions,
bringing a tribute of beer of all kinds.
All kinds of kneaded bread,
(16/2) abundant blooms of yesterday and today,
all kinds of fruit for (16/3) recreation.
Come, pass the day in pleasure.
Morning (16/4) after morning, (for) 3 days
while you sit in my shade.
Her (16/5) friend is upon her right.
She makes him drunk,
(16/6) and follows what he says.
The storeroom of beer is disordered in drunkenness,
(16/7) as she stays with her brother.
What is hers[138] is spread out (16/8) under me.
The sister is in her walk.
I am discreet[139] (17/1) (and) shall not say that
    I have seen their conversation (?).

THE CAIRO LOVE SONGS OF OSTRACON 25218[140]

(Poem One)
    (X/1) Sister for....
    (X/2) My God, my [lord]....
    (X/3) My desire is to go down

(X/4) to bathe in your presence,
that I may let you [see] my beauty
in a tunic of fine, royal linen
which is soaked in ti-$šps̆y$ oil.
(X/5) That I may go into the water with you and
I come out to you carrying a red wt fish[141]
which is well-behaved in my fingers
and lay it before you....
(X/6) Come, that you might see me.

(Poem Two)

The love of the sister is upon the other side.
The tributary is [between me and my sister].[142]
(X/7) The crocodile stands upon the sandbank.
I go down to the water.
I wade in the waves.
My heart is strong upon the lake.
(X/8) The waves are like land to my feet.
Her love makes me flourish.
Then she shall make a water-spell for me.
I am seeking (X/9) the sister as she returns,
My heart is exulting;
my arms separate to embrace her.
My heart is joyful upon its proper station
as...(X/10) eternity,
after the lady comes to me.

(Poem Three)

I embrace her.
Her arms separate.
Then I am[143] like one in Punt,
like him who possesses (X/11) ladanum (?).

(Poem Four)

I kiss her.[144]
Her lips open.
I rejoice without beer.
The time[145] of preparing [her bed] was completed.
(X/12) O servant, hurry there I tell you.

Place fine linen between her limbs,
as a bed for her,[146] with royal sheets.
Guard yourself (with) a decorated white linen...
found like one who is
(X/13) moistened with moringa oil.

(Poem Five)

Would that I were her Nubian (maid)
who is her personal servant....
She gives pleasure indeed. (X/14) The hue of every limb
has been offered to me.

(Poem Six)

Would that I were her washerman...
for a single month...
(X/15) washing the moringa oils
which are in her kerchief....

(Poem Seven)

(X/16) Would that I were her seal ring
which is [on her fingers]....
(X/17) Like one who passed her lifetime...
(X/18) reeds (?)....

THE LOUVRE C 100 LOVE SONG[147]

(16/1) Sweet, lovable[148] (is) Hathor's priestess,
   Mutiridis.
Sweet, sweet beloved by the king of Upper and Lower
   Egypt, Menkheperre, given life.
(16/2) [Sweet], lovable with all men.
A lady beloved by women.
She is the lovable princess,
fairest of women,
a girl (16/3) whose likeness has not been seen.
Blacker is her hair than the blackness of the night,
than the grapes of the $\overset{?}{\textit{id}b}$-vines.

[Whiter (are) (16/4) her teeth] than flakes of
   (white) stone at cutting.
(Two) wreaths are her breasts settled at her arm.

[1]The translation of the love songs contained in Papyrus Harris 500 is based upon the hieroglyphic transcription of the hieratic text published by Müller. In the translation, references are made to Müller's work in the following manner: (*Tafel*/line number). Places in which the text has been restored are marked with brackets, and words which have been added to enhance the translation are frequently designated by the use of parenthesis.

[2]The word *mn [dwi]*, "breasts," should be restored; see (2/5) and (2/11).

[3]Reading ⌠⌐ ⁓⁓⁓ instead of ⌠⌐ ⁓⁓⁓ , for harmony with the dual "breasts."

[4]Reading *ḥr nḥw* with Müller, *Liebespoesie*, 15 n. 9.

[5]The word ⌠⊙⅜⌠⌐ is a problem. Müller renders it "remember" and joins it to the beginning of the line: "remember to visit your sister" (*Liebespoesie*, 15). The word is apparently without a determinative. One might propose that the word is a corruption of ⌠⊙⅜⊙⧹, "hasten." Another possibility would be to read the word as a causative of *ḥȝs* (⧸ ⅜ ⚊ ⧹) which Faulkner lists as "scramble" (in which case it would have a determinative ⌐⧹); see his *A Concise Dictionary of Middle Egyptian* (Oxford: Griffith Institute, 1962) 185. Cf. Adolf Erman and Hermann Grapow, *Wörterbuch der aegyptischen Sprache* (Berlin: Akademie-Verlag, 1950) 3.234. Another possibility, and the one accepted in this translation, would be to read the word *sḥȝ·st*, a word of unknown meaning, plus a pronominal object. Although the clarity of the pronoun *st* argues for reading noun + pronoun object, the reading is still uncertain. The word ⌐⧹is to be read as the ideogram *ȝs*: "to hasten."

[6]See Müller, *Liebespoesie*, 16 n. 3.

[7]The words *mtnw* and *wgȝt* are obscure in terms of their meaning; cf. Erman and Grapow, *Wörterbuch* 2.170 and 1.376. The translation of these words follows closely that of Simpson, *The Literature*, 299.

[8]Müller, *Liebespoesie*, 16 n. 7.

[9]The text has been restored to read *rdwy m šnw*, "feet (are) in hair." I have also restored a third person, feminine suffix pronoun, "her hair." Müller suggests that instead of "feet" one should read "*Blicke*." Simpson (*The Literature*, 299) suggests "beak." Since birds were usually snared by the feet, one should read with the restored text.

[10]Müller, *Liebespoesie*, 17 n. 6.

[11]The reading *r ḥȝᶜ pȝ ȝbw·i* in Müller's transcription necessitates the elimination of either the *pȝ* or *i*. In this

text, *i̧* is frequently superfluous and, therefore, should be deleted in this instance. In cases where [glyph] or [glyph] appear to be superfluous in a given context, they have been deleted for purposes of this translation.

[12]Because there is no article, Müller correctly proposes the addition of [glyph] , "my"; see his text (4/7), note c.

[13]Reading [hieroglyphs] for Müller's [hieroglyphs] .

[14]This poem portrays a journey to Memphis, the "life of the two lands." The deities represented here are Memphite ones. See Morenz, *Religion*, 258-71.

[15]Following Simpson (*The Literature*, 300) in the restoration of *nbwt*. The Golden One is Hathor. Müller's restoration, [*snt·ỉ*] *pw* [*m*] *ršwt*, "my sister is in joy," is a difficult reading syntactically. In such a reading, Müller has made *pw* superfluous due to the presence of the adverbial predicate [*m*] *ršwt*. A reading of noun + *pw* + noun is required; thus one might restore as follows: [*nbwt*] *pw ršwt*, "The Golden One is joy."

[16]The determinative [glyph] , if correct, points out that the "one beautiful of face" is a deity.

[17]One must restore the first person pronoun, thus reading *kꜣ mr·*[*ỉ*] (on analogy of the *kꜣ sḏm·f* construction). The *kꜣ sḏm·f* is a verbal form which expresses future result of injunction and can be noted in the following two verb forms as well; see Gardiner, *Grammar*, §450, 5d.

[18]For [glyph] with suffix, see Erman, *Grammatik*, §623.

[19]Following Müller's proposed emendation, reading [hieroglyphs] instead of [hieroglyphs] (*Liebespoesie*, 19 n. 6).

[20]See Erman, *Grammatik*, §127.

[21]The meaning of [glyph] in this context is difficult to determine. One would be inclined to doubt that [glyph] is an earlier writing for [glyph], "for." Such writing is rare in New Egyptian (see Erman, *Grammatik*, §600.9). The reading "in my *bꜣ*" would be acceptable; yet, in this context, the sense of the sentence would, then, be uncertain. Müller may have captured the correct sense of [glyph] when he noted that the objects held in the arms function as a fan; see *Liebespoesie*, 20 n. 6).

[22]See Müller, *Liebespoesie*, 20.

[23][hieroglyphs] should be emended to [hieroglyphs] following ibid., 20 n. 10. This emendation, unfortunately, does not solve the translational difficulties in this problematic line. Instead of [hieroglyphs] , one should read [hieroglyphs] , "Lady of the Two Lands."

[24][hieroglyphs] should be translated as a passive *sḏm·f* form (see Erman, *Grammatik*, §§318-320), although there might be

reason to suspect a first person form from the ending 〖〗 , "[I] have created everything for you" (see §61).

[25]In (8/3), note d, Müller suggests that the textual reading ⟨hieroglyphs⟩ , db(w) should be read tb(w) (cf. the word ⟨hieroglyphs⟩ , "crate"). To support this reading, one may note that the consonantal change t/d is possible in New Egyptian. The word ⟨hieroglyphs⟩ is, however, found in Erman and Grapow, associated with "bird-snaring" and "trap." The word may have the connotation "cage."

[26]Müller translates škykt as Fangschirm and points out that it may be a loan word; see Liebespoesie, 21 n. 3.

[27]For the in·ti (in·tw) passive, see Erman, Grammatik, §270.

[28]Reading tȝyt for rt; see Müller, Liebespoesie, 22 n. 3.

[29]This is restored in Müller's text.

[30]The text reads, "Your arm lies upon my kȝbt (breast)." The restoration gbȝt, "arm," should be made, given the frequency of this phrase in love poetry and given the presence of the determinative ⟨hieroglyph⟩ . Yet, the text may betray the error of a copyist whose mind wandered as he pondered the image of the lovers' embrace!

[31]The text should be emended. Instead of reading ⟨hieroglyphs⟩ , one should read ⟨hieroglyphs⟩ , literally, "in my intestines."

[32]The text reads pȝ ib·i. One should emend it to read pȝy·i ib, "my heart."

[33]Literally, "Don't, O bird." This phrase is an ellipsis which means, "Don't make so much noise," or "Be quiet."

[34]Following Simpson, The Literature, 304.

[35]Delete ⟨hieroglyph⟩ and restore ⟨hieroglyph⟩ on analogy with ⟨hieroglyph⟩ in (10/4).

[36]These lines in (10/8) should not be understood as duplications or fragments of Poem Nineteen (cf. Müller, Liebespoesie, 24). Although the language is strikingly similar to that of Poem Nineteen, there is no internal evidence of interpolation. The similarity in theme is due to the presence of repetitions in love poetry.

[37]For this meaning of šdšd ti·i n, see Erman and Grapow, Wörterbuch, 4.569.

[38]The phrase kȝ dd is a difficult one to parse. Because the kȝ has no suffix, it might well be an old perfective of a verb kȝi ("to plan"). The phrase could read, then, "he having thought to say." One might also treat kȝ dd as an ellipsis for r dd (cf. Hebrew לֵאמֹר?). These lines about "the message" are difficult to translate due to the obscure syntax and text.

[39] Reading *gm·n·f kt.*

[40] Reading *ḥr·ỉ.*

[41] "The Song of the Harper" is an example of wisdom litera-ture. Although it is not love poetry, it has been included in this translation at the point of its occurrence in Papyrus Harris 500 because, as noted above, p. 81, in circles which preserved love songs the Harper Song was not viewed as intru-sive.

[42] Reading *ḥrt·sn* instead of *fḫt·sn.*

[43] The text should be emended to include *m,* "do not let."

[44] Read *m ḥḏ* instead of *m wḏ.*

[45] Read *n·k* instead of *n·ỉ.*

[46] See Gardiner, *Grammar,* §483 for *ỉw* + infinitive construc-tion.

[47] The next three poems form a cycle about plants. In Egyp-tian, there is a word play on the name of each flower. See above, pp. 81 and 124 n. 39.

[48] See Erman and Grapow, *Wörterbuch,* 4.370.

[49] Ibid., 2.424.

[50] The hieratic text clearly has *t3y·ỉ.*

[51] For *n* with *sḏm·f* to express the relative, see Gardiner, *Grammar,* §191.2.

[52] The text reads ⟨glyphs⟩ .

[53] See Erman and Grapow, *Wörterbuch,* 3.119.

[54] This translation is based upon Gardiner's hieroglyphic text (*Chester Beatty*). Verso, recto, and line numbers refer to Gardiner's transcription. In the first cycle of seven songs, the first and last word in each stanza is either the re-spective number or a play on words on the number of the stanza.

[55] Gardiner appears to translate *gmḥw* and *mdt* (in the fol-lowing line) as infinitives ("wherewith to gaze" and "where-with to speak") (*Chester Beatty,* 30).

[56] Faulkner, *Dictionary,* 318.

[57] This translation is an attempt to literally render the *rdỉ·f wn·f* + old perfective verb form. Gardiner attempts to clarify the translation by the gratuitous addition of "daz-zled." He renders the line as follows: "She maketh the necks of all men to be turned away dazzled at the sight of her" (*Chester Beatty,* 30).

[58]Literally: "joyful."

[59]That is, "the sun."

[60]Following Gardiner, one should relate the word *stꜣwḥ* to Coptic ⲧⲱϩ, "mix, stir, be clouded." See W. E. Crum, *A Coptic Dictionary* (Oxford: Clarendon, 1939) 453-54. The form of the Egyptian word would be an *s* causative; see Gardiner, *Chester Beatty*, 31 n. 1.

[61]Literally, "Behold he (is) as (one) whose heart (i.e., mind) does not exist."

[62]The form *mtw·f ḥꜣb(wy)* is a conjunctive construction. See Erman, *Grammatik*, §§575 and 576.

[63]That is, Hathor. The initial  is the particle of agent. See Erman, *Grammatik*, §619 and Gardiner, *Grammar*, §168.

[64]"Lusty youths" is Gardiner's translation for 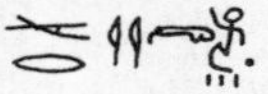.

[65]Literally, "(One) who is very ignorant (is) my heart."

[66]The root *pẖr* usually means "to turn, to turn about," but, as Faulkner notes (*Dictionary*, 93), the phrase *pẖr ỉb n* can mean "incline the heart to." One may propose the meaning "inclination" or "feeling."

[67]For a discussion of the parenthetic phrase , see Gardiner, *Grammar*, §436 and Erman, *Grammatik*, §716.

[68]The *sw* which occurs in this line (*ỉfd sw ỉb·ỉ ꜣs*) is puzzling. Although I cannot find a meaning for *ỉfd* which could use a reflexive, the *sw* could be a reflexive object of *ỉb·ỉ*: "My heart *ỉfd*'s itself."

[69]See Faulkner, *Dictionary*, 285. The preceding lines are structured by the *bw* + infinitive constructions.

[70]One should read *shꜣ*· [*ỉ*] *sw*. A characteristic feature of this text is the occasional dropping of *ỉ*, especially before a suffix pronoun such as *sw*.

[71]Since the sister is speaking to her heart, context demands that *snt* be emended to *sn*; see Gardiner, *Chester Beatty*, 32 n. 2.

[72]Simpson, *The Literature*, 318. 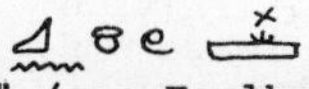 (*knw*) may be related to 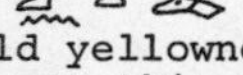, "yellowness" (see Faulkner, *Dictionary*, 279). Could yellowness of the eye describe a condition such as blindness? On this point see Ebers Medical Papyrus 431 (64, 4-5) in H. Grapow, *Die medizinischen Texte in hieroglyphischer Umschreibung autographiert* (Berlin: Akademie-Verlag, 1958) 87.

[73]For the verb *twhꜣ*, see Erman and Grapow, *Wörterbuch*, 5.255.

[74]An old perfective used in exhortation (see Gardiner, *Grammar*, §313).

[75] Literally, "How great is what is happening to me." The particle 𓂝𓏤 ⟨⟩ gives the adjectival predicate 𓄙 𓏺𓏺 𓊪𓏛 exclamatory force. See Erman, *Grammatik*, §684. The word 𓂝𓏤 ⟨⟩ is simply a variant of 𓅱 ⟨⟩ (see Gardiner, *Grammar*, §49).

[76] For the meaning of *smȝ ꜥw*, see Erman and Grapow, *Wörterbuch*, 4.125.

[77] Gardiner questions the meaning of *spdy* as "gift"; cf. his *Egyptian Hieratic Texts* (Hildesheim: Georg Olms, 1964) 16 n.7.

[78] To maintain harmony, the text should be emended from *swȝ·n·f* to *swȝ·n·i*.

[79] For a discussion of the expression 𓂋 𓄖 in the context of recognition, see Erman, *Grammatik*, §428.

[80] The construction *m swȝ* is difficult to explain syntactically. In its use as a noun subject with adverbial predicate, one might expect a construction such as *nfrwy swȝ*.

[81] 𓊃𓂝 is used as a third, feminine singular pronoun.

[82] For the use of the particle 𓌡𓏤 in a relative sentence with 𓈖𓏤 , see Erman, *Grammatik*, §462.

[83] Reading *snt* for *sn*.

[84] The future tense reflects the use of the *kȝ sḏm·f* form.

[85] See Erman's discussion of the wish particle 𓌡𓏤𓈖𓏺𓂝 in *Grammatik*, §§298 and 690. The *n·i* should be understood syntactically as an ethical dative.

[86] "You might come quickly" attempts to translate the 2nd person, masculine singular Old Perfective of the verb 𓂻𓏤 𓂽 .

[87] For discussion of the genitival 𓈖 followed by *sḏm·f*, see Gardiner, *Grammar*, §191.

[88] One should restore the text on analogy with (G^1/1).

[89] See Erman, *Grammatik*, §§409 and 410 for the use of *pȝy·f* as the subject of an infinitive and the infinitive as an object clause.

[90] The text reads *ḥnꜥ·f*, "with him."

[91] Following Simpson, *The Literature*, 322.

[92] This construction is *r* + infinitive; see Erman, *Grammatik*, §611.

[93] Literally, "are after."

[94] For Erman's discussion of participial statements, see *Grammatik*, §368.

[95] The indefinite "it" in this line is a problem for the interpretation of the scene which is being described in the lines
which follow. Gardiner suggests (using a magnificent double
negative) the following: "I am not quite certain that 'it' has
not an obscene reference; only on this supposition can I imag-
ine any sense for 'remove it' in 16, 12"; see Gardiner, *Chester
Beatty*, 36 n. 3.

[96] The text reads ⬡ which should be under-
stood as syllabic orthography for $ḥrꜥ$, a word of obscure meaning. Simpson (*The Literature*, 323) conjectures "slaughter-
house," which would require textual emendation to $ḥryt$.

[97] Because there is no determinative ⬡ , Simpson's reading "mistress of the house" for ⬡ seems unlikely.
Given the hypothesized setting of the night of love, a euphemism
for vagina would be expected. One may propose that the structure of the sentence can be clarified by textual emendation.
One should read swt instead of sw, the t having dropped out of
the text because of haplography before $tꜣy·st$. Thus, one has
the following structure in the line: Noun A = Noun B. See
Gardiner, *Grammar*, §254 for a discussion of the adversative swt.

[98] Following Gardiner, *Chester Beatty*, 36. The imagery of
intoxication is found in several places in the love poetry (see,
e.g., Harris, 14/12; Turin, 16/5) and *may* be in some way related to the "festival of inebriety for Hathor." See Bleeker,
Hathor and Thoth, 91 and H. Brunner, "Die theologische Bedeutung
der Trunkenheit," *ZÄS* 79 (1954) 81-83.

[99] Literally, "that you may intoxicate her $srgḥ$"; I have
read with Gardiner, *Chester Beatty*, 36.

[100] For the verb $mnḫ$, see Erman and Grapow, *Wörterbuch*, 2.89.

[101] One should read ⬡ instead of ⬡ "they."

[102] The determinative ⬡ on the word $ḥgꜣ$ demands the connotation "wood." The word "thicket" has been proposed, again
a possible euphemism for the female genital region. The word
appears to be a loan word, akin to Hebrew חֲגָו (see Cant 2:14).

[103] See Erman, *Grammatik*, §386.

[104] The meaning of the word ⬡ ($ꜣnr$) is uncertain. It apparently means "noose."

[105] Literally, this line reads, "without giving birth to the
cattle-tax." Such a reading, however, makes no sense in context. I have read msw as a form of ⬡ ms, "surely, indeed."
The meaning of $ꜣrw$, given the context, is unknown.

[106] This time clause construction is discussed in Erman,
Grammatik, §810 under the word ⬡ . The particle ⬡
as a replacement of ⬡ is discussed in §§625, 664, and 726.

[107] The text reads $n(?)$ stn. The n is problematic and,
moreover, may evidence that something is missing in the text.

Gardiner reads *siͨn* ("to wait for") for *stn* (*Chester Beatty*, 37 n. 4). The form may be old perfective, but given the suspicion of a missing element in the text, nothing conclusive can be proposed. I have read *st̲n*, "to honor," for *stn*.

[108]One should read [hieroglyphs] (*inm*, "flesh," "skin") for [hieroglyphs] .

[109]"Release" should be understood as ejaculation, a meaning conveyed by the determinative in the word *whͨ* ([hieroglyphs]).

[110]Reading *i* instead of *k*.

[111]This line is introduced by [hieroglyph] which is written for the interrogative particle [hieroglyph] ; see Erman, *Grammatik*, §739.

[112]For *pnͨt* ("threshold"), cf. Coptic [Coptic] (Crum, *Dictionary*, 266).

[113][hieroglyphs] Based upon the context, one might conjecture that [hieroglyphs] refers to a wooden part of the door, perhaps "door-step" or "lock."

[114]Emend [hieroglyphs] "we" to [hieroglyphs] "they." The converse emendation was noted in (R[16/11]), above, n. 101. [hieroglyphs] has [hieroglyphs] as its antecedent.

[115]Cf. the translation of the preceding lines by Suys, "Chants," 225.

[116]Reading [hieroglyphs] for [hieroglyphs] .

[117]This translation of the Turin Papyrus is based upon the hieroglyphic transcriptions of Maspero. References are made to his page and line numbers.

[118]The form [hieroglyphs] , is a pronoun before an adverbial predicate, and is mentioned in Gardiner, *Grammar*, §124 and Erman, *Grammatik*, §479.

[119]Reading *irwy* with Müller.

[120]In Maspero's transcription, the dot which marks verse division is incorrectly placed after the number "12" in the text. One should read with Müller, placing the verse point after *3bd(w)*; see *Liebespoesie*, 38 n. 5.

[121]Reading *ptry* as the form in Erman, *Grammatik*, §364. Recognizing the difficulty of this line, Müller suspects damage in the text and wishes to restore an *nw*, "they," thus reading as follows: "They regarded me as second class" (Müller, *Liebespoesie*, 38 n. 8).

[122]See Maspero, *Chants*, 10 n. 2.

[123]Following Caminos' identification of *s͏šny*, *prḫ*, and *nhmw*; see Ricardo A. Caminos, *Late-Egyptian Miscellanies* (London: Oxford University, 1954) 213.

[124]Reading _dsrw_ as "costly (oil)" or "holy (oil)," with Müller, _Liebespoesie_, 38 n. 13. Maspero is incorrect when he attempts to develop an etymology from Coptic ⲤⲀⲓⲡⲉ. Cf. Caminos, _Miscellanies_, 425.

[125]Following Erman and Grapow, _Wörterbuch_, 1.326 and Müller, _Liebespoesie_, 38 in reading ⟨glyphs⟩, _wndwt_, as "kinds."

[126]See Erman, _Grammatik_, §362.

[127]For the interrogative particle ⟨glyph⟩ in a conditional sentence, see Erman, _Grammatik_, §§676 and 815.

[128]See Faulkner, _Dictionary_, 53. Cf. Müller's understanding of _w3ḥ_ as a word for libation (_Liebespoesie_, 39 n. 7).

[129]A _bw sdm·n·f_ form; see Erman, _Grammatik_, §722.

[130]Literally: "I was found to be made healthy because of laughing." Schott _Liebeslieder_, 59 and Müller (_Liebespoesie_, 39), translate "amusing."

[131]See Müller, _Liebespoesie_, 39.

[132]Erman, _Grammatik_, §392, translates this relative phrase.

[133]See Caminos, _Miscellanies_, 424-25. Hebrew אַחְלָמָה (Exod 28:19; 39:12) appears to be a loan word related to _ḥnm·t_; see Lambdin, "Loan Words," 147.

[134]See, however, Müller, _Liebespoesie_, 40 n. 5.

[135]Reading _rdiw·st_; see ibid., n. 6.

[136]Maspero has restored an [r] which is admittedly strange syntax. Müller denies Maspero's reconstruction and reads as follows: "Die Aue voll Gebüsch feiert (?) ihren Tag." Unfortunately, Müller does not provide textual emendation for this reading or evidence for his reconstruction.

[137]The construction _iw bw ir·t_ expresses the circumstance of "not yet." Compare the Coptic ⲘⲡⲀⲧⲩ (Crum, _Dictionary_, 179); see Erman, _Grammatik_, §445.

[138]See Erman, _Grammatik_, §179.

[139]See Gardiner, _Admonitions of an Egyptian Sage From a Hieratic Papyrus in Leiden_ (Leipzig: J. C. Hinrichs, 1909) 104.

[140]This translation is based upon the transcription of Spiegelberg, "Sammlung," 117-21. Recently, Posener has published the text of Ostracon Deir el-Medineh 1266 which augments the text of Cairo Ostracon 25218. While Ostracon 1266 does appear to aid in the reconstruction of portions of the hieratic text of Cairo Ostracon 25218, the text is generally fragmentary and does not aid our understanding of the topoi of Egyptian love lyrics; see Posener, _Catalogue_, Vol. II/3, 75-79.

[141]Identified by Caminos, *Miscellanies*, 77-78.

[142]Reading with Müller's restoration of the text (*Liebes-poesie*, 42).

[143]Reading with Spiegelberg, "Sammlung," 120 n. 1.

[144]See Erman, *Grammatik*, §§307-11 for a discussion of the emphatic *sḏm·f*.

[145]Ibid., §667.

[146]Reading with Müller, *Liebespoesie*, 43; see n. 4.

[147]The hieroglyphic transcription of H. P. Hurd has been used for this translation.

[148]The phrase *bnr mrwt* is translated "lovable" by Faulkner (*Dictionary*, 83).

SELECTED BIBLIOGRAPHY

A. Texts

De Boer, Piet. A. H., and W. Baars, eds. *The Old Testament in Syriac, Sample Edition: Song of Songs, Tobit, 4 Ezra.* Leiden: Peshiṭta Institute, 1966.

Daressy, M. Georges, ed. *Catalogue général des antiquités égyptiennes du musée du Caire.* Cairo: L'institut français d'archéologie orientale, 1901.

Ebeling, Erich. *Keilschrifttexte aus Assur religiosen Inhalts* 1. Wissenschaftliche Veröffentlichungen der deutschen Orient-Gesellschaft 28. Leipzig: Hinrichs, 1919.

Erman, Adolf. "Bruchstuck eines Liebesliedes." *ZAS* 39 (1902) 147.

Gardiner, Alan H. *Admonitions of an Egyptian Sage from a Hieratic Papyrus in Leiden.* Leipzig: Hinrichs, 1909.

_____. *Egyptian Hieratic Texts.* Hildesheim: Georg Olms, 1964.

_____. *The Library of A. Chester Beatty: Descriptions of a Hieratic Papyrus with a Mythological Story, Love Songs, and Other Miscellaneous Texts.* London: Oxford University, 1931.

Gordon, Cyrus H. *Ugaritic Textbook.* Rome: Pontifical Biblical Institute, 1965.

Grapow, Hermann. *Die medizinischen Texte in hieroglyphischer Umschreibung autographiert.* Berlin: Akademie-Verlag, 1958.

Horst, Friedrich, ed. "Canticum Canticorum." In *Biblia hebraica.* 3d ed. Ed. Rudolph Kittel. Stuttgart: Württembergische Bibelanstalt, 1937.

Hurd, H. Page. *The World's Oldest Love Poem: Louvre C 100.* Newark: n.p., 1954.

Maspero, Gaston C. C. "Les chants d'amour du papyrus de Turin et du papyrus Harris." *JA* ns (1883) 5-47.

Müller, W. Max. *Die Liebespoesie der alten Ägypter.* Leipzig: Hinrichs, 1899.

Posener, Georges. *Catalogue des ostraca hiératiques littéraires de Deir el Médineh.* 2 vols. Cairo: L'institut français d'archéologie orientale, 1938-1972.

Rahlfs, Alfred. *Septuaginta.* 2 vols. Stuttgart: Württembergische Bibelanstalt, 1935.

Spiegelberg, Wilhelm. "Eine neue Sammlung von Liebesliedern."
Pp. 117-21 in *Aegyptiaca*: Festschrift for G. Ebers.
Leipzig: Wilhelm Engelmann, 1897.

B. Reference Works

Brown, Francis; Driver, S. R.; and Briggs, Charles A., eds.
A Hebrew and English Lexicon of the Old Testament.
Oxford: Clarendon, 1907.

Cowley, Arthur E., trans.; Kautzsch, E., ed. *Gesenius' Hebrew
Grammar*. 2d Eng. ed. Oxford: Oxford University, 1910.

Crum, W. E. *A Coptic Dictionary*. Oxford: Clarendon, 1939.

Erman, Adolf. *Neuägyptische Grammatik*. Hildesheim: Georg
Olms, 1933.

_____, and Grapow, Hermann. *Wörterbuch der aegyptische
Sprache*. 5 vols. Berlin: Akademie-Verlag, 1950.

Faulkner, Raymond O. *A Concise Dictionary of Middle Egyptian*.
Oxford: Griffith Institute, 1962.

Gardiner, Alan H. *Egyptian Grammar*. 3d rev. ed. London:
Oxford University, 1973.

Holladay, William L. *A Concise Hebrew and Aramaic Lexicon of
the Old Testament*. Leiden: E. J. Brill, 1971.

Joüon, Paul. *Grammaire de l'hébreu biblique*. Rome: Pontifical
Biblical Institute, 1947.

Köhler, Ludwig H., and Baumgartner, Walter. *Lexicon in Veteris
Testamenti libros*. 3d ed. 2 vols. Leiden: E. J. Brill,
1967-1974.

_____. *Supplementum ad Lexicon in Veteris Testamenti libros*.
Leiden: E. J. Brill, 1958.

C. General Works

Albright, William F. "Archaic Survivals in the Text of Canticles." Pp. 1-7 in *Hebrew and Semitic Studies*. Ed. D. W.
Thomas and W. D. McHardy. Oxford: Clarendon, 1963.

_____. *From Stone Age to Christianity*. 2d ed. Garden
City: Doubleday, 1957.

_____. "The Old Testament and the Canaanite Language and
Literature." *CBQ* 7 (1945) 5-31.

Alonso-Schökel, Luis. *Estudios de poetica Hebrea*. Barcelona:
J. Flors, 1963.

Angénieux, Joseph. "Le Cantique des Cantiques en huit chants à refrains alternants." *ETL* 44 (1973) 87-140.

_____. "Note sur les trois portraits du Cantique des Cantiques." *ETL* 42 (1966) 582-96.

_____. "Structure du Cantique des Cantiques en chants encadrés par des refrains alternants." *ETL* 41 (1965) 96-142.

Audet, Jean-Paul. "Love and Marriage in the Old Testament." Trans. F. Burke. *Scr* 10 (1958) 65-83.

_____. "Le sens du Cantique des Cantiques." *RB* 62 (1955) 197-221.

Batto, Bernard F. *Studies on Women at Mari*. Baltimore: Johns Hopkins University, 1974.

Bausinger, H. *Formen der "Volkspoesie."* Berlin: E. Schmidt, 1958.

Bea, Augustin. *Canticum Canticorum Salomonis*. Rome: Pontifical Biblical Institute, 1953.

Ben-Amos, Dan. "Analytical Categories and Ethnic Genres." *Genre* 2 (1969) 275-301.

Bergsträsser, Gotthelf. "Das hebräische Prafix ש." *ZAW* 29 (1909) 40-56.

Biggs, Robert S. *ŠA.ZI.GA. Ancient Mesopotamian Potency Incantations*. Locust Valley, NY: J. J. Augustin, 1967.

Blackman, Aylward M. "On the Position of Women in the Egyptian Hierarchy." *JEA* 7 (1921) 8-30.

_____. "The Use of the Egyptian Word *h·t* 'House' in the Sense of 'Stanza.'" *Or* 7 (1938) 64-67.

Bleeker, Claas J. *Hathor and Thoth*. Leiden: E. J. Brill, 1973.

_____. "Der religiöse Gehalt einiger Hathor-Lieder." *ZÄS* 99 (1973) 82-88.

Broadribb, Donald. "Thoughts on the Song of Solomon." *AbrN* 3 (1961-62) 11-36.

Brown, J. P. "The Mediterranean Vocabulary of the Vine." *VT* 19 (1969) 160-64.

Brunner, Hellmut. *Altägyptische Erziehung*. Wiesbaden: Harrassowitz, 1957.

_____. "Gerechtigkeit als Fundament des Thrones." *VT* 8 (1958) 426-28.

Brunner, Hellmut. *Grundzüge einer Geschichte der altägyptischen Literatur*. Darmstadt: Wissenschaftliche Buchgesellschaft, 1966.

_____. "Das Herz als Sitz des Lebensgeheimnisses." *AO* 17 (1954-55) 140-41.

_____. "Das hörende Herz." *TLZ* 79 (1954) 697-700.

_____. "Die theologische Bedeutung der Trunkenheit." *ZAS* 79 (1954) 81-83.

Budde, Karl F. R. *Das Hohelied*. HSAT 2. 4th ed. Tübingen: J. C. B. Mohr, 1923.

Buzy, Denis. *Le Cantique des Cantiques*. Paris: Letouzey et Ané, 1949.

Caminos, Ricardo A. *Late-Egyptian Miscellanies*. Brown Egyptological Studies 1. London: Oxford University, 1954.

Carniti, Cecilia. "L'Unita' Letteraria del Cantico dei Cantici." *BeO* 13 (1971) 97-106.

Černý, Jaroslav. "Consanguineous Marriages in Pharaonic Egypt." *JEA* 40 (1954) 23-29.

_____. "Egypt: From the Death of Ramesses III to the End of the Twenty-first Dynasty." *CAH*. 3d ed. Ed. I. E. S. Edwards, C. J. Gadd, and N. G. L. Hammond. Fasc. 27. Cambridge: Cambridge University, 1965.

Cooper, Jerrold S. "New Cuneiform Parallels to the Song of Songs." *JBL* 90 (1971) 157-62.

Cothenet, Édouard. "L'interprétation du Cantique des Cantiques." *AmiCl* 73 (1963) 529-40, 545-52.

Cross, Frank M., and Freedman, David N. "The Pronominal Suffixes of the Third Person Singular in Phoenician." *JNES* 10 (1951) 228-30.

Dahood, Mitchell J. "Canaanite-Phoenician Influence in Qoheleth." *Bib* 33 (1952) 33-52, 191-221.

_____. "Hebrew-Ugaritic Lexicography II." *Bib* 45 (1964) 393-412.

_____. "The Phoenician Contribution of Biblical Wisdom Literature." Pp. 128-34 in *The Role of the Phoenicians in the Interaction of the Mediterranean Civilizations*. Ed. W. A. Ward. Beirut: American University, 1968.

_____. *Psalms I*. AB 16. Garden City: Doubleday, 1965.

_____. *Psalms II*. AB 17. Garden City: Doubleday, 1968.

Černý, J. "Egypt: From the Death of Ramesses III to the End of the Twenty-first Dynasty." Pp. 606-57 in *CAH* 2/2. 3d ed. Ed. I. E. S. Edwards, C. J. Gadd, and N. G. L. Hammond. Cambridge: Cambridge University, 1975.

Dahood, Mitchell J. *Psalms III*. AB 17a. Garden City: Doubleday, 1970.

_____. Review of *Seven Books of Wisdom*, by Roland E. Murphy. *Bib* 42 (1961) 235-37.

_____. *Ugaritic-Hebrew Philology*. Rome: Pontifical Biblical Institute, 1965.

_____. "Ugaritic Studies and the Bible." *Greg* 43 (1962) 55-79.

Davies, Nina M., and Gardiner, Alan H. *Ancient Egyptian Painting*. 3 vols. Chicago: University of Chicago, 1936.

Delitzsch, Franz J. *Commentary on the Song of Songs and Ecclesiastes*. Trans. M. Easton. Edinburgh: T. & T. Clark, 1891.

Dornseiff, F. "Ägyptische Liebeslieder, Hoheslied, Sappho, Theokrit." *ZDMG* 90 (1931) 588-601.

Doty, William G. "The Concept of Genre in Literary Analysis." In *Proceedings*. Ed. L. C. McGaughy. Missoula, MT: Society of Biblical Literature, 1972.

Driver, Godfrey R. *Canaanite Myths and Legends*. Edinburgh: T. & T. Clark, 1956.

Dubarle, André M. "L'amour humain dans le Cantique des Cantiques." *RB* 61 (1954) 67-86.

_____. "Le Cantique des Cantiques dans l'exégèse récente." Pp. 139-52 in *Aux grands carrefours de la révélation et de l'exégèse de l'Ancien Testament*. RechBib 8. Paris: Desclée de Brouwer, 1967.

Eissfeldt, Otto. *The Old Testament: An Introduction*. Trans. P. R. Ackroyd. New York: Harper & Row, 1965.

Erman, Adolf. *The Literature of the Ancient Egyptians*. Trans. A. M. Blackman. London: Methuen, 1927.

Exum, J. Cheryl. "A Literary and Structural Analysis of the Song of Songs." *ZAW* 85 (1973) 47-79.

Faulkner, Raymond O. "Egypt: From the Inception of the Nineteenth Dynasty to the Death of Ramesses III." Pp. 217-51 in *CAH* 2/2. 3d ed. Ed. I. E. S. Edwards, C. J. Gadd, and N. G. L. Hammond. Cambridge: Cambridge University, 1975.

_____, trans. *The Ancient Egyptian Pyramid Texts*. Oxford: Clarendon, 1969.

Feuillet, André. *Le Cantique des Cantiques*. Paris: Les Editions du Cerf, 1953.

_____. "Einige scheinbare Widersprüche des Hohenliedes." *BZ* 8 (1964) 216-39.

_____. "La formule d'appartenance mutuelle (2,16) et les interprétations divergentes du Cantique des Cantiques." *RB* 68 (1961) 321-53.

_____. "Note sur la traductión de Jer XXXI, 3c." *VT* 12 (1962) 122-24.

Fischer, Johann. *Das Hohe Lied*. Würzburg: Echter-Verlag, 1950.

Fisher, Loren R., ed. *Ras Shamra Parallels* 1. Rome: Pontifical Biblical Institute, 1972.

Fitzmyer, Joseph A. *The Genesis Apocryphon of Qumran Cave I*. BibOr 18a. Rome: Pontifical Biblical Institute, 1971.

Foster, John L. *Love Songs of the New Kingdom*. New York: Charles Scribner's Sons, 1974.

Frye, Northrop. *Anatomy of Criticism*. Princeton: Princeton University, 1957.

Gerleman, Gillis. "Bemerkungen zum Brauteslied der Thomasakten." *ASTI* 9 (1973) 14-22.

_____. *Ruth, Das Hohelied*. BKAT 18. Neukirchen-Vluyn: Neukirchener Verlag, 1965.

Gilbert, Pierre. "La composition des recueils de poèmes amoureux égyptiens et celle du Cantique des Cantiques." *CE* 45 (1948) 22-23.

_____. "Le grand poème d'amour du papyrus Chester Beatty I." *CE* 34 (1943) 186-87.

_____. *La poésie égyptienne*. Brussels: P. F. Merckx, 1943.

Ginsburg, Harold L. "Ugaritic Studies and the Bible." *BA* 8 (1945) 41-58.

González, A. "El lenguaje de la naturaleza en el 'Cantar de los Cantares.'" *SBE* 26 (1969) 397-433.

Gordis, Robert. "The Asseverative Kaph in Ugaritic and Hebrew." *JAOS* 63 (1943) 176-78.

_____. *The Song of Songs*. New York: Jewish Theological Seminary of America, 1954.

Grdseloff, G. "Zum Vogelfang." *ZÄS* 74 (1938) 52-55, 136-39.

Haller, Max. *Die Fünf Megilloth*. HAT 18. Tübingen: J. C. B. Mohr, 1940.

Hallo, William, and Simpson, William K. *The Ancient Near East: A History.* New York: Harcourt Brace Jovanovich, 1971.

Hamp, Vinzenz. "Zur Textkritik am Hohenlied." *BZ* 1 (1957) 197-214.

Harris, John R. *Lexicographical Studies in Ancient Egyptian Minerals.* Berlin: Akademie-Verlag, 1961.

Harris, Rivkah. "The Case of Three Babylonian Marriage Contracts." *JNES* 33 (1974) 363-69.

_____. "Woman in the Ancient Near East." Pp. 960-63 in *The Interpreter's Dictionary of the Bible, Supplement.* Ed. L. R. Bailey, K. Crim, and V. Furnish. Nashville: Abingdon, 1976.

Hatto, A. T. "Das Tagelied in der Weltliteratur." *DtVi* 36 (1962) 489-506.

Hayes, John H., ed. *Old Testament Form Criticism.* San Antonio: Trinity University, 1974.

Hayes, William C. "Chronology: I. Egypt--to the End of the Twentieth Dynasty." Pp. 173-92 in *CAH* 1/1. 3d ed. Ed. I. E. S. Edwards, C. J. Gadd, and N. G. L. Hammond. Cambridge: Cambridge University, 1973.

_____. "Egypt: Internal Affairs from Tuthmosis I to the Death of Amenophis III." Pp. 313-416 in *CAH* 2/1. 3d ed. Ed. I. E. S. Edwards, C. J. Gadd, and N. G. L. Hammond. Cambridge: Cambridge University, 1973.

Held, Moshe. "A Faithful Lover in an Old Babylonian Dialogue." *JCS* 15 (1961) 1-26; 16 (1962) 37-39.

Hermann, Alfred. *Altägyptische Liebesdichtung.* Wiesbaden: Harrassowitz, 1959.

_____. "Beiträge zur Erklärung der ägyptischen Liebesdichtung." Pp. 118-39 in *Ägyptologische Studien.* DAWBIO 29. Ed. O. Firchow. Berlin: Akademie-Verlag, 1955.

Hermann, Wilhelm. "Gedanken zur Geschichte des altorientalischen Beschreibungsliedes." *ZAW* 75 (1963) 176-96.

Hermisson, Hans-Jürgen. *Studien zur israelitischen Spruchweisheit.* WMANT 28. Neukirchen-Vluyn: Neukirchener Verlag, 1968.

Herrmann, Siegfried. *Untersuchungen zur Überlieferungsgestalt mittelägyptischer Literaturwerke.* DAWBIO 33. Berlin: Akademie-Verlag, 1957.

Hillers, Delbert R. "Paḥad Yiṣḥaq." *JBL* 91 (1972) 90-92.

Hintze, Fritz. *Untersuchungen zu Stil und Sprache neuägyptischer Erzählungen.* DAWBIO 2. Berlin: Akademie-Verlag, 1950.

Hornung, Erik. *Untersuchen zur Chronologie und Geschichte des Neuen Reiches.* Wiesbaden: Harrassowitz, 1964.

Horst, Friedrich. "Die Formen des althebräischen Liebesliedes." Pp. 176-87 in *Gottes Recht.* Ed. H. W. Wolff. Munich: C. Kaiser Verlag, 1961.

Jacob, Edmond. *Theology of the Old Testament.* Trans. A. W. Heathcote and P. J. Allcock. New York: Harper & Row, 1958.

Jacobsen, Thorkild. "Mesopotamian Gods and Pantheons." Pp. 16-38 in *Toward the Image of Tammuz and Other Essays on Mesopotamian History and Culture.* Ed. W. L. Moran. Cambridge: Harvard University, 1970.

_____. "The Sister's Message." *JANESCU* 5 (1973) 199-212.

James, T. G. H. "Egypt: From the Expulsion of the Hyksos to Amenophis I." Pp. 289-312 in *CAH* 2/1. 3d ed. Ed. I. E. S. Edwards, C. J. Gadd, and N. G. L. Hammond. Cambridge: Cambridge University, 1973.

Jepsen, Alfred. "Pardes." *ZDPV* 74 (1958) 65-68.

Jolles, André. *Einfache Formen.* 3d ed. Tübingen: Niemeyer, 1965.

_____. "Die literarischen Travestien." *BdP* 6 (1932) 281-94.

Kayser, W. *Das sprachliche Kunstwerk.* 12th printing. Bern: Francke Verlag, 1967.

Knierim, Rolf. "Form Criticism: The Present State of an Exegetical Discipline." Paper presented to the Form Criticism Seminar--Hebrew Scriptures. SBL Annual Meeting, New York, October 27, 1970.

_____. "Old Testament Form Criticism Reconsidered." *Int* 27 (1973) 435-68.

Koschaker, Paul. "Fratriarchat, Hausgemeinschaft und Mutterrecht in Keilschrifttexten." *ZA* 23 (1933) 1-89.

Kramer, Samuel N. "The Biblical Song of Songs and the Sumerian Love Songs." *Ex* 5 (1962) 25-31.

_____. *The Sacred Marriage Rite.* Bloomingtin, IN: University Press, 1969.

_____. "The Sacred Marriage: A Panoramic View of the Sumerian Evidence." *Proceedings* of the XXVth International Congress of Orientalists 2 (1968) 28-32.

Krinetzki, Leo. *Das Hohe Lied.* Düsseldorf: Patmos-Verlag, 1964.

Krinetzki, Leo. "'Retractationes' zu früheren Arbeiten über das Hohe Lied." *Bib* 52 (1971) 176-89.

Kuhl, Curt. "Das Hohelied und seine Deutung." *TRu* 9 (1937) 137-67.

Lambdin, Thomas O. "Egyptian Loan Words in the Old Testament." *JAOS* 73 (1953) 145-55.

Lambert, Wilfred G. "Divine Love Lyrics from Babylon." *JSS* 4 (1959) 1-15.

Landsberger, Franz. "Poetic Units Within the Song of Songs." *JBL* 73 (1954) 203-16.

Lerch, D. "Zur Geschichte der Auslegung des Hohenliedes." *ZTK* 54 (1957) 257-77.

Loretz, Oswald. *Das althebräische Liebeslied*. AOAT 14/1. Neukirchen-Vluyn: Neukirchener Verlag, 1971.

_____. "Die theologische Bedeutung des Hohenliedes." *BZ* 10 (1966) 29-46.

_____. "Zum Problem des Eros im Hohenlied." *BZ* 8 (1964) 191-216.

Luft, Ulrich. "Zur Einleitung der Liebesgedicht auf Papyrus Chester Beatty I rº XVI, 9ff." *ZÄS* 99 (1973) 108-16.

Lys, Daniel. *Le plus beau chant de la creation*. Paris: Les Editions du Cerf, 1968.

Meek, Theophile J. "Babylonian Parallels to the Song of Songs." *JBL* 43 (1924) 245-52.

_____. "Canticles and the Tammuz Cult." *AJSL* 39 (1922-23) 1-14.

_____. "The Song of Songs and the Fertility Cult." Pp. 48-79 in *The Song of Songs: A Symposium*. Ed. W. H. Schoff. Philadelphia: Commercial Museum, 1924.

_____. "The Song of Songs: Introduction and Exegesis." Pp. 91-148 in *The Interpreter's Bible* 5. Ed. G. A. Buttrick. Nashville: Abingdon, 1956.

Millet, Nicholas B. "A Fragment of the Hatshepsut Punt Relief." *JARC* 1 (1962) 55-57.

Morenz, Siegfried. *Egyptian Religion*. Trans. A. E. Keep. Ithaca: Cornell University, 1973.

Morgenstern, Julian. "Beena Marriage (Matriarchat) in Ancient Israel and its Historical Implications." *ZAW* 6 (1929) 91-110; 8 (1931) 46-58.

Morgenstern, Julian. "David and Jonathan." *JBL* 78 (1959) 322-25.

———. *Rites of Birth, Marriage, Death, and Kindred Occasions among the Semites*. Cincinnati: Hebrew Union College, 1966.

Moscati, Sabatino, ed. *An Introduction to the Comparative Grammar of the Semitic Languages*. Wiesbaden: Harrassowitz, 1969.

Muilenburg, James. "Form Criticism and Beyond." *JBL* 88 (1969) 1-18.

———. "The Linguistic and Rhetorical Usage of the Particle *Kî* in the Old Testament." *HUCA* 32 (1961) 135-60.

Murphy, Roland E. "Form-Critical Studies in the Song of Songs." *Int* 27 (1973) 413-22.

———. "The Hebrew Sage and Openness to the World." Pp. 219-44 in *Christian Action and Openness to the World*. Villanova University Symposia 2-3. Ed. J. Papin. Villanova, PA: Villanova University, 1970.

———. "Recent Literature on the Canticle of Canticles." *CBQ* 16 (1954) 381-92.

———. "The Structure of the Canticle of Canticles." *CBQ* 11 (1949) 381-91.

Nolli, Gianfranco. *Cantico dei Cantici*. SaBi. Rome: Marietti, 1968.

Ohly, Friedrich. *Hohelied-Studien*. Wiesbaden: Steiner, 1958.

Van den Oudenrijn, M. A. *Het Hooglied*. Roermond: Romen & Zonen, 1962.

Patai, Raphael. *Sex and Family in the Bible and the Middle East*. Garden City: Doubleday, 1959.

Peet, Thomas E. *A Comparative Study of the Literatures of Egypt, Palestine, and Mesopotamia*. London: Oxford University, 1931.

Petsch, R. "Die Lehre von den 'Einfache Formen.'" *DtVi* 10 (1932) 335-69.

Pflüger, K. "The Private Funerary Stelae of the Middle Kingdom and their Importance for the Study of Ancient Egyptian History." *JAOS* 67 (1947) 127-35.

Pope, Marvin H. "A Mare in Pharaoh's Chariotry." *BASOR* 200 (1970) 56-61.

Pope, Marvin H. "Pleonastic Waw Before Nouns in Ugaritic and Hebrew." *JAOS* 75 (1953) 95-98.

Porter, Bertha, and Moss, Rosalind L. B. *Topographical Bibliography of Ancient Egyptian Hieroglyphic Texts, Reliefs, and Paintings* 2. Oxford: Clarendon, 1927.

Pouget, Guillaume, and Guitton, J. *The Canticle of Canticles.* Trans. J. L. Lilly. n.p.: Delcom X. McMullen, 1946.

Von Rad, Gerhard. *Old Testament Theology* 1. Trans. D. M. G. Stalker. New York: Harper & Row, 1962.

Redford, Donald B. *History and Chronology of the Eighteenth Dynasty.* Toronto: University of Toronto, 1967.

_____. "On the Chronology of the Egyptian Eighteenth Dynasty." *JNES* 25 (1966) 113-24.

Ricciotti, Giuseppe. *Il Cantico dei Cantici.* Torino: Societa Editrice Internazionale, 1928.

Ringgren, Helmer. *Israelite Religion.* Trans. David E. Green. Philadelphia: Fortress, 1966.

_____; Weiser, Artur; and Zimmerli, Walther. *Prediger, Das Hohe Lied, Klagelieder, Das Buch Esther.* ATD 16. Göttingen: Vandenhoeck & Ruprecht, 1962.

Robert, André. "Les appendices du Cantique des Cantiques." *RB* 55 (1948) 161-83.

_____. *Le Cantique des Cantiques.* SBJ. 2d ed. Paris: Les Editions du Cerf, 1958.

_____. "La description de l'Epoux et de l'Epouse dans Cant. V, 11-15 et VII, 2-6." Pp. 211-23 in *Mélanges É. Podechard.* Lyon: Facultés Catholiques, 1945.

_____. "Le genre littéraire du Cantique des Cantiques." *RB* 52 (1943-44) 192-213.

_____; Tournay, Raymond; and Feuillet, André. *Le Cantique des Cantiques.* Paris: Gabalda, 1963.

Römer, Willem H. Ph. *Frauenbriefe über Religion, Politik und Privatleben in Mari.* AOAT 12. Neukirchen-Vluyn: Neukirchener Verlag, 1971.

Rowley, Harold H. "The Interpretation of the Song of Songs." Pp. 197-245 in *The Servant of the Lord.* 2d ed. Oxford: Blackwell, 1965.

Rowton, M. B. "Chronology: II. Ancient Western Asia." Pp. 193-239 in *CAH* 1/1. 3d ed. Ed. I. E. S. Edwards, C. J. Gadd, and N. G. L. Hammond. Cambridge: Cambridge University, 1973.

Rudolph, Wilhelm. *Das Buch Ruth, Das Hohe Lied, Die Klage-lieder*. KAT 17/1-3. Gütersloh: Gerd Mohn, 1962.

Rundgren, Frithiof. "אפריון 'Tragsessel, Sänfte.'" *ZAW* 74 (1962) 70-72.

Sasson, Jack M. "Biographical Notices on Some Royal Ladies from Mari." *JCS* 25 (1973) 59-78.

Schäfer, Hans. *Von ägyptischer Kunst*. Wiesbaden: Harrasso-witz, 1963.

Schmid, Hans H. *Wesen und Geschichte der Weisheit*. BZAW 101. Berlin: Töpelmann, 1966.

Schmökel, Hartmut. *Heilige Hochzeit und Hohes Lied*. AKM 32/1. Wiesbaden: Steiner, 1956.

_____. "Zur kultischen Deutung des Hohenliedes." *ZAW* 64 (1952) 148-55.

Schneider, Heinrich. *Die Heilige Schrift*. Bd. 7/1. Freiburg: Herder, 1962.

Schott, Siegfried. *Altägyptische Liebeslieder*. Zürich: Artemis Verlag, 1950.

_____. "Ein Fall von Pruderie aus der Ramessidenzeit." *ZÄS* 75 (1935) 100-106.

Schoville, Keith N. "The Impact of the Ras Shamra Texts on the Study of the Song of Songs." Ph.D. dissertation, University of Wisconsin, 1969.

Schröder, F. R. "Sakrale Grundlagen der altägyptischen Lyrik." *DtVi* 25 (1951) 273-93.

Schwarz, Leo W. "On Translating the 'Song of Songs.'" *Judaism* 13 (1964) 64-76.

Segal, Morris H. "The Song of Songs." *VT* 12 (1962) 470-90.

Sellin, Ernst, and Fohrer, Georg. *Introduction to the Old Testament*. Trans. David E. Green. Nashville: Abingdon, 1968.

Sethe, Kurt. *Ägyptische Lesestücke*. Darmstadt: Wissenschaft-liche Buchgesellschaft, 1959.

_____. *Erläuterungen zu den ägyptischen Lesestücken*. Hildesheim: Georg Olms, 1960.

Simpson, William K. *The Literature of Ancient Egypt*. New Haven: Yale, 1972.

Smith, W. S. "The Land of Punt." *JARC* 1 (1962) 59-61.

Smither, P. C. "The Prince Mehy of the Love Songs." *JEA* 34 (1948) 116.

_____. "A Ramesside Love Charm." *JEA* 27 (1941) 131-32.

_____. "The Report Concerning the Slave Girl Senket." *JEA* 34 (1948) 31-34.

Soulen, Richard N. "The *Waṣfs* of the Song of Songs and Hermeneutic." *JBL* 86 (1967) 183-90.

Speiser, E. A. "The Wife-Sister Motif in the Patriarchal Narratives." *Biblical and Other Studies*. ST 1. Ed. A. Altmann. Cambridge: Harvard University, 1963.

Staerk, Willy O. N. *Lyrik*. SAT 3/1. Göttingen: Vandenhoeck & Ruprecht, 1920.

Stephan, Stephen H. "Modern Palestinian Parallels to the Song of Songs." *JPOS* 2 (1922) 199-278.

Suys, E. "Les chants d'amour du Papyrus Chester Beatty I." *Bib* 13 (1932) 209-27.

Thrall, W. F.; Hibbard, A.; and Holman, C. H. *A Handbook to Literature*. New York: Odyssey, 1960.

Tournay, Raymond. "Abraham et le Cantique des Cantiques." *VT* 25 (1975) 544-52.

_____. "Les chariots d'Aminadab (Cant VI: 12): Israël, peuple théophre." *VT* 9 (1959) 288-309.

Veit, W. "Toposforschung: Ein Forschungsbericht." *DtVi* 37 (1963) 120-63.

Volten, A. "Der Begriff der Maat in den ägyptischen Weisheitstexten." Pp. 78-80 in *Les sagesses du Proche-Orient Ancien*. Paris: Presses Universitaires de France, 1963.

Van de Walle, B. Review of *Altägyptische Liebeslieder*, by S. Schott. *BO* 9 (1952) 105-108.

Watson, W. "More on Shared Consonants." *Bib* 52 (1971) 44-50.

_____. "Shared Consonants in North West Semitic." *Bib* 50 (1969) 525-33.

Wegner, M. "Die Stilentwicklung der thebanischen Beamtengräber." *MDAI* 4 (1933) 56-57.

Wernberg-Møller, Preben. "Pleonastic Waw in Classical Hebrew." *JSS* 3 (1958) 321-26.

Wetzstein, Johann G. "Die syrische Dreschtafel." *ZE* 5 (1873) 270-302.

White, John B. "Conversing with the Text." *Duke Divinity School Review* 39 (1974) 153-80.

Widengren, Geo. *Sakrales Königtum im Alten Testament und im Judentum.* Stuttgart: Kohlhammer, 1955.

Wilson, John A. *The Burden of Egypt.* Chicago: University of Chicago, 1951.

_____, trans. "Egyptian Secular Songs and Poems." Pp. 467-69 in *Ancient Near Eastern Texts Relating to the Old Testament.* Ed. James B. Pritchard. Princeton: Princeton University, 1955.

Winandy, Jacques. *Le Cantique des Cantiques.* Maredsous: Casterman, 1960.

Woldering, I. *The Art of Egypt.* Trans. A. E. Keep. New York: Crown, 1963.

Wolf, W. *Kulturgeschichte des alten Ägypten.* Stuttgart: Alfred Kröner Verlag, 1962.

_____. "Über die Gegenstandsbezogenheit des ägyptischen Denkens." Pp. 403-10 in *Ägyptologische Studien.* DAWBIO 29. Ed. O. Firchow. Berlin: Akademie-Verlag, 1955.

Würthwein, Ernst. *Die Fünf Megilloth.* HAT 18. Tübingen: J. C. B. Mohr, 1969.

_____. "Zum Verständnis des Hohenliedes." *TRu* 32 (1967) 177-212.

Yamauchi, E. "Tammuz and the Bible." *JBL* 84 (1965) 283-90.

Zimmerli, Walther. "The Place and Limit of Wisdom in the Framework of Old Testament Theology." *SJT* 17 (1964) 146-58.

216